PRE-GED
READING SKILLS
FOR SOCIAL STUDIES
AND SCIENCE

REVISED

GLENCOE

Macmillan/McGraw–Hill

New York, New York   Columbus, Ohio   Mission Hills, California   Peoria, Illinois

GED • GED • GED • GED • GED

ILLUSTRATION ACKNOWLEDGMENTS

Unless otherwise acknowledged, all photographs are the property of Glencoe Publishing Co.

3 Graph "Comparing Wheat, Corn, and Cotton Production" adapted from INVITATION TO ECONOMICS, Teacher's Annotated Ed., Third Ed., by Lawrence Wolken et al. Scott, Foresman and Company, 1988, p. 336. **5** Map "The African Slave Trade" adapted from AMERICA PAST AND PRESENT by Joan Schreiber et al. Scott, Foresman and Company, 1983, p. 131, and LAND OF PROMISE: A HISTORY OF THE UNITED STATES by Carol Berkin and Leonard Wood. Scott, Foresman and Company, 1983, p. 101. CATHY® cartoon by Cathy Guisewite. Reprinted by permission of Universal Press Syndicate. **13** Behavior swings illustration adapted from CHILD'S BODY by The Diagram Group. Copyright © 1977 by Diagram Visual Information Ltd. Reprinted by permission of Diagram Visual Information Limited. **14** Calorie needs illustration adapted from CHILD'S BODY by The Diagram Group. Copyright © 1977 by Diagram Visual Information Ltd. Reprinted by permission of Diagram Visual Information Limited. **15** Friends vs. Parents adapted figure 10, from FIVE CRIES OF PARENTS by Merton P. Strommen and A. Irene Strommen. Reprinted from Harper & Row, Publishers, Inc. **35** Jeannie Taylor/TexaStock. **36** Comparing standards of living chart adapted from INVITATION TO ECONOMICS, Teacher's Annotated Ed., Third Ed., by Lawrence Wolken et al. Scott, Foresman and Company, 1988, p. 436. **37** "Number of Men and Women Workers in the United States 1950–1980" from Bureau of Labor Statistics, U.S. Dept. of Labor. **42** Copyright © Michael C. Witte. **51** "How Many People Vote?" graph adapted from data from Bureau of the Census, U.S. Dept. of Commerce and Committee for the Study of the American Electorate, as it appeared in "Clinton Climbs to Power On Broad, Shaky Base" by Rhodes Cook in CONGRESSIONAL QUARTERLY WEEKLY REPORT, January 2, 1993. Reprinted by permission of Congressional Quarterly Inc. **52** Copyright © Brent Jones. **55** As reported in THE 1993 WORLD ALMANAC AND BOOK OF FACTS. Copyright © 1992 by Pharos Books. Published by Pharos Books, a Scripps Howard Company. **57** G. French/H. Armstrong Roberts. **59** "The Economic Cycle in a Market System" adapted from INVITATION TO ECONOMICS, Third Ed., Teacher's Resource Book: Consumer Guide Activities on Blackline Masters by Lawrence Wolken et al. Scott, Foresman and Company, 1988, p. vii. **60** As reported in THE 1993 WORLD ALMANAC AND BOOK OF FACTS. Copyright © 1992 by Pharos Books. Published by Pharos Books, a Scripps Howard Company. **61** Jobs chart from HUMAN BEHAVIOR: STATUS AND CONFORMITY by Richard W. Murphy and the Editors of Time-Life Books © 1976 Time-Life Books Inc. Reprinted by permission. **61** Bureau of the Census, U.S. Dept. of Commerce, CURRENT POPULATION REPORTS: *MONEY INCOME OF HOUSEHOLDS, FAMILIES AND PERSONS IN THE UNITED STATES, 1988 AND 1989* (1991). **62** Bureau of the Census, U.S. Dept. of Commerce, CURRENT POPULATION REPORTS. **63** Electing a President chart from AMERICA YESTERDAY AND TODAY, Teacher's Annotated Ed. worksheet. Scott, Foresman and Company, 1988, p. 30. **64** Bureau of the Census, U.S. Dept. of Commerce, CURRENT POPULATION REPORTS. **65** *Signing of the Constitution*, painted by Howard Chandler Christy. Photograph courtesy U.S. Capitol Historical Society National Geographic Society photographer George F. Mobley. **70** "Passing an Amendment" from AMERICA YESTERDAY AND TODAY, Teacher's Annotated Ed. worksheet. Scott, Foresman and Company, 1988, p. 30. **73** Reproduced from the collections of The Library of Congress. **75** "The Southern United States" map from GEOGRAPHY: OUR COUNTRY AND OUR WORLD by Barbara J. Winston. Scott, Foresman and Company, 1988 p. 148. **76** "The United States: Census Regions" map from GEOGRAPHY: OUR COUNTRY AND OUR WORLD by Barbara J. Winston. Scott, Foresman and Company, 1988, p. 36. **78** United States Population map from GEOGRAPHY: OUR COUNTRY AND OUR WORLD by Barbara J. Winston. Scott, Foresman and Company, 1988, p. 68. **79** "Time Zones" from AMERICA YESTERDAY AND TODAY, Teacher's Annotated Ed. Scott, Foresman and Company, 1988, p. 82. **81** Copyright © 1989 by Norman Prince, San Francisco, CA. All rights reserved. **82** "The Midwest: Tornado Areas" map from GEOGRAPHY: OUR COUNTRY AND OUR WORLD by Barbara J. Winston. Scott, Foresman and Company, 1988, p. 224. **82** "The West: Natural Vegetation" map from GEOGRAPHY: OUR COUNTRY AND OUR WORLD by Barbara J. Winston. Scott, Foresman and Company, 1988, p. 57. **87** "Columbus's Four Voyages to America" map from AMERICA YESTERDAY AND TODAY by Carol Berkin et al. Scott, Foresman and Company, 1988, p. 76. **88** Institute Nacional de Anthropologia e Historia, Mexico. **89** "Where Major Indian Groups Lived" map from REGIONS OF OUR COUNTRY AND OUR WORLD, Indiana Ed., by Joan Schreiber et al. Scott, Foresman and Company, 1985, p. 51. **90** "Diagram of Woodland Society" from WESTERN HEMISPHERE: LATIN AMERICA AND CANADA, Teacher's Ed., by Joan Schreiber et al. Scott, Foresman and Company, 1986, p. 105. **95** Courtesy Ford Motor Company. **100** Paul Sequeira. **103** Copyright © 1989 Bob Thomason: Tony Stone Images. **108** Adapted from NOISE POLLUTION by Shan Finney. Copyright © 1984 by Shan Finney. Reprinted by permission of Franklin Watts Inc. **109** Adaptation of "Reston: A Planned Community" compiled by Travelers Insurance Company, as it appears in OLD CITIES & NEW TOWNS: THE CHANGING FACE OF THE NATION by Alvin Schwartz. Copyright © 1968 by Alvin Schwartz. **112** "Value of Trade Between U.S. and Selected Countries" from AMERICA PAST AND PRESENT by Joan Schreiber et al. Scott, Foresman and Company, 1983, p. 409. **114** "The South: Points of Interest" map from GEOGRAPHY: OUR COUNTRY AND OUR WORLD by Barbara J. Winston. Scott, Foresman and Company, 1988, p. 207. **123** © 1989 Robert Frerck: Tony Stone Images. **150** "Drug Abuse Cases in Emergency Rooms" adapted from THE WORLD BOOK MEDICAL ENCYCLOPEDIA. Copyright © 1988 World Book, Inc. Reprinted by permission. **151** Copyright © Wolfgang Kaehler 1989. **160** "Speeds of Animals" adapted from THE WORLD BOOK ENCYCLOPEDIA. Copyright © 1988 World Book, Inc. Reprinted by permission. **167** Diagram of population/farmland/forestland adapted from ECOLOGY 2000: THE CHANGING FACE OF EARTH by Tom Burke, ed. by Sir Edmund Hillary. Copyright © 1984 by Multimedia Publications. Reprinted by permission of Kampman and Company. **171** NASA. **188** National Oceanic & Atmospheric Administration. **211** Milt and Joan Mann/Cameramann International, Ltd. **214** Milt and Joan Mann/Cameramann International, Ltd. **223** Courtesy of International Business Machines Corporation. **225** Milt and Joan Mann/Cameramann International, Ltd.

Cover Photo: Peter Arnold/Peter Arnold, Inc.

TEXT ACKNOWLEDGMENTS

3 Barbara J. Winston, GEOGRAPHY: OUR COUNTRY AND OUR WORLD. Scott, Foresman and Company, 1988, p. 77. **4** Adapted from REGIONS OF OUR COUNTRY AND OUR WORLD, Indiana Ed., by Joan Schreiber et al. Scott, Foresman and Company, 1985, p. 192. **12** Excerpt from "Caring, Loving Mom in S. Carolina" by Ann Landers, Los Angeles Times Syndicate, from THE CHICAGO TRIBUNE, June 9, 1988. Copyright © 1988 by Los Angeles Times Syndicate. Reprinted by permission of Ann Landers. **14** Excerpt from THE THOUGHT-A-WEEK-GUIDES: HOW TO LIVE WITH YOUR TEENAGER by Jack Clarke. Copyright © 1987 by Blue Cliff Editions. Reprinted by permission of Blue Cliff Editions. **21** Horatio Alger, Jr., RAGGED DICK AND MARK, THE MATCH BOY. Ragged Dick Series, 1867. **23** Judy Dunn, SISTERS AND BROTHERS. Copyright © 1985 by Judy Dunn. Reprinted by permission of Harvard University Press. **24** From THE BODY LANGUAGE OF SEX, POWER, AND AGGRESSION by Julius Fast. Copyright © 1977 by Julius Fast. Reprinted by permission of the publisher, M. Evans and Company, Inc., New York. **34** Adapted from "On the Assembly Line" by Gene Richards, ed. by Warren Susman, CULTURE AND COMMITMENT 1929–1945. George Braziller, Publishers. Copyright © 1973 by Warren Susman. All rights reserved. **42** Adapted from INVITATION TO ECONOMICS, Teacher's Annotated Ed., Third Ed., by Lawrence Wolken and Janet Glocker. Scott, Foresman and Company, 1988, p. 513. **43** Bureau of Labor Statistics, U.S. Dept. of Labor. **45** Adapted from FLORIDA: THE STUDY OF OUR STATE by Kathleen Kain. Scott, Foresman and Company, 1986, p. 112. **51** Adapted from FLORIDA: THE STUDY OF OUR STATE by Kathleen Kain. Scott, Foresman and Company, 1986, p. 126. **52** Adapted from REGIONS OF OUR COUNTRY AND OUR WORLD, Indiana Ed., by Joan Schreiber et al. Scott, Foresman and Company, 1985, p. 232. **53** Adapted from LOUISIANA: THE STUDY OF OUR STATE by Kathleen Kain. Scott, Foresman and Company, 1986, and Huey P. Long, EVERY MAN A KING. New Orleans: National Book Co., Inc., 1933. **58** Adapted from INVITATION TO ECONOMICS, Teacher's Annotated Ed., Third Ed., by Lawrence Wolken and Janet Glocker. Scott, Foresman and

Send all inquiries to
GLENCOE DIVISION
Macmillan/McGraw-Hill
936 Eastwind Drive
Westerville, OH 43081

ISBN 0-02-802068-5

2 3 4 5 6 7 8 9   HESS   99 98 97 96 95 94

Consultants to the Program

Jeff Bishop
New Brunswick Adult Learning Center
New Brunswick, NJ

Kathryn Boesel-Dunn
Columbus Public Schools
Columbus, Ohio

Toby G. Cannon
Cohn Adult Learning Center
Nashville, Tennessee

Charmaine M. Carney
Hawkeye Institute of Technology
Waterloo, Iowa

Mary S. Charuhas
College of Lake County
Grayslake, Illinois

Lee Chic
Sequoia Adult School
Redwood City, California

James R. Fryxell
College of Lake County
Grayslake, Illinois

Marcia Harrington
D.C. Public Library
Washington, D.C.

Cynthia A. Green
Lincoln Instructional Center
Dallas, Texas

Esther Gross
Petit Jean Technical College
Morrilton, Arkansas

Theodore M. Harig
Ellsworth Correctional Center
Union Grove, Wisconsin

Chuck Herring
GED Institute
Seattle, Washington

Linda L. Kindy
Little Rock Adult Education Center
Little Rock, Arkansas

Claudia V. McClain
South Suburban College
South Holland, Illinois

Ed A. Mayfield
Fayette County Adult Education
Center
Lexington, Kentucky

Valerie Meyer
Southern Illinois University
Edwardsville, Illinois

Pat Mitchell
Dallas Independent School District
Dallas, Texas

Laura Morris
Center for Community Education
Tallahassee, Florida

Evelyn H. Nunes
Virginia Commonwealth University
Richmond, Virginia

Ann Kuykendall Parker
Cohn Adult Learning Center
Nashville, Tennessee

Jill Plaza
Reading and Educational Consultants
Palatine, Illinois

John H. Redd
Dallas Independent School District
Dallas, Texas

Gail Rice
Adult Basic Education Program
Palos Heights, Illinois

Karen Samson
Chicago State University
Chicago, Illinois

Yvonne E. Siats-Fiskum
Gateway Technical College
Elkhorn, Wisconsin

Sheldon Silver
Truman College
Chicago, Illinois

Robert T. Sutton
Central Piedmont Community College
Charlotte, North Carolina

Dee Swanson
Minnesota Correctional Facility
Stillwater, Minnesota

Glencoe Pre-GED Reading Skills
for Social Studies and Science
Scope and Sequence

Diagnostic Tests — Parts A and B: Measuring What You Know

Vocabulary Development

Context clues and word-part analysis — Taught in Working with Words and reinforced in Reading on Your Own in each lesson in the book

Reading Strategies

Self-appraisal and self-correction — Part A: The Active Reader preceding Lesson 2

Locating information — Part A: The Active Reader preceding Lesson 3

Self-questioning — Part B: The Active Reader preceding Lesson 6

Using prior knowledge — Part B: The Active Reader preceding Lesson 8

Taught in Before You Read at beginning of each lesson in the book

Previewing — Part A: Lessons 4, 5, 10, 11
Part B: Lessons 1–11

Reading Skills*

Literal comprehension

Stating the main idea — Part A: Lessons 1, 2
Part B: Lesson 9

Summarizing — Part B: Lesson 9

Seeing patterns of ideas — Part A: Lessons 1, 4
Part B: Lesson 1

Interpreting tables — Part A: Lessons 6, 7
Part B: Lesson 3

Interpreting graphs — Part A: Lessons 6, 7
Interpreting diagrams — Part B: Lesson 2
Interpreting maps — Part A: Lessons 8, 11

Inferential comprehension

Inferring the main idea — Part A: Lessons 2, 3, 5

Predicting outcomes — Part A: Lesson 5
Drawing conclusions — Part A: Lesson 11
Part B: Lesson 4

Applying ideas — Part A: Lesson 5
Part B: Lesson 5

Analysis

Cause and effect — Part A: Lesson 4
Part B: Lesson 7

Recognizing point of view — Part A: Lesson 9

Facts, opinions, hypotheses — Part B: Lesson 11

Evaluation

Assessing supporting data — Part B: Lesson 10

Recognizing values — Part A: Lesson 10

Evaluative Test — Parts A and B: Measuring What You've Learned

*Taught in The Active Reader preceding the first lesson listed for each skill, and reinforced in the lessons

Contents

Part B
Reading Skills for Science / 117

How to Use This Book

This book will give you a start in reading articles about social studies and science. It is divided into two parts. In Part A, you'll read social studies topics. In Part B, you'll read science topics.

The book does not cover every area of these subjects. But it will give you a foundation in reading and thinking about important ideas in social studies and science.

This book will help you in two ways. First, you'll see that topics in social studies and science touch your life. You'll learn information you can use. Second, you'll learn skills to help you read with better understanding. The reading skills you'll learn will give you a strong start for further study.

Measuring What You Know

Each part starts with a survey of what you know. Use this survey to guide you. Your answers will help you plan your study time.

The Active Reader

Before each lesson, you'll find a two-page tip. Here you'll learn to *do* something as you read. You'll learn to work with the information you read.

The Lessons

The lessons have interesting articles to read. You'll also build your reading skills. Each lesson follows the same order.

Before You Read This section helps you find out how much you already know about a subject. Don't worry if you don't know a lot. What is important is that you are thinking about the subject. You will answer a few questions. You'll also look over the articles that follow. This will give you ideas about what you want to find out as you read.

Finally, you'll study some words that are in the articles. You'll learn how to figure out the meaning of the words on your own. Then you can look at the definitions in **Word Power** to see if you were right. You can use the word skills you learn to figure out other words you will read.

Reading on Your Own This section will give you seven to ten short articles on a general topic. The articles were chosen with adult interests in mind. Questions help you check your understanding. You'll also use the skill you learned in The Active Reader.

After the last article, you'll find a **GED Warm-up.** This gives you a chance to try a multiple-choice question. The questions are like the ones on the GED

Test. In many lessons, **A Test-Taking Tip** offers a suggestion on how to answer test questions.

Answer Explanations

All the answers are explained at the back of the book. This section helps you know *why* your answer is right. It also helps you know why you answered wrong.

Measuring What You've Learned

Each part ends with a test. The test shows how much you've learned. It also helps you see what you need to review.

Goals are important to learning. This book can help you reach two goals: (1) to enjoy reading social studies and science articles, and (2) to improve your reading skills. With these goals reached, you'll be ready to study for the GED Test.

Part **A**
Reading Skills for Social Studies

In **Part A**, you will build skills in reading social studies. In **Unit 1**, you'll read about people and groups. Some articles are on raising children. In others, you'll learn about different personality types—including your own! In one lesson, you'll read about how people make moral decisions and how leaders use their authority.

In **Unit 2**, you'll read about money and power. You'll read tips on how to use and save your money. You'll read about social classes in America. You'll also learn about the United States government and Constitution.

Unit 3 has articles on the past and the land. You'll use maps and articles to learn about regions of the United States. You'll read about the discovery of America from the point of view of the Europeans and Native Americans. You'll learn how workers fought for rights in the workplace. And finally, you'll learn about some problems of city life today.

Measuring What You Know

The following test has three articles, a bar graph, a map, and sixteen questions. This test will show you what you already know about social studies. It also will tell you what you need to study. So relax when you take the test. Finding out what you don't know will help you.

Carefully read each article, and study the graph and map. Then answer the questions that follow. Take your time. When you finish, turn to page 233 to check your answers. Next, look at the table on page 6. It will help you plan your study time.

Items 1–4 refer to the article below.

Charles Horton Cooley wrote *Human Nature and Social Order.* In this book, Cooley explains how a child learns to live with others. First, says Cooley, the child forms a looking glass self. This is done in three steps:

1. The child decides how he or she appears to others.
2. The child decides how he or she feels about the way others see him or her.
3. Then the child acts accordingly. For example, if people seem to value the child, he or she develops self-worth.

In short, Cooley believes that children see themselves as they think others see them.

1. Cooley says a child first decides how others see him or her. What does the child do next?

   _____

2. What is the main idea of the passage?

   _____

3. Copy the sentence below that you think Cooley would agree with.

   a. Parents help mold their child's character.

   b. A person's personality is set at birth.

   _____

4. What is the "looking glass" a child uses to develop his or her *looking glass self*?

   _____

Items 5–7 refer to the graph below.

The bar graph below shows one way new farm machines changed farming between 1800 and 1980.

Comparing Wheat, Corn, and Cotton Production

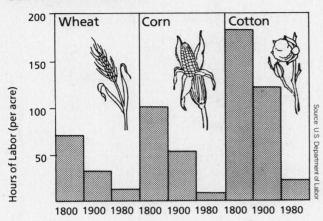

Source: U.S. Department of Labor

5. Which crop needed the most hours of labor in 1980?

_____

6. Crops needed fewer hours of labor in 1980 than in 1800. For which crop was the difference in hours the greatest?

_____

7. When do you think farmers produced more wheat, corn, and cotton—in 1900 or in 1980?

_____

Items 8–11 refer to the article below.

Along with their rights as citizens, Americans share certain responsibilities. In our nation, for example, people choose representatives to make laws. In return, people agree to obey the laws that are made. Obeying laws is one of the responsibilities, or duties, of being a citizen.

Laws are needed to keep peace and order in a country. For example, the United States has laws about how fast people may drive their cars. What would happen if people could drive at any speed they wanted? Some people might drive too fast, even when it is unsafe to do so. They might speed by a crosswalk and not see someone stepping off the curb. Other people might drive too slowly. They might cause traffic jams. Laws about speed limits make sure that people drive in a safe and orderly way.

8. According to the passage, what may happen if people drive too slowly?

_____

9. Copy the sentence below that states the main idea of the second paragraph.

   a. Laws keep peace and order.

   b. Driving too fast is unsafe.

_____

10. What may happen if a driver goes too fast to see someone step off a curb?

_____

11. What word from the passage means the same as *responsibilities*?

_____

Items 12–13 refer to the article below.

By the 1700s, French explorers claimed a large part of North America. New France included what is now the midwestern United States, as well as parts of Canada.

The English and the French went to war. The English won. In 1763, France gave up its land in North America to England. Many English people wanted to move to the new land. These colonists hoped to start new settlements. The settlements would be colonies ruled by England.

This made the Indians who lived in North America angry. The Indians did not want English colonists settling the land. So, to keep peace with the Indians, the government in England passed a law. The law closed the land west of the Appalachian Mountains to new settlers.

The law made the English colonists angry. They felt England had cheated them of land that was rightfully theirs. The difference in feeling about this law helped start the American Revolution.

12. "Fighting the Indians would cost too much to be worthwhile." Which of the following groups most likely thought this way? Copy your answer on the line below.

   a. French Americans

   b. English lawmakers

   c. English colonists

   _____

13. Why were the English in America called *colonists*?

   _____

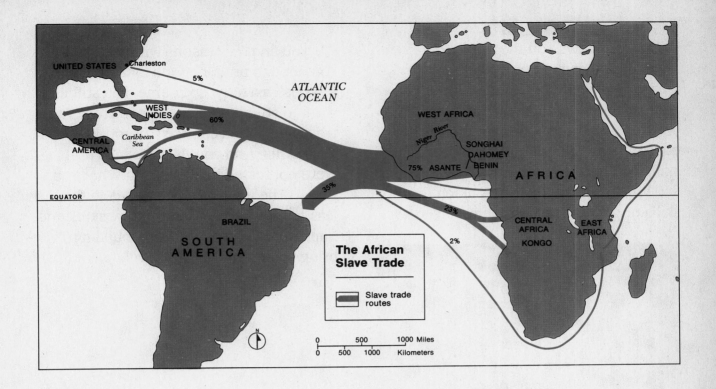

The African Slave Trade

Slave trade routes

0   500   1000 Miles
0 500 1000 Kilometers

UNITED STATES Charleston   5%   ATLANTIC OCEAN
WEST INDIES   60%
CENTRAL AMERICA   Caribbean Sea
EQUATOR
BRAZIL
SOUTH AMERICA
35%
WEST AFRICA   Niger River   SONGHAI   DAHOMEY   BENIN
75%   ASANTE   AFRICA
23%
2%
CENTRAL AFRICA   EAST AFRICA
KONGO

Items 14–16 refer to the map above.

14. Most slaves came from what part of Africa?

_____

15. More slaves were taken to _____ and _____ than to other places.

16. What percentage of the total number of slaves was taken to the southern United States?

_____

You can check your answers to this test on page 233.

Using Your Results

This table shows you the main skill needed to answer each question in Measuring What You Know. Did you have problems with some questions? If you did, find the numbers of those questions on the table. You'll see which skills you need to practice. You'll also find which lessons in Part A teach these skills or give practice in them.

Did you find the lessons with the skills you need to practice? You can study those lessons carefully. Of course, you still will want to study the other lessons too. That way, you'll get a chance to improve all your skills. And you'll learn skills that were not tested in Measuring What You Know. The interesting passages in the lessons will help you learn new skills and improve old ones. Your skill building will bring you up to the GED level.

Question	Skill	Lesson
1	Seeing patterns	1
2	Stating the main idea	1,2
3	Using inferences	2,3,5
4	Understanding vocabulary	all
5	Reading a graph	6,7
6	Reading a graph	6,7
7	Using inferences	2,3,5
8	Cause and effect	4
9	Stating the main idea	1,2
10	Predicting outcomes	5
11	Understanding vocabulary	all
12	Point of view	9,10
13	Understanding vocabulary	all
14	Reading a map	8,11
15	Reading a map	8,11
16	Reading a map	8,11

People and Groups

Looking for Patterns in Social Studies

cathy®   **by Cathy Guisewite**

Picture It

In the cartoon above, Cathy has her hands full with baby Zenith. Cathy has a plan for how they will spend the evening. But Zenith has other ideas.

Have you ever been in this kind of trouble? Maybe it was the first time you baby-sat. Most likely, the baby's parents gave you a plan for the baby: Bathe her at four o'clock. Feed her at six. Put her to bed at seven.

In similar ways, social studies authors help their readers. Authors want you to understand what you read. They want you to remember what you read. So to help you, authors use **patterns.** In other words, they order what they write.

As a reader, you need to look for those patterns. Reading is more than looking at words. It is more than knowing all the words you read. Reading is an active process. As you read social studies, look for the patterns that shape what you read.

Here's an Example

This paragraph gives directions in a **step-by-step order.**

■ When you feed the baby, first tilt the bottle. After five minutes, take away the bottle. Then gently pat the baby until he or she burps. Repeat these steps until the baby won't take any more milk.

Step-by-step order tells you how to do something. It tells you in the same order as you should do it. Words like *first, after,* and *then* often are clues to this pattern.

Sometimes authors write items in **time order.** Words such as *six o'clock* and *three years* often show time order. They tell you when something happened.

The following example has a time-order pattern. Find out what children can draw at different ages. The words that can help you are underlined or in dark print.

■ No one can draw when he or she is born. But as children grow, so do their skills. Newborns can't even hold pencils. Their wrists are too weak. By age two, children's wrists are stronger. So they can draw **up-and-down lines.** At two and a half, most children can copy **left-to-right lines.** At three, they can copy **circles.** They usually add eyes and mouths to the circles to make faces. By four, children are connecting up-and-down and left-to-right lines to make **crosses.** By five, children are putting together several lines to make **boxes.**

The words in dark print list the kinds of things children draw. The underlined words tell the order in which children learn to draw them.

For example, when do children begin to draw up-and-down lines? Look for **up-and-down lines** in dark print. The underlined words in the same sentence tell you that children learn to draw up-and-down lines at age two.

Working It Out

Read the following passage. Then answer the questions below it. The list and the order of the directions should help you find the correct answers.

■ Jenny began to prepare for Danny's bath. First she gathered these things: a tub of warm water, soap, cotton, a washcloth, a bath towel, baby oil, a diaper, clothing, and a bottle for after the bath. Next she undressed Danny and lowered him into the water. He opened his eyes wide with surprise. Smiling, Jenny rubbed Danny's neck, chest, arms, hands, and even his hair with the bar of soap. She used the cotton balls to clean the creases behind his neck and knees. With a warm cloth, she washed off the soap. Then Jenny removed Danny from the tub and patted him dry. In her hands, she warmed a dab of baby oil. Then she rubbed the oil on Danny's legs, arms, and tummy. Finally Jenny dressed Danny and held him close to smell his skin.

Answer the following questions. Try to use sentences. You may also use parts of sentences.

1. What steps did Jenny follow after putting Danny in the tub and before taking him out?

_____

_____

2. What did Jenny do after she took Danny out of the tub?

_____

Raising Children

Before You Read:
Thinking About Raising Children

The following pages include articles on raising children. They cover some of the latest thinking by doctors, teachers, and parents. They are samples of what you might read in child psychology books.

Before you read the articles, think of what you already know about raising children. Then you can draw on what you know as you read. This will help you focus on new ideas. It will help you connect new ideas with what you already know.

Almost everyone has ideas about how to raise children. You may have children of your own. Even if you don't, you probably have friends who are parents. And you can also think about your own family and how *you* were raised.

Take one area of child rearing: punishment. Some parents think children should be spanked when they are bad. Others think children should never be hit or spanked. What do you think? Write your ideas in a sentence or two below.

_____

_____

Here's another case. Suppose a teenager is in serious trouble. The problem might be drugs, poor grades at school, or an unwanted pregnancy. What do *you* think parents can do to help the teenager?

_____

_____

Today many families use day care for their children. What do you think a good day care center needs to have? Why?

_____

_____

As you wrote about children, did any questions come to mind? Asking your own questions will help you get involved in what you read. Below, write down any questions you have about raising children.

_____

_____

As you read, look to see if your questions are answered.

Working with Words

Some words from the articles in this lesson are used in the sentences below. These words may be new to you. Or you may have seen them before. Try to figure out what the words mean. Use what you already know. Also use hints from the sentences.

Swimming lessons **stimulate** babies to move quickly and surely.

Annette knew mumps hurt, so she had **empathy** for Clare.

That umpire takes a lot of **abuse**.

What hint does the first sentence give for the meaning of *stimulate*? The sentence tells you that stimulating "helps babies move." What do you think *stimulate* means? List ways besides swimming that you think would stimulate babies.

_____

You may want to attack *empathy* in a different way. Divide the word into parts—em•path•y. What word do you know that has the same last parts? Most likely you answered *sympathy*. You

probably have sent a sympathy card to a friend who lost someone close. The card told your friend that you "felt" for him or her. Now add this hint to others in the second sentence. Use them to make up a meaning for *empathy*. Write it below.

_____

_____

Abuse can be a verb or a noun. It is said differently as a noun than it is as a verb. The verb means "to treat cruelly or roughly." How do baseball fans "abuse" an umpire? Sometimes they throw bottles at him. Sometimes they call him names. However, *abuse* in the third sentence is a noun. Have you figured out its meaning? Write it below.

_____

Maybe you could not come up with a meaning for a word. Then check a dictionary. Next look at the meanings below. Are yours similar?

Word Power

stimulate to stir up
empathy the ability to feel what someone else is feeling
abuse cruel or rough treatment

Look for these words in the articles that follow. You may also read other difficult words. Try to figure out the meaning of new words just as you did here. Look at how the word is used. Look at the words around it. And look at the parts of the word. This way you'll begin to build your "word power."

Reading on Your Own

Carried Babies

I think carrying babies brings them closer to their parents. They learn how we move and see things. They're a part of our world because they do what we do. I wear Tad at home and out walking. He hears, smells, and sees more than he would from a crib or buggy. Baby-wearing seems like a great way to stimulate learning.

Some worry that being so close makes children depend too much on their parents. But many children's doctors say this isn't true. Carried babies become more independent than other children. Why is this so? Maybe because carried babies feel more sure of their parents' love.

Write a few words to answer each question.

1. Why does the passage call carrying babies *baby-wearing*?

_____

2. Why does the author think that carried babies become independent?

_____

What's Wrong with Today's Youth?

Dear Ann Landers: If you want to know what is wrong with today's youth, I can tell you. It's the adults.

I am a 45-year-old woman with three children and three grandchildren, not exactly a kid. In the four years that I have been working with the public I have seen it all. The way some parents treat their children is a disgrace. No wonder the children turn out hostile, angry, and destructive, a problem to society and themselves.

I've seen parents hit, kick, beat, curse and scream at their children. . . . If they treat them like that in public, I can just imagine how they treat them at home.

Children need to be respected and loved. They treat others the way they are treated. They learn what they live. Isn't there enough suffering in this world without heaping abuse and humiliation on those we are supposed to value? . . .
Caring, Loving Mom in S. Carolina

In a few words answer these questions.

1. "They learn what they live." Can you explain this sentence in your own words?

_____

2. How might a parent who screams at his or her child answer this letter?

_____

_____

Typical Swings in Behavior

One way to show facts is with a **diagram.** It uses words and pictures. The diagram below gives facts about how children act as they grow. The numbers tell you the children's ages.

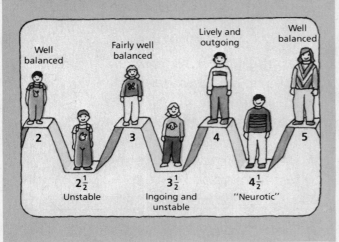

Follow the directions below.

1. Explain how children from age two to age three behave. In your answer, use time-order words such as *then* and *later.*

_____

_____

_____

2. In the space below, draw a diagram. Show how parents might feel during the first five years of their children's lives. Don't worry about your artwork. If you like, use the picture above as a model.

Showing Love

LaToya sinks into a chair and sighs.

"LaToya," her mother says. "Nothing can be that bad. Go out and play."

"Ma. Not now. I want to sit and think."

"LaToya, when I say jump, you jump."

Manuel has been lying on his bed for hours.

"How are you feeling, Manuel?" his father asks. Manuel doesn't answer.

"You know, once I stayed in my room all weekend. I had failed a math test."

Manuel turns to his father. "The band picked another guy for lead guitar," he says.

"There are other bands."

"I know," says Manuel. "I still don't like it."

Manuel's father rests his hand on Manuel's arm. "I know," he says.

The mother wants her daughter to be happy. But she doesn't know why LaToya is sad. And she doesn't seem to care.

The father also wants to see his son happy. He listens to Manuel's spoken and unspoken messages. He shows empathy for his son.

Which child do you think feels loved?

1. In a sentence or two, sum up the main point the author makes.

_____

2. How could LaToya's mother have helped her daughter feel loved? Write a new conversation for them.

Mother: _____

LaToya: _____

Mother: _____

LaToya: _____

Daily Calorie Needs

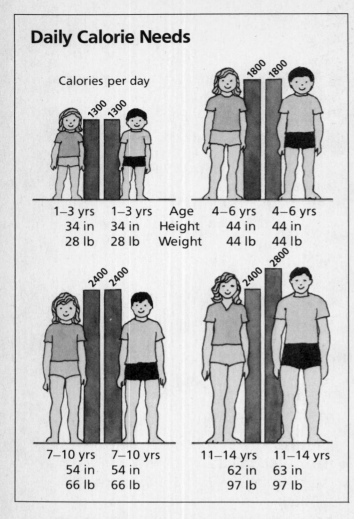

Calories per day

		Age		
1–3 yrs 34 in 28 lb	1–3 yrs 34 in 28 lb	Age Height Weight	4–6 yrs 44 in 44 lb	4–6 yrs 44 in 44 lb
7–10 yrs 54 in 66 lb	7–10 yrs 54 in 66 lb		11–14 yrs 62 in 97 lb	11–14 yrs 63 in 97 lb

Each sentence below is false. Correct the words that are wrong. Then write the new sentence on the lines that follow.

1. For the first fourteen years, boys and girls need the same amount of food.

    _____

    _____

2. In general, fourteen-year-old girls are heavier and taller than fourteen-year-old boys.

    _____

    _____

Secrecy Breeds Dis-ease

Jessie is in tenth grade. She loves English, but today her mind is far away.

She's scared.

Last night her mom and dad were louder than usual. The fights are getting worse. Yesterday some woman called and asked for Dad. She wonders who that was.

Last night Jennifer came in her room crying and asked to sleep with her. She heard, too.

She knows Mom cries when she's alone. She can see it in her eyes when she comes home from school. She tried to talk to her, but she said, "It's not your problem, honey. It's nothing. It will pass." She wonders. She's worried. She hates to go home now. It's like a funeral parlor.

Every secret has a smell of its own that teenagers pick up like hound dogs. They know, and usually suspect the worst. In the end, secrecy always causes greater pain and hardship than telling the truth. It robs everyone of closeness. So isn't it better to share some of our problems with our children?

Write a few words to answer each question below.

1. Why was Jessie's mother upset?

    _____

2. What is the author's main point?

    _____

3. What do *you* think? Should a parent be open with a child? Why or why not?

    _____

    _____

Friends vs. Parents

Another way to show facts in picture form is a **graph**. This one is called a bar graph. It shows how students answered this question.

■ You have to decide something very important. Whom would you ask for help—your friends or your parents?

The white bars stand for those who said *parents.* The gray bars stand for those who said *friends.* The dotted bars stand for those who said *both.*

Find the numbers at the top of the bars. They tell how many students out of one hundred gave that answer.

Now find the numbers along the bottom of the graph. They show what grade the students were in.

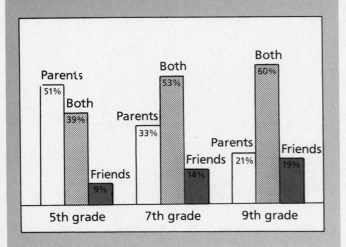

Write a short answer to each question.

1. According to the graph, how are fifth graders and ninth graders different?

_____

2. Note the changes the graph shows. Based on what you see, do you think most third graders turn to their parents or friends for help? Explain.

_____

The Day Care Debate

Most psychologists say a good day care center will not harm a child. But are some children too young for day care? Many experts say yes. Others say no.

Many psychologists argue that children under three should be at home. A young child needs constant love from one person. That love helps the child learn to trust others. It may confuse a child to be cared for by several people.

Others believe even babies will do fine in day care. What matters is that someone loves and cares for the child. It is best to have one adult for every two to three children. That way, each child gets more attention.

It's also good if the center is small. If one baby is sick, others may get sick, too. Children in day care get sick more often than children at home. In a small center, a baby is less likely to get sick.

Most experts say day care is fine for a child over three. But for younger children, the debate goes on.

Write a short answer to each question.

1. What is the main idea of the passage?

_____

_____

2. Why do children in day care get sick more often than children at home?

_____

3. Suppose you had to find a day care center for a baby. According to the passage, what kind of center should you look for?

_____

_____

Finding a Good Day Care Center

A good day care center can have many benefits for children. In a group, children learn how to get along with others. They play with toys that help develop body movements and visual skills. They may get a head start on numbers or reading.

Young children need lots of attention. One adult can care for 4 to 6 two-year-olds. By the time children are five, an adult can care for 8 to 10 children.

Do you have a child who needs day care? Here is a checklist of things to look for.

_____ Is the center licensed with the state or an agency?

_____ Can parents visit at any time?

_____ Are there enough adults so that each child will get attention?

_____ Is the indoor space big enough?

_____ Can children play outdoors?

_____ Are the adults warm and friendly?

_____ Do the adults talk a lot with the children?

_____ Are there stimulating toys that the children will enjoy?

Answer the following questions with a few words or a sentence.

1. In the first paragraph above, what three benefits of day care are listed?

   a. _____

   b. _____

   c. _____

2. A day care center in your city is always low on money. How might this affect the quality of the center?

   _____

   _____

   _____

A Test-Taking Tip

The GED Social Studies Test will have readings and graphs like the ones in this lesson. The questions will be multiple-choice. You can get ready for the test by trying a few multiple-choice questions.

Read all the answer choices. Choose the best one to answer the question. Fill in the circle for the answer you chose.

GED Warm-up

According to the article above, the best day care center is one that has
(1) a friendly staff with people who can spend time with each child
(2) a well-paid staff with people who have studied child psychology

The Active Reader

Self-Checking and Self-Correcting

Picture It

Roy quickly looks over his company's ad for a new salesperson. "Do I fit the bill?" Roy wonders. "Neat. Friendly. Get goer." Roy does a double take. "Get goer?" he thinks. "That can't be right." So he reads the ad again, this time more slowly. On the fourth line, he finds *go-getter*. "That's more like it," thinks Roy.

The better Roy understands what the company wants, the better his chances are for landing the job. It pays for him to check his understanding of the ad. Then he can correct his mistake.

You, too, can improve your understanding of what you read. Just follow the steps Roy used.

1. Set a purpose for reading.
2. Check your understanding.
3. Correct your mistakes.

Here's an Example

Read the title of the paragraph below to find out its subject. Then ask yourself what you want to know about this subject. For example, you might ask "Do any of my friends behave like show-offs?"

Show-offs

■ Show-offs try to appear important. They brag about their wealth, then prove it by telling the cost of their home and furniture. They buy fancy cars to show off, not for transportation. In general, they look for well-known labels rather than for well-made goods. After all, labels impress them. Their goal is to impress everyone they meet.

Now check your understanding by answering the following questions:

■ Do I know what the paragraph is about?

If I do, then I can underline the sentence that states the main idea.

The **main idea** is the most important point the author is making. You can usually state it in a sentence. It sums up all the pieces in the paragraph.

- Do I understand all the major points it makes?

If the answer is yes, then I can put numbers next to the major points.

- Do I understand all the important words in the paragraph?

If the answer is yes, then I can circle those words and define them.

Did you answer *no* to any of the above questions? Then read the tips below.

- Read the paragraph again. This will give you a second chance to find its main idea.

In this case, the main idea is stated in the first sentence: *Show-offs try to appear important.*

- Read more carefully than the first time.

Divide the reading into parts. For instance,

1. show-offs brag about their wealth
2. they buy cars for show
3. they buy well-known labels to impress people

- Figure out the meanings of new words.

If you don't know the meaning of *impress,* for example, use hints in the reading to help you. Or find the meaning in the dictionary.

- If you need it, get help from someone, such as a teacher or family member.

For example, you may not understand how labels can impress people. Someone else can point out that many jeans, scarves, and even sheets have the names of their famous designers on them. These names are in full view. They also mean a high price tag.

Finally, answer the question you asked before you started reading. Do your friends brag about the cost of their homes and furniture? Do they buy cars for show? Do all their things have well-known labels?

Working It Out

Claire also read the paragraph under Here's an Example. After reading the title, Claire asked herself, "How do show-offs behave?" Before answering her question, however, Claire felt she needed to understand the reading better.

1. For instance, Claire was not sure what *transportation* meant. So she looked it up. On the lines below, write what Claire found. Look for clues in the sentence. Use a dictionary. Or put down the meaning if you already know it.

_____

_____

2. Claire thought the paragraph said that show-offs look for well-made labels. But that didn't make sense. So Claire read the paragraph again. On the lines below, copy the sentence that would help Claire clear up her mistake.

_____

_____

3. Claire wanted to know how show-offs behave. How do you think Claire answered her question?

_____

_____

Personality

Before You Read: Thinking About Personality

In this lesson, you will read about personality. It is the quality that makes one person different from another. As you read, you will learn how personalities are formed. You'll see how they show up in what people do and say. You even may discover something about your own personality.

What do you think when you read the word *personality*? Does *shy* pop into your head? In the circles below, write all the words that come to mind. Add circles if you need more.

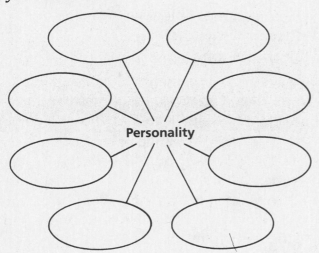

Personality

Probably you could come up with some words for the circles. Personality is a topic most people like to discuss.

Everyone wants to know what makes other people tick. Maybe sometimes you want to know what makes *you* tick, too!

Here's a way to organize the ideas you came up with. Take one of the words you wrote in the circles. Write it in the first blank below.

1. Some people are _____; but

   other people are _____ .

Fill in the other blank with a word that describes a different kind of personality. Here's one done for you.

Some people are <u>shy</u>; but other people are <u>outgoing</u>.

Try this with other words you wrote in the circles.

2. Some people are _____; but

   other people are _____ .

3. Some people are _____; but

   other people are _____ .

4. Some people are _____; but

   other people are _____ .

When you read the passages, look for the words you used on this page. You may find the authors used them too.

Working with Words

Some words in this lesson may be new to you. They are used in the sentences below.

She has all the personality **traits** to make a good actress.

He lined up his tools in **order** of their size.

Ahmed is often alone; he's an **introvert**.

Muma is an **extrovert**; she's never alone.

Maybe you have read or heard these words before. However, words can take on different meanings. These meanings often depend on the subject being covered. To find out what meanings are used in this lesson, add what you already know to the hints in the sentences.

Look at the first sentence again. Picture your favorite actors in your mind. Why do you like them? Is it their looks? their talent? the way they dress? All these could be called the actors' traits. Now try to write a meaning for *trait* below.

_____

_____

Perhaps you have heard *order* used in "law and order." In this phrase, *order* means "the state of things in which the law is obeyed." Or maybe you think of "command" when you read *order.* In the above sentence, *order* has a different meaning. Use the hints in the sentence to discover what order means here. Then write the meaning below.

_____

_____

The key clue to the meaning of *introvert* is its beginning—*in-.* Use this and the clues in the third sentence to help you finish these sentences. Circle the choice that makes more sense.

An introvert directs his or her thoughts (inward, outward).

An introvert is interested in his or her (friends' ideas, own thoughts).

Have you figured out what an introvert is? Write a meaning for *introvert* below.

_____

_____

The beginning of *extrovert* can help you figure out its meaning. *Ex-* means "out," as in *exit.* Can you guess what the opposite of an extrovert is? Now use this clue and the fourth sentence to help you figure out the meaning. Write the meaning below.

_____

_____

The definitions below are from the dictionary. Are they similar to the meanings you wrote?

Word Power

trait a quality of mind or character; feature; characteristic

order the way one thing follows another

introvert a person who is more interested in his own thoughts than in what is going on around him

extrovert a person more interested in what is going on around him than in his own thoughts and feelings

Reading on Your Own

A Successful Writer

It was something that most Americans dreamed of. Even from the earliest days of the country's history, it was true. All that anyone asked for was a chance at it. It was what America was all about: success!

During the 1860s and 1870s, Horatio Alger wrote about this idea. In all, he produced more than one hundred "rags to riches" stories. The following paragraphs are from one of those stories.

The scene: New York City. Dick Hunter is an orphaned teenager. He is trying to make his own way in the world. He is discussing his future with Mr. Whitney.

"You know in this free country poverty in early life is no bar to a man's advancement. I haven't risen very high myself," he added, with a smile, "but have met with moderate success in life; yet there was a time when I was as poor as you."

"Were you, sir?" asked Dick, eagerly.

"Yes, my boy. I have known the time when I have been obliged to go without my dinner because I didn't have enough money to pay for it."

"How did you get up in the world?" asked Dick, anxiously.

"I entered a printing-office as an apprentice, and worked for some years. Then my eyes gave out and I was obliged to give that up. Not knowing what else to do, I went into the country, and worked on a farm. After a while I was lucky enough to invent a machine, which has brought me a great deal of money. But there was one thing I got while I was in the printing-office which I value more than money."

"What was that, sir?"

"A taste for reading and study. During my leisure hours I improved myself by study, and acquired a large part of the knowledge which I now possess. Indeed, it was one of my books that first put me on the track of the invention, which I afterwards made. So you see, my lad, that my studious habits paid me in money, as well as in another way."

Write a few words to answer each question below.

1. What does the author say that Americans as a group value? Do you agree? Give reasons for your answer.

   _____

   _____

2. Mr. Whitney begins his story by saying that poverty is no bar to success in life. Do you agree? Why or why not?

   _____

   _____

3. Which of the following words describe the personality of Mr. Whitney in his early years? Explain your answers with facts from the reading.

   secure   hardworking   studious   clever

   _____

   _____

   _____

   _____

A Secure Way of Life

For thousands of years in India, the future of village people was pretty much decided at birth. Sons followed in their fathers' footsteps. If the father was a barber, for example, the son became a barber. In fact, the son served the same families that his father once served. Also, parents in Indian villages arranged the marriages of their sons and daughters. In short, the people in Indian villages had little say in the important decisions of their life. If they went along with this system, they were rewarded with support and respect.

Social scientists who studied the village people noted that they shared many of the same traits. For one, they showed little desire to change their life. Also, they didn't worry about making choices. The village people were sure of their place in the world. They were at peace with themselves.

Write a few words to answer each question below.

1. Would a potter from a village in India be likely to invent something new and make a fortune? Explain your answer.

   _____

   _____

   _____

2. Would a person from a village in India fit in a Horatio Alger story? Why or why not?

   _____

   _____

   _____

Birth Order and Personality

Some of the best-known ideas about personality came from Alfred Adler. Adler lived in the early 1900s. He believed that birth order plays a major part in shaping personality. Birth order is a person's place—oldest, middle, or youngest—among the family's children. Because of a person's place in the family, Adler reasoned, he or she is likely to be treated a certain way. As a result, the person is likely to treat others in certain ways. So a person's childhood decides, at least in part, how he or she behaves later in life. In general, oldest children grow up to be responsible achievers. Middle children often are skilled at dealing with people. Many youngest children have sunny outlooks. They expect people to take care of them. People, in turn, often do just that!

Explain why Adler's ideas about birth order might be correct. Use what you know about what happens in families.

1. Why would the oldest be the most responsible?

   _____

   _____

2. Why would the middle child be good with people?

   _____

   _____

3. Why would the youngest expect to be cared for?

   _____

   _____

The Responsible Oldest

From the time I was five, I can remember taking care of the children. I used to lie on my mother's bed and push my little brother back and forth in his carriage until he fell asleep. . . . By the time I was in third grade, I was always helping mother while the others played with the neighboring children. This made me old beyond my years, serious, and quite responsible for all that went on in the household. . . . Each Saturday, my mother went into the city six miles away for the groceries and stayed for the day. In the evening she and dad visited friends and came home at about midnight. From age fifteen to nineteen, I found myself responsible for seeing that the housework was finished, cooking lunch and dinner for the children, and caring for the newest baby. At night, I bathed six children, washed their heads, and tucked them into bed.

Write a few words to answer each question.

1. What kind of person does the author of this passage say she is?

_____

_____

_____

2. How do you think her younger brothers and sisters would describe her?

_____

_____

_____

What Being Shy Can Do

Shy people hold themselves back in many ways.

- They are afraid to meet new people and try new things.
- They follow the crowd rather than voice their own ideas.
- They hide their talents and strengths from others.
- They become wrapped up in how they're acting and feeling. Then they don't see how others are acting and feeling.
- Because they find it hard to speak up, they sometimes do poorly in school.
- They often feel sad and lonely.
- They bottle up their anger, which may someday explode.
- They often appear cold and unfriendly.

On the lines below, copy any of the following tips that would help people overcome shyness.

1. Hide your feelings.
2. Talk loudly enough to put your message across.
3. Take a dancing or acting class.
4. Pay closer attention to how you behave.

_____

_____

_____

_____

Using Eyes to Overcome Being Shy

I like a girl I go to school with, but I'm too shy to tell her how much she means to me. I've heard that you can tell someone whether or not you like them with your eyes alone. Is this true, and, if it is, how can I do it?

Studies have shown that when we like someone, or are interested in someone, we tend to look at them more often. We signal our likes and dislikes with our eyes. Literature is full of expressions that confirm this. "Her eyes never left his face." "He devoured her with his eyes." "He couldn't see enough of her." And so on. . . .

The less you like someone, the more you avoid looking at them. "I couldn't bear to look at her. I couldn't meet his eyes."

In a few words answer each question.

1. According to the reading, what are the eyes in the following picture "saying"? Copy the correct answer.

   a. "Wow! Am I surprised!"

   b. "I don't like you."

   c. "Be my friend."

   _____

2. Some people think looking straight at someone is disrespectful. What do you think? Do you use your eyes in the ways described in the reading? Give examples.

   _____

   _____

Extrovert or Introvert?

Underline the sentence that better describes you in each pair below.

1. **a.** I like to work with others.
   b. I like to work alone.
2. **a.** I often try new things.
   b. I stay with the tried and true.
3. **a.** I keep my feelings to myself.
   b. I eagerly share my feelings.
4. **a.** I am easily bored.
   b. I enjoy working on one thing for a long time.
5. **a.** I pay attention to details.
   b. I am interested in results.
6. **a.** I'd rather write than talk.
   b. I'd rather talk than write.
7. **a.** I enjoy big parties.
   b. I enjoy a movie with a friend.
8. **a.** I think before I act.
   b. I dive right into things.
9. **a.** I do most things to please others.
   b. I do most things to please myself.
10. **a.** I have many friends.
    b. I have a few very good friends.
11. **a.** I ask questions to find out what others want.
    b. I ask questions to understand things.

Answers and points: (1) a–1 b–2 (2) a–1 b–2 (3) a–2 b–1 (4) a–1 b–2 (5) a–2 b–1 (6) a–2 b–1 (7) a–1 b–2 (8) a–2 b–1 (9) a–1 b–2 (10) a–1 b–2 (11) a–1 b–2

Add up the points to your answers. Then match your total to the kind of personality your answers suggest.

11–16 points: You are an extrovert. You are interested in things, events, and people. You appear sure of yourself and are easy to get to know.

17–22 points: You are an introvert. You are interested in thoughts and ideas. You appear deep and a little mysterious.

Unhappy People

You can spot unhappy persons by the way they behave. Often the things these people do hide their true feelings. For example, a person who feels small tries to appear bigger than others. A person who feels worthless asks for everything he or she sees. Two other kinds of unhappy personalities are described below.

1. *The Empty Shell:* This kind of person always needs more. She eats whole batches of raw cookie dough in one sitting. And then does it again and again. She watches old movies until dawn. She buys and buys—shoes, makeup, jewelry, and everything else she can.

   The Empty Shell has trouble becoming close to people because she doesn't like herself. She thinks life with one person would be boring. So she says good-bye to a boyfriend as soon as he says "I love you." She's really afraid he'll find out she's worthless. Naturally, she always feels empty and bored. This makes her touchy. She blows up anytime life slows down. She starts to feel that she actually is no good!

2. *The Martyr:* This kind of person needs to impress people with how bad things are for him. When someone asks "How are you?" the Martyr says "I could be better." He drags himself around and always seems sad and tired. For the Martyr, the world is ugly. Every task is a chore. After a while, things get harder for him. He tells himself he can't: he can't enjoy, he can't work, he can't go on living.

A Test-Taking Tip

Some passages, like the one you just read, describe people or ideas. On the GED Test, you may be asked if someone else fits the description. Sum up the description in your mind. This will make finding the correct answer easier. For instance, you might say, ''The Empty Shell wants more. She feels empty and bored. And she may blow up at any time.'' You might sum up the Martyr this way: ''The Martyr is a drag to talk to. He feels sad and tired. And he has given up on life.''

GED Warm-up

Either the Empty Shell or the Martyr might make each statement below. Choose the type of person who would more likely make the statement.

1. "I feel like throwing things." Who probably said this?
   (1) the Empty Shell
   (2) the Martyr
   ① ②

2. "I just can't shop because nothing ever looks good on me." Who probably said this?
   (1) the Empty Shell
   (2) the Martyr
   ① ②

Locating Information

Picture It

There it was: the perfect bathing suit. Rosa spotted it in an ad for a new store. She rushed to the mall. Once there, however, Rosa didn't know which way to go. The mall had hundreds of stores. Where was the new shop?

Finally, Rosa noticed a directory. It listed stores under groups. She saw groups for food, clothing, shoes, and books. Rosa looked at the group called "Women's Clothing." It listed all the stores **alphabetically,** from A to Z. Each store on the list had a number. This number was used to show where the store was on the map of the mall. Now Rosa knew where to go.

When you look for information, do you ever feel the way Rosa did? It helps to know that information is often listed in a central place. You can find a phone number in the telephone book. You can find a word's meaning in a dictionary. You can find more information in a book. In every library, a list of books is kept in a **card catalog.** A card catalog is like the mall directory in many ways.

The card catalog holds cards for every book in the library. There are at least three cards for each book. These cards are filed alphabetically by subject, by author's name, and by the title of the book.

Here's an Example

Suppose you wanted a book about home repairs called *Complete Do-It-Yourself Manual.* Begin by finding the title card. It looks like this:

```
643.8   COMPLETE DO-IT-YOURSELF
REA     MANUAL
        Reader's Digest
           Pleasantville, New York,
           Reader's Digest Association
           (1983) 600 p.
             1. Tools   2. Home repairs
             3. Decorating inside and outside
```

The call number in the upper left-hand corner of the card matches one on the spine of the book. To find the book, go to the shelves that hold the books marked with 600 numbers. (Some libraries have put their card catalog information on computer. A librarian can help you learn to use this system.)

Sometimes you will want to find more than one book. Don't just note the first one you want. Write down each title and call number. Then look for the books all at once. This will save you time.

Once you have found a book, how do you find certain facts? Try looking at the Table of Contents. This is near the beginning of the book. The Table of Contents lists the chapter or section titles. The titles often tell what is in the book.

Working It Out

Below is part of the Table of Contents from the *Complete Do-It-Yourself Manual.*

Contents

In which section would you find the correct way to use a hammer? A hammer is a hand tool. So the right answer would be ''Section 1: Hand tools: How to choose and use them.''

The following questions ask for other facts you would expect to be in the book. Write the title of the section where you would find each answer.

1. Why should you replace a dull blade on your electric band saw?

_____

2. Is a folded wood rule or a steel tape rule better for measuring curves?

_____

3. Why are washers used under screw heads?

_____

4. How do you fell a tree with a gas-powered chain saw?

_____

5. When do you use a tack hammer?

_____

6. How is a flooring nail different from a common nail?

_____

7. Why do Phillips head screws have crossed slots?

_____

8. What jobs can an electric drill do?

_____

9. What is the best kind of bolt for hanging heavy mirrors?

_____

Society

Before You Read: Thinking About Society

Society is people living together. In this lesson, you will read about how people in society act toward one another.

Two social sciences study how people act. **Psychology** deals with the acts, feelings, and thoughts of individuals. **Sociology** deals with how people act with each other and in groups.

Don't let the long names scare you. Believe it or not, you already know something about these two sciences. Prove it to yourself by answering the following questions.

1. Some researchers watched groups of people talk to each other. They found that the most powerful person in the group always talked the most. Were they doing psychology or sociology?

   _____

2. Do you think people with power talk the most in groups? Base your answer on what you have noticed when people talk.

   _____

   _____

3. Another study found that beautiful people are treated better than plain

people in American society. What kind of study was this—psychology or sociology?

   _____

4. Do you think beautiful people are treated better than everyone else? Explain why you think as you do.

   _____

   _____

5. Another study showed children often feel guilty when their parents divorce. They blame themselves for the divorce. What kind of research was this—psychology or sociology?

   _____

6. What would you say to a child whose parents were divorcing?

   _____

   _____

You were right if you answered *psychology* for question 5. In the last lesson, you read passages about psychology. The answer to questions 1 and 3 was *sociology*. This lesson discusses sociology.

Working with Words

Some words you'll see in this lesson are used in the sentences below. They may be new to you. Or you may have come across them before. Try to figure out each word's meaning. Use what you already know about the word. Also, use the other words in the sentence to help you. And try to find a root word. A root word is a smaller word from which the longer word was made. It may give you a hint about the meaning of the new word.

An **authoritarian** boss believes that the most important trait in a worker is obedience.

A **democratic** boss treats workers as equals.

Children learn how to behave as they go through stages of **moral development.**

The root word in *authoritarian* is *authority. Authority* means "the power or right to give commands and enforce obedience." What other words do you think can be used in place of *authoritarian*? Make sure the new words do not change the meaning of the sentence. Write the words below.

_____

_____

Democratic is a form of *democracy.* Most likely, you connect *democracy* with the government of the United States. In a *democracy,* the government is supposed to treat everyone equally. What do you think *democratic* means when it describes a person rather than a government? On the lines below, describe someone as *democratic* in your own sentence.

_____

_____

Moral development is two words with one meaning. In your reading you will come across many such "combined words." Look at the words and sentences around the new term. They will help you guess how the words are used in your reading.

You may not be able to figure out the meaning of a term in a book you're reading. Then the best place to find the meaning is in the Glossary at the back of the book. A Glossary is a list of hard words with their meanings.

Look in the Table of Contents to see if a book has a Glossary. Suppose the book has no Glossary. Then look up each word of the term in the dictionary.

Try these steps to figure out what *moral development* means. Write your meaning below.

_____

_____

Look at the following definitions. Are the meanings you came up with close to these?

Word Power

authoritarian favoring obedience to authority rather than individual freedom
democratic treating other people as one's equals
moral development the stages in which people learn how to behave in society

---

Reading on Your Own

Moral Development in Children

In the 1950s Lawrence Kohlberg was a student at the University of Chicago. There he read that, as children grew, their views on right and wrong changed. Kohlberg wanted to test this idea. He also wanted to know the reasoning behind their views.

Kohlberg talked with fifty-eight boys. They were 10, 13, and 16 years old. To each boy, Kohlberg told a story such as the following:

■ The wife of a man named Heinz was dying. She needed a certain drug to save her life. The town druggist had just lately discovered this drug. So he was the only person who sold it. His price was $2,000 a dose. Heinz could raise only $1,000. He told the druggist that his wife would die without the drug. Then Heinz begged the druggist to lower his price. The druggist refused. So Heinz broke into the drugstore and stole the drug.

After telling this story, Kohlberg asked the boys: "Should Heinz have stolen the drug? Was it right or wrong? Why?"

Kohlberg was little interested in the answers to the first two questions. He was more interested in the answer to "Why?"

For example, suppose two boys answered, "Yes, Heinz should have stolen the drug." The first boy explained that Heinz needed his wife to cook and clean for him. The boy based his answer on how Heinz's action helped Heinz. Kohlberg thought this kind of thinking showed a low level of moral development. The second boy said the wife's life was in Heinz's hands. So he had to save her. This boy believed Heinz had a duty to his wife. Kohlberg thought this kind of thinking showed a high level of development.

Kohlberg divided the boys' answers into three levels. The levels were like steps. They went from a low level of moral thinking to a high level.

Kohlberg talked to the same boys every three years for the next twenty years. He asked them the same questions. Most of the boys changed their reasoning over time. Fifty-six of the 58 boys moved to a higher level of moral development. Kohlberg concluded that people did go through stages of moral development.

Write a short answer to each question.

1. Was Heinz right or wrong to steal the drug? Why?

_____

_____

2. Which of the following words describes the reasoning behind the first boy's answer? Explain your choice.
   a. selfish   b. caring

_____

_____

3. Do you agree that people's views of right and wrong change over time? Why or why not?

_____

_____

Lawrence Kohlberg's Levels of Moral Development in Children

Behavior

Level I

Children obey because they fear being punished.

Children value "pleasing myself" most highly. They sometimes want to help others too.

Level II

Children please and help people to win their approval.

Children respect authority. They value "law and order."

Level III

Children believe that laws decide what is right and wrong. Duty to others comes before the children's own needs and desires.

Children know laws and rules. But they decide right and wrong based on their own principles.

Write the level of moral development that each act described below shows.

1. Timmy ate his carrots rather than go without his dessert.

   _____

2. Stash took the blame for the spitballs rather than tell on his friends.

   _____

3. Janet often gave her mother flowers because they made her mother smile.

   _____

A Woman's Point of View

Carol Gilligan taught at Harvard with Kohlberg. She noticed that Kohlberg based his findings on the thinking of boys only. She also noticed that girls scored low when measured on Kohlberg's scale of moral development.

In 1982 Gilligan wrote *In a Different Voice.* In this book, Gilligan argues that Kohlberg did not take girls' views into account. So measuring girls on Kohlberg's scale was unfair.

Men, Gilligan wrote, are interested in rights and justice. Women, on the other hand, are more interested in caring and responsibility.

Gilligan used the following example to make her point: An eleven-year-old boy and an eleven-year-old girl were told Heinz's story. The boy believed that Heinz had a right to steal the drug. The boy reasoned that the wife's right to life was more important than the druggist's right to payment.

The eleven-year-old girl said that Heinz should not have stolen the drug. He might go to jail for stealing. Then he could not care for his sick wife. The girl believed that the druggist should have tried to help. In other words, Heinz had a responsibility to his wife. The druggist had a responsibility to others.

According to Kohlberg, the boy was on the highest level of moral development. The girl was only on level two.

Gilligan claims the girl was as developed as the boy. But the girl, like most women, viewed right and wrong in terms of caring rather than rights.

Write a few words to answer each question.

1. Why do you think Gilligan titled her book *In a Different Voice*?

_____

_____

2. Do you think the boy's or the girl's answer is better? Why?

_____

_____

3. In one or two sentences, state Gilligan's main idea.

_____

_____

4. Reread the last paragraph of the passage. Do you agree with Gilligan's claim? Why or why not?

_____

_____

Authoritarian and Democratic People

Listed below are two kinds of personalities. Brief descriptions tell how the people with these personalities treat others.

Democratic individuals treat people equally. In general, they are patient. They try to understand the desires of both sides when dealing with problems.

Authoritarian individuals favor powerful people. They may mistreat people who are less powerful than themselves. They want to give orders but also like to take them. They see people as either friends or enemies, all good or all bad. They fear people who are different from themselves.

Each statement below was made by either an authoritarian or a democratic person. Choose the more likely speaker. Write your choice on the line that follows.

1. "Children can make important points when talking to their parents."

_____

2. "The world has two kinds of people — the weak and the strong."

_____

The next questions ask for your opinion.

3. Are there problems with the democratic point of view? Explain.

_____

_____

4. Are there problems with the authoritarian point of view? Explain.

_____

_____

People Who Carry Orders Too Far

During the 1960s Stanley Milgram began a group of experiments. He wanted to find out how far people would go in obeying an authority.

The leaders of the experiments chose subjects to take part in the experiment. They placed subjects in front of clearly marked switches. Each switch was supposed to send a different level of electric shock. Really, no shocks were sent. But the subjects were told that persons in a nearby room would be shocked.

Many subjects pulled "high-power" (300-volt) switches. Then the persons in the nearby room pounded the wall. This signaled that they were in pain. Really, they had felt nothing.

At this point, the leaders ordered the subjects to raise the level of shocks. Most subjects thought they were causing real pain. But they raised the power anyway. The persons in the nearby room then became silent. They seemed to have passed out.

The leader told the subjects to keep on sending shocks. Most obeyed. More than six of every ten subjects kept shocking the persons in the next room.

Write a few words to answer each question.

1. What kind of personality do you think most of the subjects had? Why?

_____

2. Our country's safety depends on soldiers obeying their officers. When is obedience dangerous even in the army?

_____

Leaders Make or Break Boys' Clubs

In 1939 three researchers did an important study of groups. They trained several leaders of boys' clubs to act either authoritarian or democratic.

The authoritarian leaders planned and watched over the work that the boys did. The boys were allowed to talk to the leaders. But they could not talk to the other boys. Under authoritarian leaders, the boys worked very hard. But they did little on their own. When the leaders left the room, the boys dropped their tasks and horsed around. Working with one another was hard. Often the boys teased the weaker ones in the group.

The democratic leaders helped the boys but did not plan for them. These leaders worked with the boys as equals. They also welcomed give-and-take among the members. The boys with democratic leaders did not work as hard. But they were more interested in their work. When the leaders left the room, the boys kept on with their tasks. Yet they talked often and worked well with one another. The members almost never picked on the weaker boys.

Write a few words to answer each question.

1. Which kind of leader helped the boys make decisions? How?

_____

2. Would you prefer to work for an authoritarian or a democratic boss? Why?

_____

_____

The Foreman

Today the foreman walked up to my group as we were working. Then he began to lecture:

"Listen. I can't kick about your work. You turn out them rods fast enough and do a fine job. But you rush, so you can take time out to gab.

"You guys can't stand around and talk. Maybe you don't know how that looks to the big bosses who come down here. It looks like everything is going to hell. When they don't like what they see, I take the heat. And I'm not going to take it all. I'll pass it along to you guys if you don't help me out.

"Like I said, I can't kick about your work. All I'm saying is take it slower if you have to—so there ain't no time to loaf."

We hung our heads. Then we quietly went back to work. I felt guilty for slacking off. Still, I thought the foreman had singled us out unfairly. Then I saw him stopping at all the stations. "At least we're not the only ones," I said to myself. It struck me then that I was feeling and thinking like a kid. This boring work (painting stripes on rods) must be dulling my mind.

A Test-Taking Tip

When answering questions on the GED Social Studies Test, draw on what you already know. This could be general knowledge or facts from other readings on the test. For the questions that follow, think about other readings in this lesson. That may help you choose the correct answers.

1. How did the foreman show that he was an authoritarian leader?
   (1) He praised the workers' output.
   (2) He treated the workers as equals.
   (3) He told the workers to stop talking.
   (1)   (2)   (3)

2. How did the workers show they ranked lower than the foreman?
   (1) They painted rods.
   (2) They hung their heads.
   (3) They stood around and talked.
   (1)   (2)   (3)

In a few words, state your opinion about the questions below.

3. Why do you think the worker was feeling and thinking like a kid?

   _____

   _____

   _____

4. Was the foreman fair? Explain.

   _____

   _____

   _____

5. How would you handle this problem if you were the foreman?

   _____

   _____

   _____

   _____

Money and Power

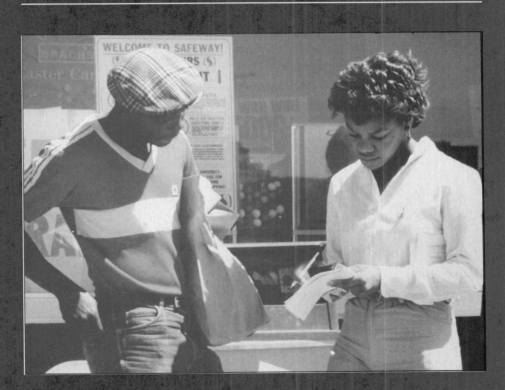

The Active Reader

Seeing Patterns in Social Studies

Picture It

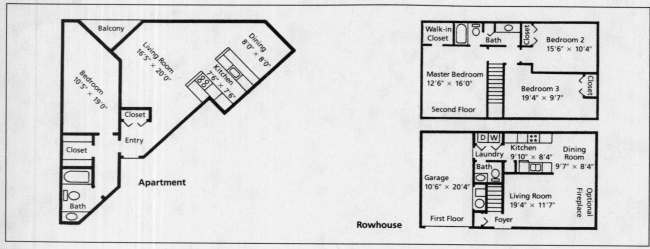

Steve and Sandy can't decide where to live. They like two places. One is a rowhouse. The other is an apartment.

Which is better? The floor plans above could help them compare the two places. For instance, the rowhouse has extra bedrooms. The apartment has a balcony.

Comparisons can help you too. You'll often see two things compared in social studies. Look for comparisons as you read.

Here's an Example

In social studies, tables often are used to compare things. (A table organizes information in rows and columns.) This table compares prices in 1945 and 1950.

You can see that prices in 1950 were higher than in 1945. You also can see that jean and gasoline prices went up about the same amount. So the table helps you see how prices in 1945 and 1950 were different and how they were the same.

Rising Prices, 1945 to 1950

	1945	1950
Monthly rent	$84.00	$107.00
Bag of groceries	6.80	10.12
Pair of jeans	7.73	9.80
Gasoline for a week	7.80	9.80

Graphs like the following also help readers to compare facts.

Number of Men and Women Employed in the United States 1960–1990

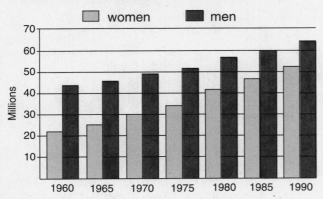

How many more men than women worked in 1990? How many more women worked in 1990 than in 1960? You can find answers to these questions and more on the graph.

Most often, comparisons are made in sentences. Look for words like these:

more In general, men earn more than women.

less Andrea eats less than her brother.

smaller This house is smaller than ours.

larger She wears a larger size than I do.

Another pattern you'll find in your reading is cause and effect. A **cause** is why something happened. An **effect** is what happened. Here's an example you might find in social studies.

■ Because more women worked in 1990 than in 1960, more day care centers opened.

What happened is that more day care centers opened. That's the **effect.** *Why* it happened is that more women worked. That's the **cause.**

The following words help you recognize cause and effect in a reading:

so We arrived late, so we sat in back.

thus Ice blocked the river; thus it overflowed.

since Since rain falls often here, crops grow fast.

because I received a raise because I work so hard.

as a result He practices every day. As a result, he plays basketball like a pro.

Working It Out

To help them decide where to live, Steve and Sandy have listed the questions below. Compare the floor plans on the facing page. Then answer each question with either *the rowhouse* or *the apartment*.

1. Which has more closets?

_____

2. Which has more room for parties?

_____

In the passage below, look for causes and effects.

■ In the 1980s, more and more women worked outside the home. As a result, the fast-food industry grew. No one had time to cook dinner anymore. So families ate out several times a week.

3. What was one effect of more women working?

_____

4. What caused families to eat out more often?

_____

Consumer Issues

Before You Read:
Thinking About Consumer Issues

The articles in this lesson give you hints on how to be a wise consumer. A **consumer** is a person who buys and uses food, clothing, or anything grown or made by someone else.

Jot down five to ten items or services you've bought in the last few weeks.

_____

_____

_____

_____

It probably didn't take you long. That's because you already are an experienced consumer.

Most likely you've handled your own money for years. Maybe you've found ways to make it stretch. Check any practices below that you follow.

_____ I look in the paper for sales before I shop for anything special.

_____ I collect discount coupons for products that I like.

_____ I compare costs when shopping for groceries.

_____ I often buy store brands because they're cheaper than name brands.

_____ I save some money each month in an interest-earning account.

Like most people, you probably welcome hints for making or saving money. So look ahead at the titles of the articles in this lesson. Which of the money facts they suggest interest you most? In the list that follows, circle the subjects you want to learn more about.

Planning for goals

Making a budget

Using credit cards

Cost of living around the world

Understanding warranties

Getting the most for your money

Buying a used car

Buying a house

Getting a loan

Now write questions about the subjects you have circled. For instance, you might write "How can I plan for my goals?"

_____

_____

_____

Look for answers to your questions as you read the articles.

Working with Words

Some words from this lesson are used in the sentences below.

The Duffys **budget** one-fourth of their money for food each month.

The **warranty** promises my new car will last 60,000 miles or 5 years.

Because of **inflation,** groceries cost one-tenth more than last August.

Read the sentences below. Circle the one that you think means the same as the first sentence above.

The Duffys spend most of their money on food each month.

The Duffys earn only enough to buy food each month.

The Duffys plan to spend the same amount on food each month.

In the first sentence above, what does *budget* mean? Write your definition below.

_____

_____

In the first sentence, *budget* is used as a verb. However, it also can be used as a

noun. An example is "Bonita hardly ever spends over her budget." Write a meaning for *budget* as a noun.

_____

_____

Most likely you have bought many things that have warranties. Read the second sentence. Then write a meaning for *warranty.* Hint: The sentence tells you that a warranty "promises."

_____

_____

The third sentence tells you that inflation has something to do with groceries costing more than in August. Now read this sentence: Because of inflation, I can no longer afford a large house. You now might guess that inflation is connected to rising costs in general. Write what you think *inflation* means.

_____

_____

Look at the following definitions. Are they close to the ones you wrote?

Word Power

budget 1) a plan that helps make the best use of money; 2) to make such a plan
warranty a promise that something is what it is claimed to be
inflation a general rise in prices

Reading on Your Own

Budgeting for Goals

What do you want over the next few years? The next fifty? You may not know exactly what your long-term goals are for the far future. But most likely you have some ideas. Perhaps you would like to marry, buy a house, or take a vacation. Your short-term goals—a new pair of shoes or a night out—may be clearer in your mind.

To reach most goals, you need money. It's likely you have more goals than money to pay for them. Budgeting will help you to reach more goals. It also will help you use your money to reach the most important goals first.

To set up a budget, first add up the money you earn or receive in a month. Subtract your *fixed costs*—costs such as rent that must be paid. Then figure out how much you spend on other costs, such as food, gas, clothing, and entertainment. You have some control over these. Are you spending too much on clothes or movies? Maybe you can cut back. This could help you save money for long-term goals.

Read the goals below. How long will each goal take to reach? Number the goals from the longest time (1) to the shortest (3).

_____ **1.** Each month Ed sets aside $40 toward the price of a new motorcycle.

_____ **2.** Twenty-six-year-old Barb deposits part of each weekly check in a retirement account.

_____ **3.** Belinda sets aside $25 each week so she can take her children out to a movie on Saturday.

Bill's Monthly Budget

The budget below sums up how Bill spends his money.

Take home pay:	$935.
Costs that are the same each month:	
Car payment/insurance	$110.
Rent	420.
Heat/electricity/telephone	60.
Savings	40.
Costs that change from month to month:	
Food	$150.
Clothing	70.
Car repairs and gas	45.
Other	40.
Total costs	$935.

Write a short answer to each question.

1. About how many years will it take Bill to save $1,500 to buy new furniture?

_____

2. Should Bill borrow from his rent or from his clothing money to pay for a date? Explain your answer.

_____

3. How do you think a budget helps Bill?

_____

_____

4. Do you think very poor people should have budgets? How about very rich people? Explain your answers.

_____

_____

Buy Now, Pay Later

Credit cards can help you in these ways:

1. You can use goods while you're paying for them.
2. Charging goods is like borrowing money. You could borrow money from a bank. But then you would have to pay interest. Interest is extra money that you pay to use the money you borrow. With a credit card, you can pay your charge account in full each month. Then you pay no interest.
3. You don't have to carry cash.
4. You can build a good credit rating. If you want a car loan or a mortgage to buy a home, you'll apply to a bank. The bank checks your credit record before deciding whether to give you a loan.
5. You use only one check to pay for several purchases. This can save you money. Often a bank will charge you money to write a check. So if you write one check instead of ten, you're ahead.
6. Checks may bounce. So many stores refuse your checks. But stores can quickly find out if your credit card company will back your charge. As a result, most stores will accept your credit card.

Credit cards have drawbacks. The following are just a few:

1. It's easy to spend more than you have with a credit card.
2. You can owe as much as 20 percent interest a month if you pay only part of your charges and end up paying more for something than if you had paid cash.
3. The interest rate may rise on your charges as the general interest rate changes at banks.
4. The amount you charge may get out of hand. Some people's monthly payments cover only their interest.

Write a few words to answer each question.

1. Sally charged most of the things she bought this month. So she saved $3 in check charges. How did she do this?

_____

_____

2. Washington pays on his charge account each month. But he has not paid yet for anything he bought last year. Why do you think this is so?

_____

_____

3. Your friend lives from payday to payday. After bills, she has $10 in her checking account. She has no savings. But she wants a fox fur coat. Right now a nice one is on sale for half price. She asks if you think she should charge it. What do you tell her?

_____

_____

_____

_____

Credit Card Slaves

Study the cartoon. Then answer each question below.

1. Compare the faces of the man signing his name and the woman at the left. Who looks greedy? Who looks frightened? Why do they look that way?

_____

_____

2. Most of the figures in the cartoon stand for consumers. Why are they shown trapped in their credit cards?

_____

3. Is the artist who drew this cartoon for or against credit cards? Explain.

_____

_____

Buying a Used Car

To get the best deal on a used car, follow these tips:

- **Buy from a dealer who has been in business a long time.**
  In general these dealers have tried to please customers. So the customers tell their friends to buy there. As a result, the dealers stay in business.
- **Hire a mechanic to look over the car.**
  If a dealer won't allow this, go elsewhere.
- **Ask about a warranty.**
  Get any promises in writing. You may get a 50/50 warranty. This means you have to split the costs of repairs that the dealer makes. You may have to buy a car "as is." Then you get what you see.
- **Look the car over closely.**
  Tires should be worn evenly. Put a penny in the tread. It should reach Lincoln's hair. Otherwise, the tires are not good. Hoses should be free of cracks. These are signs of old age. Oil spots on the ground mean a leak somewhere. Rust spots mean the car will have a short life.

For each effect below write a cause.

1. A good dealer attracts new customers because

_____

2. George had to pay one-half the cost of repairs on his used car because

_____

Checking Warranties

You save money by buying goods that last. Checking warranties can help you get your money's worth. Many products come with a warranty. In general it promises that the product will work for a certain time. Look closely at a warranty before you buy. Otherwise you may be sorry if the product breaks down.

An **implied warranty** isn't stated. It is an understanding between buyer and seller. It means that a product must work the way it is supposed to. Ovens must bake. Knives must cut. This kind of warranty does not cover goods bought "as is." These words tell the buyer that the goods may be damaged. They have no warranty.

The promises in an **express warranty** are spelled out. They are either written or spoken.

A written warranty is easier to prove than a spoken one. And you may have to prove it if something goes wrong with the product. But make sure you understand the fine points. For example, how long does the warranty last? What is covered?

Suppose a warranty is spoken. Then you must separate sales chatter from real promises. "You'll love this suit" promises nothing. "These towels are 95 percent cotton," however, has to be true. Otherwise you should get your money back.

Write a few words to answer each question.

1. What is an implied warranty?

_____

2. Which is better—a written or spoken warranty? Why?

_____

_____

Comparing Costs of Living

How would you spend your money if you lived in another area of the United States? The table below gives you some idea. It shows how much a family of three spent in 1991 to buy certain goods and services.

	Northeast	Midwest	South	West
Housing	$9,252	$7,334	$7,370	$10,142
Utilities	2,006	1,808	1,905	1,740
Food	5,020	4,214	4,140	4,727
Health Care	1,453	1,654	1,748	1,619
Clothing and Services	1,344	1,188	1,116	1,254
Entertainment	1,211	1,335	1,314	1,375

1. Which area's families spent the most on housing?

_____

2. Which two areas had health costs that were the most similar?

_____

3. Which area's families spent the least amount on clothing and services?

_____

4. If you were on a fixed income, in which two areas would your money go the furthest? Explain.

_____

_____

Buying a House

Finally, you find a house you like. You have the money for a down payment. Like most people, you don't have enough cash to pay the whole price of the house. So you go to a bank to get a mortgage.

A **mortgage** is a loan contract. It states how much money the bank or lending company will lend you. It also tells the rate of interest you'll have to pay. You agree to make payments over a certain time period. This time may be as long as 30 or 40 years.

You go to several banks. Finally, you find the kind of loan that meets your needs. So you fill out a loan application. You pay a couple hundred dollars just to ask for the loan. The bank keeps this money—even if it turns you down for the loan.

The bank loans money only to people who can make the payments. So it finds out how much money you earn and how much you owe.

The bank decides to give you a loan. But a loan does not cover all your home-buying costs. You have to use your own money for some costs. For instance, you should pay for a home inspection. The inspector will tell you what condition the property is in. You may pay for a title search. This service makes sure the present owner has the right to sell you the house. You also pay for a survey. This service tells you exactly where the land you are buying begins and ends. You also may want to pay a lawyer to look over the forms.

Now all the forms have been filled out. So the bank sets a time for the **closing**. A closing is a meeting where you sign paper after paper. These papers protect the bank first and you second. At the closing, you pay the state for recording your deed. You pay real estate taxes too. You also pay the down payment. Now the house is yours!

A Test-Taking Tip

The answers to multiple-choice questions often differ by only one or two words. Pay close attention to those few words. They could make the difference between a right answer and a wrong one. The following sentences are examples:
In times of inflation, prices decrease.
In times of inflation, prices increase.
Only the last word in each sentence is different. Yet the words have opposite meanings. The first sentence is false. The second is correct. So you see, one word can mean a lot.

GED Warm-Up

1. A mortgage is a contract that states
   (1) that you want to borrow money
   (2) where your land begins and ends
   (3) how much money the bank lends you
   ① ② ③

2. What happens if the bank turns you down for a loan?
   (1) It keeps your application money.
   (2) It returns your application money.
   (3) It doubles your application money.
   ① ② ③

3. Who most likely would meet with you at the closing?
   (1) the seller and the surveyor
   (2) the seller and an agent of the bank
   (3) the title searcher and an agent of the bank
   ① ② ③

Predicting Outcomes

Picture It

Francesca always surprises her customers. She knows their names before they tell her. She knows their plans for the future. Without magical powers, she couldn't possibly know the things she does. Or could she?

Really, magic has nothing to do with Francesca's "fortune telling." She's not a witch, she's a watcher. She notices details. Then she uses them to predict many things correctly.

You too can make predictions. You might guess the correct way to say a word. Or you might guess what comes next in a reading. Good readers are good guessers.

Good guessers can make mistakes. But they are quick to notice them. Then they correct their mistakes. How? By making another guess and checking to see if it's correct. You can expect to make a lot of mistakes before you finish reading. Only when you finish reading can you be sure about what you've read.

Here's an Example

Read aloud the following sentence: Jerzy opened his presentation with a bow. Suppose you say *bow* so that it rhymes with *toe*. Then the sentence would mean "Jerzy opened his presentation with a tied and looped piece of ribbon." However, that doesn't seem right. If you say *bow* so that it sounds like *cow*, the sentence makes more sense. The word can be read more than one way. You chose how to read it. So you made a kind of prediction.

Another way to predict is to tell what you think comes next. You base this on what you already have read. Try this kind of prediction with the next reading.

■ Rodolfo Garcia has been interested in politics since he was in grade school. After school, he would go to city hall to listen to council meetings.

He enjoyed hearing government in action. He listened to the government officials argue about the best ways to spend taxes and to help the city grow.

The rest of the reading tells what Garcia did when he grew up. Can you predict what it says? Underline hints in the reading that can help you decide.

You may make several guesses. He could have become a teacher of government. He could have become a reporter on government affairs. Or he could have run for office. The reading doesn't show that Garcia is interested in teaching or writing. So "officeholder" is the most likely choice. Now read on to see if you're right.

■ In 1984 voters in Hialeah and nearby towns elected the 21-year-old Garcia to the Florida legislature. He is the youngest lawmaker ever to serve in Florida.

Working It Out

Look at Francesca and her customer in the picture on page 45. Now read below what Francesca is saying. Use hints in the picture and in the "fortune" below to help you answer the questions that follow. Also remember that Francesca often adds what she already knows to what she sees.

■ Welcome, Mrs. Kowalski. May I call you Pamela? I can see that months of minute planning for meetings and speeches are over for you. You have helped elect a man to office. The man is your husband. His name begins with an *S*. It's Sam, Sandy—no, Stan. I see

you handing Stan a present. Around you are balloons and cheering people. It looks like some kind of gathering.

1. How did Francesca know the woman's first name?

_____

2. Why did Francesca connect the woman with the Kowalski campaign?

_____

3. Francesca already knew that Stan Kowalski ran for office and that he had a wife named Pamela. How did Francesca most likely get these facts?

   a. by looking at papers in her customer's purse

   b. by reading news articles about the election

4. Which of the following pronunciations and meanings suits *minute* as used in the second sentence of the passage?
   a. (mī nüt') detailed

   b. (min' it) 60 seconds

5. Which kind of gathering will Francesca say that the woman will attend?
   a. birthday party

   b. victory party

See if your answer to question 5 is correct. Read the ending of Francesca's "fortune."

The gathering is a victory party. Give your husband my best wishes when you see him there.

Taking Part in State and Local Government

Before You Read: Thinking About Government

The articles on the next few pages discuss voting and government. You will read about people active in state and local governments. You will read ideas and facts about voting and politics.

What do these subjects have to do with you? More than you may think. For example, what would you do if a fire started? Would you call the White House? Would you ask your neighbors to put out the fire with their garden hoses? Most likely you would do neither. You would call the fire department. The fire department is run by your local government.

State and local governments provide fire protection and many other services. And your tax money pays for these services.

You pay all kinds of taxes. Some taxes, such as your federal income tax, go to the federal government. But other taxes go to the state and city or community you live in. For example, many states collect an income tax. They also collect a sales tax when you buy goods. Towns, cities, and counties collect property taxes.

You have a right to choose the people who will spend your tax money. You can vote. Your vote helps decide who will run the government.

Look at the boxes below. Use them to list all the elected state and local officeholders you can think of. Put the most powerful officials in the top boxes. Put the lesser ones in the bottom boxes. The first box has been filled in for you.

governor

On the next page is a list of questions many voters have asked. Check any that you are interested in.

_____ Have people like me always been able to vote?

_____ Why should I take the trouble to vote?

_____ How can public officials help me?

_____ What can I do about a public official I don't agree with?

_____ What can I do about unfair laws?

Look over the titles in this lesson. Do you think the articles will have answers to the questions you checked? What other questions do the titles suggest to you? Write any new questions below.

_____

_____

As you read, try to find facts and ideas that will help answer your questions.

Working with Words

Some words you'll see in this lesson are used in the sentences below. Draw on what you know to help you define each word. But also use the clues in the sentences.

Write your **representative** to complain about the latest tax hike.

Fifty new voters were recorded during the town's latest voter **registration** drive.

The mayor's son entered **politics** just as his father had.

How many smaller words can you find in _representative_? List the ones you see on the lines below.

_____

_____

One word you may have written is _represent_. _Represent_ means "to act in place of; speak and act for." The ending _-ative_ turns _represent_ into a noun. Add these facts to the hints in the sentence. Now write a meaning for _representative_ on the line below.

_____

You can figure out the meaning of _registration_ in much the same way. It contains the verb _register_. This word means "to have one's name written in a list or record." The ending _-ation_ is often used in nouns. What do you think _registration_ means?

_____

The key to the meaning of _politics_ is in the third sentence. The son's father was a mayor. A mayor works in city government. The sentence doesn't tell you that the son's job is connected to the city. But what does it tell you about how the son makes a living? Write your answer below. It should be close to the meaning of _politics_.

_____

Look at the definitions below. Are they close to the ones you came up with?

Word Power

representative a person appointed or elected to act or speak for others
registration the act of listing or recording
politics the work of government

Reading on Your Own

American Voters Over the Years

1776 Most states limit the vote to free white men who own land and who are 21 or older.

1789 New Jersey is the only state that allows women to vote.

1807 Women lose the right to vote in New Jersey.

1860 All free white men 21 or older can vote. Only five New England states allow free African American men to vote.

1870 After the Civil War, African American men win the vote.

1900 Women in only four states—Colorado, Idaho, Wyoming, and Utah—can vote in all elections.

1920 Women win the right to vote in all states, after a long fight.

1924 The Indian Citizenship Act gives Native Americans the vote.

1965 African Americans in the civil rights movement win passage of the Voting Rights Act. It forbids states to ask voters to pass reading tests.

1971 The voting age is lowered to 18.

Write a short answer to each question.

1. Which group of Americans has been voting longest?

_____

2. How would you feel if you couldn't vote?

_____

_____

Voting Power

As a citizen of the United States, you live in a democracy. This means you have a voice in your government. You can elect representatives. You can tell them what you want done. And you can replace them if you don't like what they do.

Political leaders listen to public opinion. They read their mail. They do polls to find out what people want. Often they make decisions based on what they think most voters want.

Your vote has more power when joined with others. Many times a group of people with a common interest has elected a new leader.

Find out who is running for office in your state and city. Find out who represents your interests. Then vote. Your vote could make a difference.

In a sentence or two, answer these questions about the passage above.

1. Why are the officials mentioned in the passage called *representatives*?

_____

2. Why does the author believe your vote will make a difference?

_____

_____

3. Do you agree that your vote will make a difference? Why or why not?

_____

_____

A Voter's Registration Card

A card like the following is given to everyone who signs up to vote. It proves that a voter lives in the area where he or she votes. Registration helps stop people who live outside a city or state from voting in its elections.

```
Verification of Registration        William G. Rummel Executive Director
ISSUED BY THE BOARD OF
ELECTION COMMISSIONERS              Joseph Schneider
Room 308, City Hall,                Presiding Judge County Division
Chicago, Illinois 60602             Circuit Court of Cook County

PRECINCT
WARD 5 PRECINCT 15


JANE DOE
5201 S BLACKBERRY AV
        APT   21E
CHICAGO, IL   60615


(SIGNATURE)  Jane Doe
```

Write out your answer to each question.

1. In addition to her name, what other fact about Jane Doe is important for the voting commissioners to know? Why?

   _____

   _____

2. Which part of the city of Chicago does Jane Doe vote in?

   a. Cook County

   b. Precinct 15

   c. Illinois

   _____

Why Many People Don't Vote

One-third of all Americans do not vote. Many people vote only in national elections. For a state or local election, the voting rate is very low. Why don't people vote? Here are some reasons they give.

1. "Why should I vote? Someone else's vote will cancel out mine."

2. "Government doesn't affect me. Why should I care who's in office?"

3. "Politics is over my head. I don't understand enough about it to vote."

4. "Public officials don't care what I think. Why should I bother to vote?"

5. "Political parties are all the same. They don't offer real choices."

6. "The rich get richer and the poor get poorer. My vote isn't going to change things for people like me."

Choose three of the reasons above. Write their numbers on the lines below. Tell whether or not you agree with each one. Explain your answers.

_____

_____

_____

_____

_____

_____

How Many People Vote in Presidential Elections?

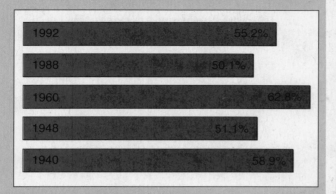

Year	Percentage
1992	55.2%
1988	50.1%
1960	62.8%
1948	51.1%
1940	58.9%

In 1992 only 55.2 percent of Americans who could vote did so. This was much lower than the percentage of people who vote in most other democratic countries.

There are several reasons for the difference. In some countries, everyone must vote, by law. Americans must register to vote, and registration can be difficult. You can't register on Election Day, so you must think early about voting. You also have to find out where to register and then get to that place. For some people, this is not an easy task.

If registration were not required, more Americans might vote.

Answer these questions in a few words.

1. In which year shown on the graph did the largest percentage of Americans vote?

_____

2. What does the author say is the main reason so few Americans vote?

_____

3. Do you agree with the author?

_____

Saving Wildlife

In the early 1970s, a group in Dade County, Florida, planned to build one of the world's biggest airports. They wanted to build it six miles north of the Everglades National Park. The builders spent $13 million laying a runway. This was only the beginning.

Alarmed citizens said draining land to build runways would draw water from the park. Also, fumes from jets would poison the air and water in the Everglades. In time, the park plants and animals might die. The builders called the concerned citizens "butterfly chasers."

The builders did not seem concerned about the park. This angered groups such as the Audubon Society who were working to preserve Florida's wildlife. These groups persuaded the national government to step in, since the Everglades is a national park. The government stopped the building of the airport.

Circle the letter by the correct answer.

1. How did the concerned groups probably persuade the government to help?

    a. by promising to vote for representatives who supported them

    b. by threatening to bomb the runways if building did not stop

2. Which is the more likely ending to the reading?

    a. Today the airport covers thirty-nine square miles.

    b. Other runways never were added on to the first.

An Indiana Mayor

In 1967 voters in Gary, Indiana, elected Richard Hatcher their first African American mayor. A major goal of Mayor Hatcher was to help the city's poor. He obtained millions of dollars from the government. The city used the money to build homes for people with low and middle incomes.

Hatcher also helped Gary's jobless and minorities. He set aside city money to train people and find jobs for them. Some trainees were put to work paving city streets. Others filled openings in the Gary fire and police departments. A 1983 report on sixty-two cities showed that, during the Hatcher years, Gary handled its money better than any of the other cities.

Write a short answer to each question.

1. How did helping Gary's jobless also help the other people in Gary?

   _____

   _____

2. Why might a taxpayer in Texas object to Mayor Hatcher's programs?

   _____

Winning Civil Rights

During the 1950s African Americans decided to change "Jim Crow" laws in Montgomery, Alabama. These laws separated African Americans and whites. One law stated that African Americans on buses had to give up their seats to whites.

On December 1, 1955, an African American woman named Rosa Parks boarded a bus. She took one of the few remaining seats. A white man entered the bus. He demanded that Parks give up her seat to him. Parks refused. She was arrested.

African Americans in Montgomery were angry about the way the bus company treated Parks and other African Americans. So they decided to boycott the bus company. They did not use the buses for about a year.

In 1956 the Supreme Court of the United States settled the problem. It ruled that the bus company had been denying African Americans their civil rights. These are rights that belong to all American citizens.

The victory in Montgomery gave African Americans across the United States courage. They joined together and demanded equal rights. As a result, they made many gains. One such gain was the Voting Rights Act of 1965. It made registering to vote as easy for African Americans as it was for whites.

Write out your answer to each question.

1. What does *boycott* mean?

   a. to not deal with a business

   b. to discuss both sides of a problem

   _____

2. What did the bus company most likely do after the Supreme Court's ruling?

   _____

Huey Long of Louisiana

In 1924 Huey P. Long was a favorite public figure in northern Louisiana. But few people in southern Louisiana had heard of Long. From 1924 to 1928, Long visited the southern part of the state. There he made speeches like the one he gave under an oak in St. Martinville.

The St. Martinville oak was a landmark. Beneath this tree, Evangeline was supposed to have waited for her true love. Evangeline was the heroine in a poem by the American poet Longfellow. Her lover never came.

In his speech, Long said:

■ . . . Evangeline is not the only one who has waited here in disappointment. Where are the schools that you have waited for your children to have, that have never come? Where are the roads and highways that you send your money to build, that are no nearer now than ever before? Where are the [hospitals] to care for the sick and disabled? . . .

1. Which of the following sentences is the most likely ending to the reading?
   (1) Words like these helped elect Long governor of Louisiana in 1928.
   (2) Louisianans were unimpressed because few knew about Evangeline.
   (3) Huey Long lost votes in northern Louisiana because he seldom spoke there.
   ① ② ③

2. What group's interest did Long address in his speech?
   (1) wealthy Louisiana taxpayers
   (2) parents of school-age children
   (3) current Louisiana officeholders
   ① ② ③

3. How did Huey Long most likely hope to win votes in St. Martinville?
   (1) by appealing to disabled veterans from World War II
   (2) by praising the town's landmark oak
   (3) by recognizing the people's problems
   ① ② ③

Interpreting Tables and Bar Graphs

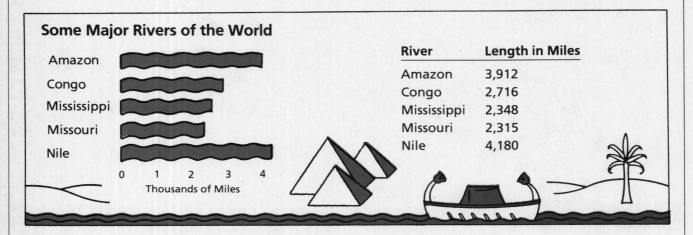

Some Major Rivers of the World

River	Length in Miles
Amazon	3,912
Congo	2,716
Mississippi	2,348
Missouri	2,315
Nile	4,180

Picture It

Look at the table and graph at the top of the page. They both show the same information. The **bar graph** on the left shows the length of five major rivers. It shows this in a picture form. Can you

pick out the longest river? _____
The Nile has the longest bar. That helps you see that it's the longest river.

    How long is the Nile? _____
Did you find this information on the bar graph or the table? It's easier to find the exact length on the **table.** It lists the lengths of each river. Tables and graphs both give information. But you read them differently.

Here's an Example

On the next page are a table and a graph that give facts about population, the number of people who live in a place. How can you tell? The words *population* or *people* are in the titles. The title almost always lets you know what kind of facts a table or graph covers.

    The numbers in the bar graph are **percents.** They stand for the number of city dwellers out of every 100 people who live in a country. For example, over 70 percent of the people in the United States live in cities. In other words, more than 70 out of every 100 Americans live in cities.

Population

Country	Total	City
	(in thousands)	
Indonesia	193,000	57,900
Japan	124,017	95,493
Kenya	25,241	6,563
Switzerland	6,783	4,070
Taiwan	20,658	14,873
United States	248,710	189,020

People Living in Cities

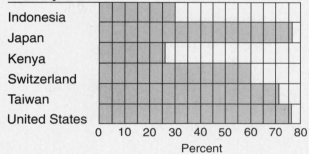

Country

Does the United States or Switzerland have a greater percentage of people who live in cities? You can quickly find the answer to this question on the bar graph. You don't even need to read the whole graph.

First, look at the length of the bar next to *Switzerland.* Then compare it to the bar next to *United States.* The bar next to *United States* is longer. So the United States has a greater percentage of city people than Switzerland does.

Suppose you wanted to know the *number* of Americans who live in cities. Then the table would be more useful than the graph. Place your finger on *United States.* Move it to the

right. Stop under the heading *City.* The number you are pointing to tells you what you want to know. More than 189 million people live in U.S. cities.

Working It Out

Study the table and bar graph again. For each question, decide where you can find the answer more quickly. Then write either *table* or *bar graph.* Also write the answer to the question.

1. Does Taiwan or Japan have a greater percentage of city people?

_____

2. Does Switzerland or Indonesia have more people living in cities?

_____

3. How many more Americans than Japanese live in cities?

_____

4. In which countries do more people live in cities than in the countryside?

_____

_____

_____

5. Does Kenya probably have more workers on farms or in factories?

_____

_____

Money and Class

Before You Read:
Thinking About Money and Class

The articles on the next few pages are about money and class. Some articles tell about how money is used. These articles are about **economic systems.** Economic systems are different ways to produce, buy, and sell goods and services. Other articles tell how money is connected to class. A **class** is a rank in society. For many years, people throughout the world have been divided into three general classes: upper class, middle class, and lower class.

Most likely you connect money with the upper class. Prove it to yourself. Read the following pairs. Then write *UC* in the blank before the item in each pair that you think is upper class.

_____ a Rolls Royce

_____ a Chevy Cavalier

_____ a French restaurant

_____ a greasy spoon

_____ a fur coat

_____ a cotton jacket

_____ a private hospital room

_____ a bed in a hospital ward

Now look over your choices. Most likely you have picked the one in each pair that costs more. What does this tell you? Maybe to you money equals class.

However, many people believe other things besides money decide a person's class. What are some of these things? Education and jobs are two factors.

You already have some ideas of how class is judged in the United States. Look at this list of jobs. Which do you think has the highest status? Number that 1. Number the next highest 2, and so on, down to the job that has the lowest status.

_____ taxi driver

_____ business leader

_____ teacher

_____ car mechanic

_____ pharmacist

_____ Supreme Court justice

_____ police officer

_____ shoe shiner

How did you rank the jobs? For instance, which did you rate higher, a police officer or a Supreme Court justice? Who was higher in your rating, a teacher or a business leader? Why? Based on your answers, what kinds of jobs do you think have the highest class in our society?

_____

_____

As you read, look for how others describe social class.

Working with Words

Some words you'll see in this lesson are used in the sentences below. You may have read or heard these words before. Feel free to use what you know to help you find the words' meanings. But also use the sentences in which the words appear to help you.

> Nicole gave the paychecks to her co-workers. At the same time, she **distributed** the summer vacation list.
> The **literate** adults in this country outnumber those who cannot read.
> Some people lost their jobs during the last **recession.**

Look at the first two sentences above. Nicole distributed the list at the same time that she gave out the paychecks. So you can guess that *distributed* means about the same as *gave.* Use the sentences to help you figure out a meaning for *distributed.* Write your meaning on the line below.

_____

The third sentence gives you a hint about the meaning of *literate.* The last few words describe the opposite of literate adults. What, then, are literate adults? Write your answer on the line below.

_____

The fourth sentence also gives you a hint. It tells you what happens during a recession. What would cause people to lose their jobs? The answer should describe a recession. Write your answer below.

_____

Look at the meanings below to see if your guesses were correct.

Word Power

distributed gave some to each; dealt out
literate able to read and write
recession a time when business activity is somewhat slow and some people are out of work

Reading On Your Own

Different Economic Systems

All people need food, clothing, and housing. But groups of people have just so many resources to meet those needs. So groups must decide what to do with their resources.

To decide, four questions must be answered. (1) What goods and services will be made or offered? (2) How many will be made? (3) How will they be made? (4) How will these goods and services be distributed?

The ways people answer these questions depend upon their economic system. The peoples of the world have many different values. So economic systems are different from country to country.

Some countries have mostly a **planned economy.** In these countries, the government decides what to make and how to make it. Imagine making a plan for all the jobs in a country. This kind of system is often called communism.

At times, the United States uses a planned system. But the United States, like many other countries, uses mostly **free markets** to answer the four questions. A market is the buying and selling of a good or service.

There are many markets. One is the labor market. In this market, business owners buy workers' time. If there are many workers and few jobs, the workers' pay will be low. If there are many jobs and few workers, pay goes up.

People who buy and sell have the most control in a market economy. No one knows for sure from day to day what goods and services will be in demand. So this kind of economy cannot be planned.

In the past many countries had a **traditional economy.** In these countries, custom decided the answers to the four questions. In other words, people did things as their families always had done. Today no country uses only a traditional economic system.

Write the kind of economy that is at work in each example below.

1. In the former Soviet Union, party leaders decided how many shoes were made and what stores would sell them.

   _____

2. Small-farm owners in Colombia raise corn and beans the same way their parents and grandparents did.

   _____

3. Many Americans bought running shoes in 1985. So factories made twice as many pairs in 1986.

   _____

4. The state of Indiana has built thousands of miles of highways since 1920.

   _____

5. In October 1929 thousands of people tried to sell their shares in companies. No one wanted to buy. So the stock market crashed.

   _____

The Economic Cycle in a Market System

3. Levi makes more jeans.

2. _____

1. Levi advertises more.

4. More fabric is ordered.

5. Work increases at fabric manufacturers.

6. _____

7. Workers work overtime on fabric.

8. Workers earn more money.

9. _____

Look at the picture above. Three steps have been left out. In their place are three blanks. After the correct number below, copy the sentence from the box that best fits each blank.

People spend more for wants.
People buy.
Workers are hired.

2. _____

6. _____

9. _____

The Changing U.S. Economy

For years, many Americans worked in factories. They built cars and machines. They worked in steel mills. They helped make clothing. Many of these jobs did not require much education. But they often paid very well. By the 1950s, most Americans had a high standard of living.

Then things began to change. Factories used more machines and fewer people. Japan and Germany sold high-quality cars and steel to Americans at low prices. Some factories closed or cut back on workers. Jobs in factories declined.

Jobs in services began to grow, however. Today, many people find work in sales. They care for the sick. They wait on tables. They program and repair computers. They work in office jobs. By the 1980s, more Americans worked in service jobs than any other jobs.

You don't need much education for some service jobs, such as work in fast-food restaurants. But pay is low in these jobs. If you want a service job that pays well, you need a GED credential, a high school diploma, or even a college degree. Education is one of the keys to moving ahead in today's work world.

Answer the following questions in a sentence or two.

1. What is the main change in the U.S. economy over the last 30 years?

_____

_____

2. Why is it often hard for an autoworker out of work to move into a service job?

_____

_____

Quality of Life

What makes a country rich or poor? One measure of a country's wealth is how well its people live. The **quality of life** in a country involves the welfare of its people: food, clothing, shelter, health, and security. As people earn more money, their quality of life tends to go up. They are able to buy goods and services they need to make their lives better.

However, several things besides income decide the quality of life in a country. One is the country's population density. This is the average number of people living in each square mile. If people are too crowded, housing may be hard to find. If people are too spread apart, the goods and services they need may be hard to get.

Health also helps decide quality of life. One measure of health in a country is the number of infants who die.

Finally, the number of people who can read is also important. Literate people can learn how to produce many kinds of goods and services. So a country with more literate people than another country generally has a better quality of life.

Use the passage and the table below to answer each question.

1. In Afghanistan, 164 out of every 1,000 infants die. In Japan, only 4 out of every 1,000 infants die. What does this suggest?

_____

_____

2. In Kenya, 50 percent of the people can read. In Taiwan, 90 percent of the people read. Which country probably produces a wider range of goods? Why?

_____

_____

3. In which country do men generally live longer than women? How do you know?

_____

_____

4. Which country does the table suggest has the highest quality of life? Explain your answer.

_____

_____

Country	Life expectancy (in years) M	F	Infant deaths 1991 (per thousand)	Persons per hospital bed	Adult literacy rate 1991 (percent)
Afghanistan	44	43	164	2,054	29
Japan	76	82	4	77	99
Kenya	59	63	70	737	50
Saudi Arabia	65	68	69	406	62
Sweden	75	81	6	148	99
Taiwan	72	78	6	232	90
United States	72	79	8.9	198	97

Jobs and Status

How a person earns a living often decides his or her class. This is in part because a certain level of income is tied to certain jobs. But it is also because people value certain kinds of work more than others.

The jobs that people value most are different in different countries. The table below shows the top twenty jobs in Sweden and the United States.

Sweden	United States
1. Professor	Supreme Court justice
2. Business leader	Doctor
3. Teacher	Nuclear scientist
4. Shipowner	Governor
5. Druggist	Professor
6. Banker	Lawyer
7. Colonel in the armed services	Architect
8. Shop owner	Business leader
9. Sea captain	Airline pilot
10. Barber	Banker
11. Jeweler	Sociologist
12. Carpenter	Teacher
13. Accountant	Accountant
14. Typesetter	Factory owner
15. Taxicab owner	Artist
16. Police officer	Labor official
17. Salesclerk	Electrician
18. Noncommissioned officer in armed forces	Machinist
19. Construction worker	Farm owner
20. Traveling salesperson	Newspaper writer

Use the "Jobs and Status" table to answer each question.

1. In what country do doctors have very low status?

_____

2. Why do you think teachers rank higher in Sweden than in the United States?

_____

_____

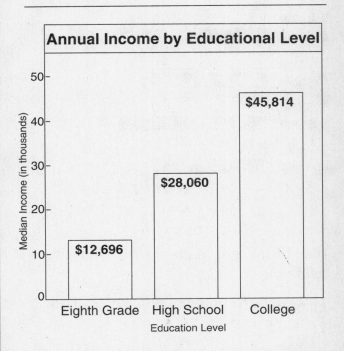

Use the bar graph above to answer the following questions.

1. On the average, how much more per year does a high school graduate make than a graduate of eighth grade?

_____

2. What general conclusion can you draw from the graph?

_____

_____

Income of Households, 1980 and 1990 (in constant 1990 dollars)

☐ = 1980
■ = 1990

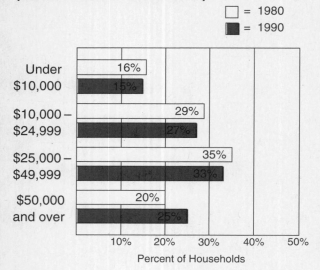

Percent of Households

Use the bar graph above to answer the following questions.

1. What percentage of households had incomes under $25,000 in 1990?

_____

2. Did the percentage of households with incomes under $10,000 increase or decrease between 1980 and 1990?

_____

3. Which income range includes more families than any other?

_____

4. According to this graph, how did household incomes change from 1980 to 1990? Explain your answer.

_____

_____

_____

_____

Are Americans Getting Richer?

Are Americans poorer or richer than they were 30 years ago? A new study has tried to settle this question. The study is not based on incomes. Instead it measures a family's present and future buying power. **Buying power** is the value of what a family buys each year and what it already owns.

The authors of the study figured wealth this way. First they averaged the value of homes, cars, furniture, bank accounts, and so on. Social security and pensions also were included. From the total, they took away the average amount American families owed and spent. They came up with the dollar worth of the average American family.

The study covers 1953 to 1987. It shows a steady rise in wealth between 1953 and 1970. In the 1970s, buying power fell. Wealth dipped because of inflation and recessions. However, in 1982, the average family's dollar worth again began to rise. It has kept on rising ever since. By 1987 the average family had a much higher buying power than in 1953.

GED Warm-up

Which of the following sentences does the study above support?

(1) Rich Americans outnumbered poor ones in the 1970s.
(2) Americans earned more money but bought less in 1953 than in 1987.
(3) Americans in general were better off in the 1980s than in the 1970s.
(4) More Americans bought houses in the 1980s than during earlier decades.

The Active Reader

Interpreting Flowcharts and Line Graphs

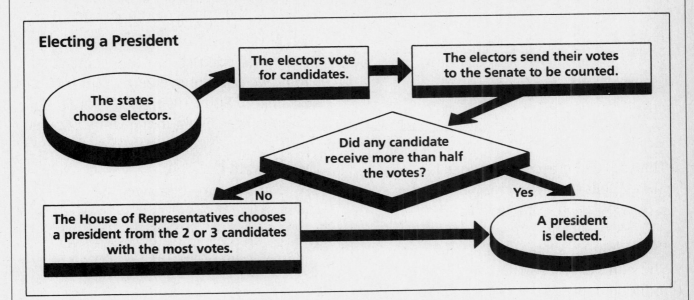

Electing a President

The states choose electors. → The electors vote for candidates. → The electors send their votes to the Senate to be counted. → Did any candidate receive more than half the votes?

No → The House of Representatives chooses a president from the 2 or 3 candidates with the most votes. → A president is elected.

Yes → A president is elected.

Picture It

Have you heard the saying: A picture is worth a thousand words? Imagine what you might learn from words *and* pictures! That's what flowcharts and line graphs are — words and pictures that explain facts and ideas.

Here's an Example

A flowchart uses words and shapes. These show the order of a set of steps.

Each of the shapes on a flowchart has a meaning. The arrows tell you in what order to read the steps. The ovals tell you where the chart begins and ends.

The boxes tell you what steps come next. Inside the diamonds are questions. Each question can be answered *yes* or *no*. The step that comes next depends on the answer to the question.

On this page is a flowchart. It shows the steps in electing the president of the United States. The first oval gives you the first step. It says, "The states choose electors."

Find the diamond. What is the question inside? The answers to the question are *yes* and *no*. What step comes next if the answer is *no*? What step comes next if the answer is *yes*?

A line graph does a different job. It shows changes over time. A line graph might track changes in a city's monthly temperatures. Or it might show a person's weight losses over several weeks.

United States Population (1986–1991)

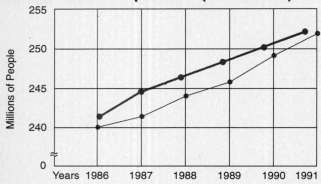

This is a line graph. What does it show? Its title tells you. The graph shows the U.S. population from 1986 to 1991.

Find the straight up-and-down line on the graph. This line is called the y-axis. The numbers along the line stand for millions of people. How can you tell? Read the label to the left of the numbers.

Look at the straight left-to-right line on the graph. This line is called the x-axis. The numbers below the line stand for years. The label tells you so.

Now look at the line that connects the dots. Notice that the line goes up from left to right. The direction of this line shows that the United States population grew between 1986 and 1991.

The graph also tells how many people lived in the United States during the

years listed along the x-axis. Here's how to find the number of Americans in 1991.

1. Place your pencil point on the line above 1991.

2. Move the pencil up to the dot.

3. Then move the pencil left to the y-axis. The pencil point now should be between 250 million and 255 million.

4. Divide the line between 250 and 255 into four equal parts.

Your pencil point should have landed about two parts above 250, or around 252 million. So in 1991, there were 252 million people living in the United States.

Working It Out

Use the flowchart to answer the questions below.

1. What step comes after the states choose electors?

_____

2. Suppose three people run for president. None receives more than half the votes. What happens next?

_____

3. What step ends the chart?

_____

Now look at the line graph.

4. How many Americans were there in 1987?

_____

5. How many more Americans were there in 1991 than in 1987?

_____

The Constitution

Before You Read: Thinking About the Constitution

Get ready to read some interesting facts about the Constitution. It is the American plan of government. Some articles in this lesson tell you how the Constitution began. Others tell what it says. And others show how it has changed.

Below is a list of events that led up to and followed the writing of the Constitution. Most likely you have heard of some of them.

Put the events in order on the time line that follows. Do not copy the words and years in dark print. But use the years in the sentences to help you.

The signing of the Constitution in 1787.

The Constitution becomes the law of the land **in 1788.**

Patriot leaders sign the Declaration of Independence **in July 1776.**

The Articles of Confederation becomes the new country's plan of government **in 1781.**

The first ten amendments are added to the Constitution **in 1791.**

1775 The Revolutionary War begins.

1776 _____

1781 _____

1783 The British surrender; war ends.

1787 The Constitution is written.

1788 _____

1789 Washington becomes President.

1791 _____

Does the time line raise questions for you? Such as, why did early American leaders get rid of the Articles of Confederation? Or what are amendments? Write any questions you may have on the lines below.

_____

_____

_____

_____

Look for answers to your questions as you read.

Working with Words

Some words you'll see in this lesson are used in the sentences below. You already may know these words. Use what you know to figure out what the words mean. But also use the sentences to help you with the words' meanings.

The central government oversees trade with other countries and **commerce** between states.
No part of the government can become too powerful because of the **checks and balances** in the Constitution.
Our state **legislature** passes hundreds of laws each year.

The first sentence has another word that means the same as *commerce*. Can you guess which one it is? Write the word on the line below.

_____

Checks has several meanings: marks, money orders, limits, restaurant bills, squares in a pattern. Which meaning is used in the second sentence?

_____

If things balance one another, they are equal in weight or amount. If parts of a government balance one another, what are they equal in? Hint: The answer is part of a word in the second sentence.

_____

Legis- is a Latin word that means "law." Add this fact to the hints in the third sentence. Then write a meaning for *legislature* below.

_____

_____

Compare what you wrote with the following meanings from the dictionary.

Word Power

commerce trade
checks and balances how the power of each of the three branches of government is limited by the other two branches
legislature a group of persons that makes laws for a state or country

Look for these words as you read. If you find other words you don't know, use the same process to figure out their meaning. Look at clues in the sentences around the word. Use what you know about the word. Make a good guess, and then see if your guess works in the sentence. If you're still stuck, look up the word in a dictionary.

Reading On Your Own

The Articles of Confederation

The first plan of government for the United States was the Articles of Confederation. Under this plan, each of the thirteen states made its own money. Each state also raised its own army. And commerce between states was not free. Each state taxed goods from other states.

The states were loosely joined under a central government. The central government could go to war and make peace. It could also set up post offices and settle trouble between states. However, the central government could not tax citizens, so it had little money.

Write a few words to answer each question.

1. Some states in the early United States did not accept other states' money. What problems could this make for traders and travelers?

_____

2. The central government under the Articles of Confederation did not have enough money to carry out its duties. Why was this so?

_____

Changing the Plan of Government

Some states had a hard time after the Revolutionary War. Massachusetts, for example, had little gold. So it could not print much paper money. People could not earn enough money for their labor. As a result, Massachusetts courts sent many people to prison for being in debt. Farmers were especially hard hit.

Many people thought the government of Massachusetts was being unfair. A Revolutionary War hero named Daniel Shays agreed with them. He led an army of farmers in debt. They wore evergreen twigs in their hats, just as they had done when they fought the British.

Shays and his followers marched to the courthouse in Springfield, Massachusetts. There they stopped the court from meeting. The governor sent an army to capture Shays and his men. Some of them got away. Shays ran to Vermont.

Many Americans felt sorry for Shays and the farmers. They blamed the trouble on the weak government under the Articles of Confederation. They thought the central government should print the country's money. The government was called a "Monster with Thirteen Heads."

In 1787 leaders from the states met to improve the Articles of Confederation. Instead, they wrote a new plan of government. This plan is the Constitution, which still rules our country today.

Write a few words to answer each question.

1. Do you think Shays and the farmers were right? Why or why not?

_____

2. Why would Americans call the government a "Monster with Thirteen Heads"?

_____

Representing the People

The Constitution set up a national legislature—the Congress—to make laws. The two houses of Congress are the House of Representatives and the Senate. The number of representatives each state sends to the House depends on the number of people in the state. But every state sends only two senators to Congress.

Over the past 200 years, the House of Representatives has increased from 59 to 435 members. The graph below shows how the Senate has grown.

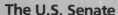

The U.S. Senate

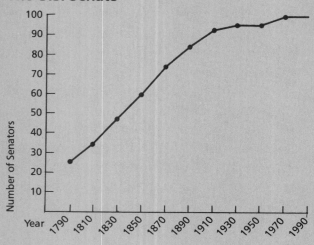

Now answer these questions.

1. Why has the size of the House of Representatives increased in the past 200 years?

_____

2. Why has the size of the Senate increased in the past 200 years?

_____

3. How many senators were there in 1850?   in 1970?

_____

Watergate and the Constitution

In 1972 five men tried to steal from an office in a Washington apartment and office complex. The office belonged to the Democratic party. The burglars worked for a group of Republicans. The crime—and the scandal it caused—came to be known by the name of the building: Watergate.

To many other people, Watergate went beyond an office burglary. Watergate tested the strength of the Constitution of the land.

The United States Constitution of 1787 set up **three branches,** or parts, **of government:** the executive, the legislative, and the judicial. It also set up a system of checks and balances among the branches. No one branch can become more powerful than the others.

In 1972, President Richard Nixon was head of the **executive branch.** The burglars were trying to get Nixon reelected. People began to believe members of the executive branch knew about the burglary and other crimes. Charges of a cover-up by Nixon and his men were heard.

Congress belongs to the **legislative branch.** A special group of senators in Congress met to study Watergate. The group asked Nixon for tapes of White House conversations. These tapes might show if crimes were planned and covered up at the White House. But Nixon refused to turn over the tapes. He said the Constitution gave the president the right to keep such tapes private.

The Supreme Court was asked to decide who was right. The Court is part of the **judicial branch.** Judges of the Court are picked by the president and approved by Congress. The judges of the Supreme Court ruled against Nixon. They said the president had to turn over the tapes.

The tapes and other evidence led many people to believe Nixon knew of crimes and tried to cover them up. In 1974 part of Congress voted to impeach Nixon, or put him on trial. Nixon resigned before the full Congress could vote. Watergate showed that the system of checks and balances works. It showed that no one—not even the president—is above the law.

Now write a few words to answer each question.

1. According to the article, what is one way the president has power over the Supreme Court?

_____

_____

2. According to the article, what is one way Congress has power over the president?

_____

_____

3. How did Watergate show the Constitution's system of checks and balances works?

_____

_____

Senator Sam Ervin (right) led the Senate hearings on Watergate.

The Rights of the Accused

"You have the right to remain silent. Anything you say can and will be used against you. You have the right to a lawyer. If you cannot afford a lawyer, one will be provided for you."

How many times have you heard police say that on TV shows or in movies? In three separate cases, the Supreme Court has ruled that the Constitution gives Americans these rights.

1963: Clarence Earl Gideon had been sent to prison for burglary. He had been too poor to afford a lawyer at his trial. The Supreme Court ruled that all accused people have the right to a lawyer in court. If a person can't afford a lawyer, the state must provide one.

1964: Danny Escobedo was in prison for murder. He had asked to see his lawyer when he was first arrested. But the police had not allowed him to. The Supreme Court ruled that police must allow accused people to see their lawyers. People must also be allowed to remain silent until they do see a lawyer.

1966: Ernesto Miranda was in prison for kidnapping and rape. Miranda had confessed to police, but he had not known he had the right to remain silent. The Supreme Court ruled that police must *tell* accused people their rights. This statement of rights is called the Miranda warning.

Answer these questions in a few words.

1. Why is the statement of a person's rights called the Miranda warning?

_____

2. Why did the Supreme Court rule that accused people had these rights?

_____

Passing an Amendment

An amendment is a change in a law or in the Constitution. Below is a flowchart showing the steps needed to pass an amendment to the Constitution.

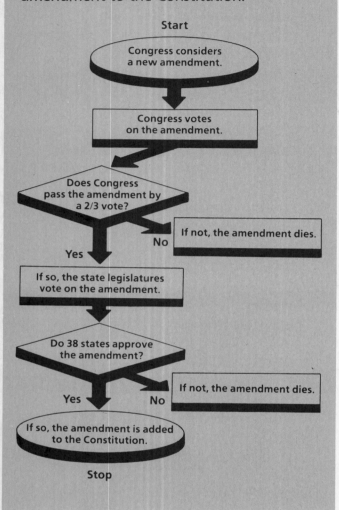

Start

Congress considers a new amendment.

Congress votes on the amendment.

Does Congress pass the amendment by a 2/3 vote?

No → If not, the amendment dies.

Yes

If so, the state legislatures vote on the amendment.

Do 38 states approve the amendment?

Yes   No → If not, the amendment dies.

If so, the amendment is added to the Constitution.

Stop

Answer these questions in a few words.

1. How might voters help decide whether an amendment is passed?

_____

2. Since 1790, only 26 amendments have been added to the Constitution. Why do you think so few have passed?

_____

_____

Women in the Central Government

Copyright 1981 by Herblock in The Washington Post.

Circle the correct answer to each question.

1. Which news story is the above cartoon about?

   a. Sandra Day O'Connor Becomes the First Woman Supreme Court Justice

   b. First Lady Goes to Capitol Hill to Speak Out Against Drug Abuse

2. Which speaker would the cartoonist more likely agree with?

   a. Arthur Calhoun: "A woman's name should appear in print but twice—when she marries and when she dies."

   b. Gail Sheehy: "If women had wives to keep house for them . . . just imagine . . . the offices that would be held by women."

The Equal Rights Amendment

Many American women in the 1960s and 1970s felt that they were "going nowhere in a hurry." For many women it was harder to get well-paying jobs than it was for men.

Some women joined groups like the National Organization for Women (NOW). Such groups wanted women to get the same rights and chances as men. They worked to change the laws of the United States government and the state governments.

In March 1972, Congress passed one such change, or amendment. It was known as the Equal Rights Amendment, the ERA. It was meant to be an amendment to the Constitution. At least 3/4 of the states had to approve it before it became law. Congress gave the amendment ten years to get approved. By November 1972, 21 states had approved the amendment.

The amendment was only one sentence long. "Equality of rights under the law shall not be denied by the United States or any state on account of sex." By 1980, though, many people often did not agree about what that sentence meant.

Many of those against the amendment were women. Some women felt that they already had equal rights. Others worried that women would have to serve in the army and navy. Both men and women wondered what would happen to families if even more mothers worked outside the home.

By 1982, only 35 states had approved the ERA. The amendment had failed. Still, many people felt that women had gained more respect and power.

Circle the correct answer.

1. The Equal Rights Amendment stated that
   a. both sexes were equal under the law
   b. all women should work outside the home
   c. women would have to join the army and navy
   d. men and women would share public washrooms
   e. all of the above

Write a sentence or two to answer the next question.

2. Do you think the ERA should have been approved? Why or why not?

_____

_____

A Test-Taking Tip

Sometimes several answers on a multiple-choice question will be taken from the reading passage. Don't choose an answer simply because you read the same word or number in the passage. Be sure the option you choose really answers the question.

GED Warm-up

How many states had to approve the ERA before it could become a law?

(1) 21
(2) 35
(3) 38
(4) 50

The Past and the Land

Interpreting Maps

Picture It

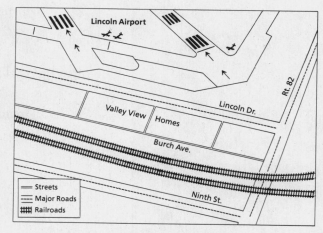

This photograph shows a view of a city— from several thousand feet in the air. It was taken on an airplane.

Could you use this photo to find your way around? Probably not. That's why people usually use maps to find where they're going.

Next to the photograph is a map of the same area. Symbols stand for some of the things in the photograph. The key shows what the symbols mean.

You know that maps tell the names of places and show how to get from one point to another. They help you get around in a city or region. They also help you understand geography. Geography deals with the earth's surface and the

people who live there. Maps are the geographer's tools.

To use a map, however, you must know its parts and what its symbols mean.

Here's an Example

Look at the map on the next page. Each part of the map is labeled. Read the labels. Then read the following hints on how to read a map.

The **title** tells you what area the map covers. This map is of the southern United States. The title may also tell you what kind of map you are looking at. This one is a **political map.** It shows boundaries between political areas, such as cities, states, and countries.

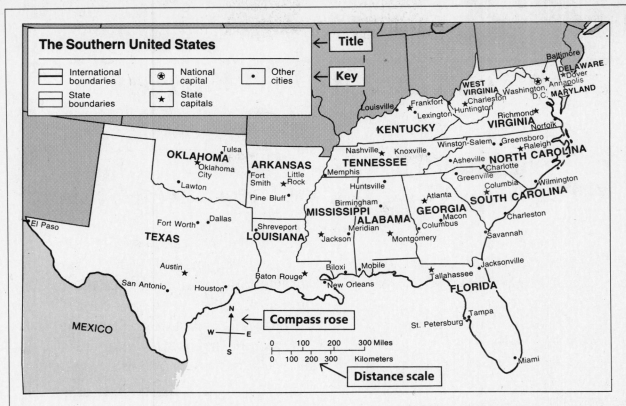

The Southern United States

| International boundaries | National capital | Other cities |
| State boundaries | State capitals | |

Title

Key

Compass rose

Distance scale

0 100 200 300 Miles
0 100 200 300 Kilometers

Another map you'll sometimes see is a **physical map.** It shows land features such as lakes, rivers, and mountains. Finally, **special purpose maps** show such things as land use or population.

The **directional symbol** shows you the directions on the map. The symbol can be a **compass rose** like the one here. It shows the four directions—north, south, east, and west. Some maps show only an arrow pointing north. Then you have to fill in the other directions.

The **key** tells you the meanings of colors and symbols on the map. This key tells you what the lines, dots, and stars mean.

The **distance scale** shows you how many miles each inch on the map stands for. Many map scales also show kilometers. A kilometer is the metric measure closest to a mile.

Working It Out

Use the map to answer the questions.

1. What area does the map cover?

_____

2. Which state is farthest west?

_____

3. What two states are farthest south?

_____

4. What is the capital of Tennessee?

_____

5. About how many miles apart are the cities of Montgomery and Richmond?

_____

6. What state probably has the largest number of immigrants from Mexico?

_____

Regions of the United States

Before You Read:
Thinking About Regions of the United States

In this lesson you'll read about regions, or areas, of the United States. Most of the articles discuss **census regions.** These are the regions the government uses when it takes a census, or counts its people. The census regions are the Northeast, the South, the Midwest, and the West. This map shows what states are in each region. Do you know the abbreviations for all the states? If you don't, look at the list on page **261.**

Try to find a few states on the map. Draw a circle around the letters for California, Ohio, Florida, and Vermont.

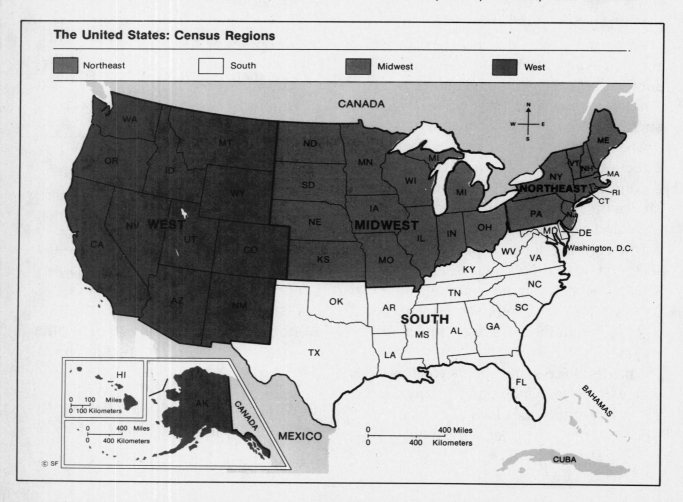

The United States: Census Regions

Northeast | South | Midwest | West

Find the state you live in on the map. Draw an X on it. What region do you live in? _____

Test your knowledge. Read the following list. In the blank before each item, write NE if it reminds you of the Northeast, S if it reminds you of the South, MW if it reminds you of the Midwest, or W if it reminds you of the West.

_____ cotton

_____ New England

_____ Pacific Standard Time

_____ plantations

_____ tornadoes

_____ high mountains

What region do you know the most about?

_____

What region do you know the least about?

_____

You'll find out more about all the regions of the United States as you read.

Working with Words

Some words from the readings are used in the sentences below.

The **climate** in much of Hawaii is hot and wet.

The major **vegetation** in Minnesota is evergreen trees.

Our friends in Arizona live in an **adobe** house.

The first sentence tells you that the climate in Hawaii is hot and wet. But the climate in parts of Alaska is cold and dry. What are these words such as *hot* and *dry* generally used to describe? Write your guess below. It probably will be close to the meaning of *climate.*

_____

To figure out the meaning of *vegetation*, study the following sentence. *The major vegetation in Kansas is prairie grass.* This sentence uses *vegetation* in the same way as the second sentence above. It tells you that prairie grass is vegetation too. What describes both evergreen trees and prairie grass? The word you come up with probably will be close in meaning to *vegetation.* Write the word below.

_____

Use the hints in the third sentence to finish the meaning for *adobe* below. You are given two choices for each blank. Copy the correct one in the blank.

Adobe is a material used in building

_____ in a _____
   (roads, homes)   (warm, cold)
region.

The following meanings are from the dictionary. How close did your meanings come to the correct ones?

Word Power

climate the kind of weather a place has over many years

vegetation plant life

adobe 1 a brick made of clay baked in the sun. **2** built or made of adobe.

Reading on Your Own

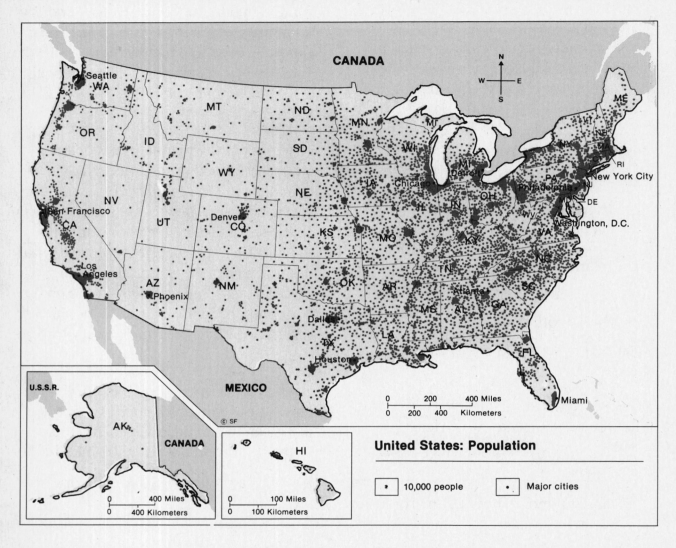

United States: Population

•	10,000 people
▫	Major cities

A Population Map

The map above shows how people are spread out in the United States. Each dot stands for 10,000 people. The areas where the dots run together have the greatest population density, or number of people per square mile.

Use the map to answer each question.

1. Which region of the country has the greatest population density?

_____

2. Do you notice any patterns to where people live? Complete this sentence.

   Many people settle near _____ .

How Standard Time Began

In the middle 1800s, the United States had about 60 time zones. So many time zones existed because people told time by the sun. When the sun reached its highest point in the sky, people's watches were set at 12 o'clock noon. But the sun reaches its highest point in the east before it does in the west.

Boston, Massachusetts, for example, is east of Washington, D.C. So noon came sooner in Boston than in Washington. In fact, the time in Boston was ahead of the time in Washington all day.

Time presented a big problem for train passengers. They had to reset their watches five times between Boston and Washington. Only then would their watches agree with the times on the railroad timetables.

In 1883 railroad companies set up standard time to make their timetables simpler to follow. They divided what was then the whole United States into only four zones. Every place within a zone had the same time. Soon everyone, not just the railroads, was using standard time.

Write a short answer to each question.

1. In the 1800s railroads were the fastest way to travel. Before they existed, different time zones were not a big problem. Why do you think this was so?

_____

2. Suppose standard time had never caught on. How would the times of national programs in TV guides be different today?

_____

A Time Zone Map

Look at the map below. The time zones in the United States, except those in which Alaska and Hawaii fall, are listed across the bottom of the map. The time in each zone is one hour different from the time in the neighboring zones. The hours are later to the east and earlier to the west. Notice that the boundaries of the zones jog in some places. This is so that nearby places can have the same time.

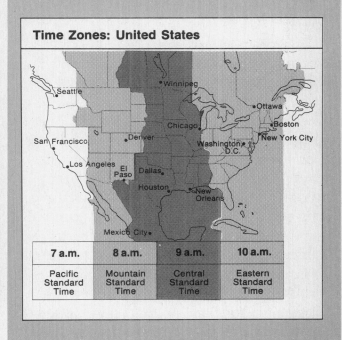

Time Zones: United States

7 a.m.	8 a.m.	9 a.m.	10 a.m.
Pacific Standard Time	Mountain Standard Time	Central Standard Time	Eastern Standard Time

Use the map to answer each question.

1. What time zone do you live in?

_____

2. It is 2 P.M. in San Francisco. What time is it in New York City?

_____

3. If you flew from New York to Denver, how would you reset your watch?

_____

Raising Cotton Down South

On southern farms in the 1920s, mules pulled the plows and hoes broke up the soil. Hundreds of workers picked the crops on large farms called plantations. Producing one bale of cotton took 150 hours of labor. Today the job takes only five hours.

How do southern farmers work so quickly? Rodalton Hart and his brothers raise cotton in Lexington, Mississippi. Read on to find out how they produce their crop.

As Rodalton Hart explains it, "Cotton is extremely, extremely hard to raise—kind of like a baby." When the cotton is ready to harvest in October, the Harts use their mechanical cotton pickers. "The two-row picker has two hands on each side, just like you have a right arm and a left arm," Hart says. "Each side has spindles like fingers at the end of your hand. Those are what pick the cotton." As the spindles turn, they pull cotton from the plants. Then the cotton is sucked into a container attached to the machine.

After the cotton is picked, it goes to a cotton gin for cleaning. Hart says today's cotton gin is about 200 feet square. After ginning, the cotton is formed into bales.

Write a few words to answer each question.

1. Why can a bale of cotton be produced so quickly today?

_____

2. Far fewer southerners live on farms today than in 1920. Based on the reading, how would you explain this change?

_____

Houses in New England

Do old houses fascinate you? Do you think about horse-drawn carriages when you see high-peaked roofs? Do you imagine families reading by firelight when you see a stone chimney? Then you would like the part of the Northeast called New England. It was named by the English colonists who settled there. For 200 years, builders throughout the United States have been copying the houses that the colonists left behind.

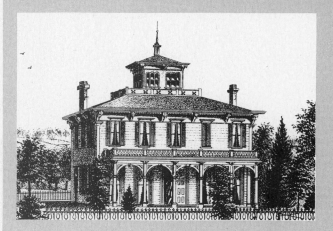

In New England seaports, for example, there are fine two- and three-story houses. Wealthy traders and sea captains built these during the 1700s. Most of the houses have rooftop balconies called "widow walks." From them, captains' wives looked out to sea and waited for their husbands. Many husbands never returned.

The simpler houses of New England show the settlers' English roots. Like houses in England during the 1600s, the houses have steep roofs. These roofs easily shed rain and snow. The chimneys are in the center of the houses rather than on outside walls. This saves heat in winter.

Write a short answer to each question.

1. What businesses does the reading suggest made money in early New England? Do you think these businesses are still important in the Northeast today?

_____

2. What do you think the climate of New England is like? What clues in the reading help you?

_____

Missions in California

In 1769, more than two hundred years after Cortés came to Mexico, Father Junipero Serra arrived in California. Father Serra was from Spain. He wanted to teach the Native Americans about the Catholic religion. He wanted them to help him build missions. A mission was like a small town. It had a church, homes, and farmland.

For the missions, the Native Americans made adobe bricks from mud and straw. With the bricks they built thick walls. These walls kept the insides of the buildings cool. They had few windows to let in the hot sun. The walls were painted white so the rays of the sun would bounce off. The roofs of the buildings were flat and covered with tiles. The tiles were made of clay and baked until dry.

In all, Serra and other priests founded twenty-two missions along California's coast. The missions included San Diego, San Francisco, San José, and Santa Barbara. They were named for Catholic saints like Saint Francis (San Francisco) and Saint Joseph (San José).

Today, some people say Father Serra was a saint. They say he loved and protected

the Native Americans. But others say the Native Americans were treated like slaves. They had to do what the Spanish commanded. If they ran away, they were beaten. They had to give up their old way of life. Whatever Father Serra was, his work still stands. It is a testament to his zeal and devotion.

Write a short answer to each question.

1. The article on page 80 gave clues about the climate in New England. Based on the clues in this article, how would you describe the climate in California?

_____

2. What do you think stands today where many missions once were? Why do you think as you do?

_____

_____

Tornadoes in the Midwest

Tornadoes are whirlwinds that destroy everything in their path. They hit the Midwest more often than other regions in the country. Why? Most tornadoes form where cool, dry air from the north meets warm, wet air from the Gulf of Mexico. In the Midwest, there are no mountains to the north or south to stop the cool air and the warm air from meeting. Tornadoes in the Midwest usually occur in spring or early summer, when temperature differences are greatest.

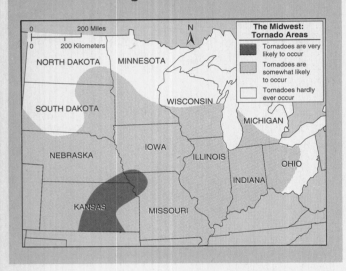

Use the map to answer each question.

1. Tornadoes are most likely to occur in which states?

_____

_____

2. In the northern areas around the Great

   Lakes, tornadoes _____

   _____ .

The West: Natural Vegetation

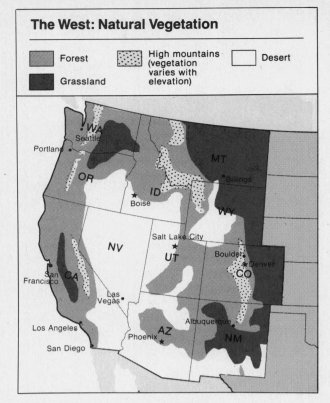

This map shows vegetation in the West. Use it to answer the questions below.

1. Which western state is least likely to have large cattle ranches?
   a. Nevada   b. Montana
   c. Wyoming   d. California

2. Which city probably has the highest elevation?
   a. Boise   b. Las Vegas
   c. Denver   d. San Francisco

GED Warm-up

Which city is most likely a center of the lumbering industry?

(1) Seattle

(2) Boise

(3) Las Vegas

(4) Salt Lake City

The Active Reader

Recognizing Point of View

Picture It

A tale from India shows how differently people can think about the same thing. In the story, six blind men came up to an elephant. They wanted to find out what the animal was like. The first man bumped into the elephant's huge side. He decided an elephant was like a wall. The second man felt the elephant's pointed tusks. He cried that an elephant was like a spear. The third man took hold of the elephant's long trunk. He said an elephant was like a snake. The fourth man circled one of the elephant's thick legs. He said an elephant was like a tree.

The fifth touched the elephant's large ears. He said an elephant was like a fan. The last man grabbed the elephant's tail. He said an elephant was like a rope. The six men had six different points of view on how an elephant looked!

In your social studies reading, you will come across many points of view. People in history often see the same event in different ways. The people who record history also see events differently. Recognizing points of view will help you better enjoy and understand your reading.

Here's an Example

Two groups who wrote about their lives were the Spanish and the Aztecs. In the 1500s, the Spanish began exploring North and South America. Hernando Cortés led several hundred Spaniards into what is now Mexico in 1521. There they met a group of Indians called the Aztecs. Montezuma was the Aztecs' leader. In the following paragraphs, a Spaniard and an Aztec describe the same event. How are their views different?

■ Cortés ordered our gunners to load the cannons with a great charge of powder so that they should make a great noise when they were fired off, and he told Pedro de Alvarado that all the horsemen should get ready so that these servants of Montezuma might see them gallop. . . . All this was carried out in the presence of the two Aztecs. Cortés made as though he wished again to speak to them and the cannons were fired off. The stones went flying through the forest making a great noise, and the two Aztecs and all the other Indians were frightened by things so new to them.

■ A thing like a ball of stone comes out of its belly. It comes out shooting sparks and raining fire. If the cannon is aimed against a mountain, the mountain splits and cracks open. Their arms are all made of iron; they dress in iron. Their deer carry them on their backs wherever they wish to go. Those deer are as tall as the roof of a house. The strangers' bodies are completely covered, so that only their faces can be seen. Their skin is white, as if it were made of lime. They have yellow hair, though some of them have black. Their beards are long and yellow. As for their food, it is large and white and not heavy. It is something like straw.

As you read, did you guess who wrote each paragraph? A Spaniard wrote the first. An Aztec wrote the second.

Look at the second paragraph. How does it show you that an Aztec wrote it? It uses things like deer and straw to describe horses and bread. Few Indians had seen horses or bread. However, they had seen deer and straw. The speaker uses what he knows to describe what he doesn't know.

Working It Out

Use the readings to help you answer each question below.

1. Why did Cortés fire the cannon and have the horsemen ride by?

_____

2. Did Cortés' plan work the way he wanted? How do you know?

_____

3. Do you think the Spanish viewed Cortés as clever or as amazing?

_____

4. How did the Aztecs view Cortés?

_____

In the box are names of things that the Spanish brought to Mexico. How did the Aztec describe these things in the second paragraph? Match the words from the box with the words from the Aztec's paragraph. Write the letter of each word in the correct blank.

a. bread	b. gunpowder	c. armor	d. horses

_____ 5. shooting sparks and raining fire

_____ 6. they dress in iron

_____ 7. deer carry them on their backs

_____ 8. large and white and not heavy

The New World

Before You Read: Thinking About the New World

This lesson is about early people in the Americas. The Vikings were the first Europeans to arrive in what is now Canada. They left behind remains of their buildings and other proof of their visit. They did not stay, though.

The next Europeans to arrive in the Americas were Christopher Columbus and his crew. They came in 1492. Many other Europeans soon followed. One of these was Cortés, who came in 1521. Europeans gave the Americas the name "New World."

To the Native Americans, however, the Americas were not new. The Native Americans had lived there in much the same way for thousands of years. The Europeans changed America more than it had changed in a long time.

How did the Native Americans view the Europeans? Suppose you were an early Native American. Large ships land in your country. Aliens, who seem to be human, get off the ships. They have frightening military weapons. How friendly and helpful would you want to be?

_____

_____

Now, how do you think the Native Americans viewed the Europeans who came to their land?

_____

_____

What did early Europeans think of the New World? Suppose you were a sailor on one of Cortés' ships. After months at sea, you arrive in a strange new land. What would you want to do?

_____ settle down and make a home here

_____ make a lot of money and go back to Europe rich

_____ teach the Aztecs your way of life, to help make life better for them

_____ teach the Aztecs your religion

_____ learn about the Aztecs' way of life

_____ overthrow the Aztec rulers and set up a new government over them

All of these were aims of Europeans coming to America. Some wanted to settle down, others wanted to get rich quick. Some came to convert the Native Americans to the Christian religion. Others wanted to rule the people.

The readings that follow will help you see history through the eyes of early people in America. You will read original accounts of historical events. You will draw your own conclusions about what took place. Already, you have read about Cortés meeting the Aztecs. You read first-hand accounts. You decided for yourself what happened in a meeting that took place over 350 years ago. Now you'll read other accounts of the early history of the settling of America.

Working with Words

Some words from the readings are used in the sentences below. These words may be new to you. Or you may have seen them before. Use what you already know as well as the hints in the sentences to figure out what these words mean.

Children are **artless** when they speak.

The town **council** met to discuss the school problem.

The **immigrant** traveled thousands of miles to the United States.

Divide *artless* into parts—*art-* and *-less.* The ending *-less* means "without." If you look in the dictionary, you will find that *art* has several meanings. Some of these are: (1) a branch of learning; (2) paintings, drawings, sculptures, or other works of art; (3) skill; and (4) trickery. Place *without* before each of these meanings. Which combination fits the first sentence? Finish the meaning below.

"without _____

You may confuse *council* with its sound-alike *counsel. Counsel* means "advice." Advice is also part of the meaning of *council.* The second sentence tells you that its meaning involves people too. Use these hints to write a meaning for *council* below.

_____

_____

A smaller word inside *immigrant* is *migrate. Migrate* comes from the Latin word *migratum,* which means "move." The word part *im-* comes from the Latin word *in.* This means "into." Put these words together. Then use hints from the sentence to finish up the meaning of *immigrant.* Write your meaning below.

_____

_____

Now read the following definitions from the dictionary. Do they match the ones you wrote?

Word Power

artless honest; without trickery

council a group of people called together to give advice and to settle questions

immigrant a person who comes into a foreign country to live

Reading on Your Own

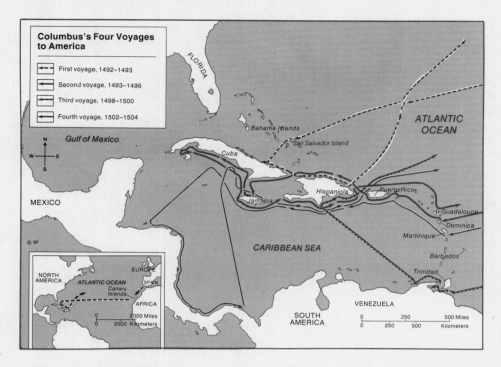

Columbus's Four Voyages to America

- First voyage, 1492–1493
- Second voyage, 1493–1496
- Third voyage, 1498–1500
- Fourth voyage, 1502–1504

FLORIDA
Gulf of Mexico
Bahama Islands
San Salvador Island
Cuba
ATLANTIC OCEAN
MEXICO
Hispaniola
Puerto Rico
Jamaica
Guadeloupe
Dominica
Martinique
CARIBBEAN SEA
Barbados
Trinidad
VENEZUELA
SOUTH AMERICA
© SF

NORTH AMERICA
EUROPE
ATLANTIC OCEAN
SPAIN
Canary Islands
AFRICA
0 2000 Miles
0 2000 Kilometers

0 250 500 Miles
0 250 500 Kilometers

The map above shows where Christopher Columbus sailed during his four voyages to the New World. Study the map. Then circle the answer to each question below.

1. During which voyage did Columbus sail along part of the South American coast?

    a. first   **b.** second   **c.** third

2. Which of the following areas did Columbus explore the most?

    a. what is now Florida

    b. the Caribbean Islands

    c. Mexico's eastern coast

A Case of Mistaken Identity

"Thirty-three days after my departure from Spain, I reached the Indian Sea, where I discovered many islands. To the first of these islands I gave the name San Salvador (The Savior). I proceeded along its coast and found it to be so large that I could not suppose it to be an island, but the continental province of China."
Christopher Columbus

Compare what Columbus wrote with the map above. Then write three wrong ideas Columbus had.

1. _____

_____

2. _____

_____

3. _____

The Arawak Indians

In 1492 Columbus also visited the island now called Cuba. There he met the Arawaks, the early people of Cuba. Columbus described them this way:

"It is true that after they have been reassured and have lost this fear, they are so artless and so free with all they possess, that no one would believe it without having seen it. Of anything they have, if you ask them for it, they never say no; rather they invite the person to share it, and show as much love as if they were giving their hearts."

From the box, choose three words that Columbus would have used to describe the Arawaks. Write your choices on the lines below. Next to each choice, copy a line from the reading that supports your answer.

- friendly
- tricky
- generous
- honest
- warlike
- frightening
- greedy

1. _____

_____

2. _____

_____

3. _____

_____

The Amazing Aztec City

On the Caribbean Islands, Spaniards had heard stories about a great city with a fabulous treasure of gold in a land called Mexico. In 1519 Hernando Cortés set out to find this city.

After hearing about the Aztecs, Cortés decided they must be the ones with all the gold. Cortés and his soldiers set out for the Aztec capital city of Tenochtitlán (te nôch´ tē tlän´).

Tenochtitlán was a fabulous place. It was built on an island in a lake. The island was connected to land by raised roadways made of stone. The city had more people and riches than any city at home in Spain.

One of Cortés' men later wrote, "We were amazed . . . on account of the great towers and temples and buildings rising from the water, and all built of masonry [stonework or brick]. And some of our soldiers even asked whether the things that we saw were not a dream."

Write a few words to answer each question below.

1. Why did Cortés go to Tenochtitlán?

_____

2. What about the city surprised the Spaniards?

_____

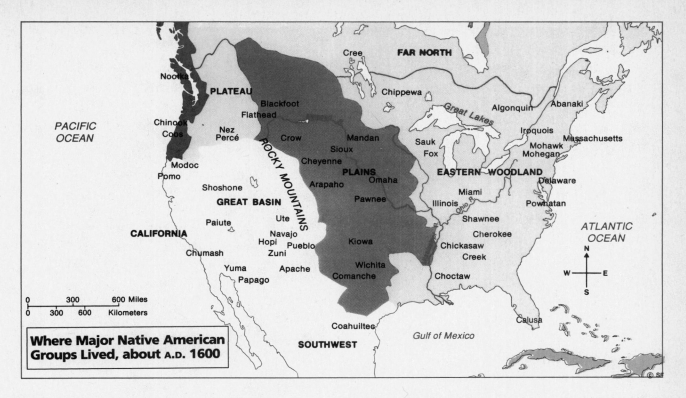

Where Major Native American Groups Lived, about A.D. 1600

This map shows names of early Native American groups and where they lived. Study the map. Then copy the correct answer to each question. Explain your answer.

1. Which of the following groups probably ate the most fish?

   a. Kiowa

   b. Apache

   c. Chinook

2. Which of the following groups probably had the earliest contact with Europeans?

   a. Ute

   b. Powhatan

   c. Chippewa

Eastern Woodland Indians

Eastern Woodland Indians did not live in small families made up of just parents and children. Instead several small families lived together in an extended family. Parents, grandparents, aunts, uncles, and cousins were all under one roof. All these family members helped raise children. They also planted crops and took care of one another.

The families of Woodland Indians made up clans. All the people in a clan shared at least one family member who had lived long before them. Members of a clan helped defend one another from enemies.

Each clan had a chief. Often chiefs became clan leaders because their fathers and grandfathers were chiefs. However, they had no more rights than anyone else. They could lead the people but not rule them.

The clans made up bigger groups called tribes. Each tribe also had a chief. Even the chief of a tribe could not make laws on his own. Before deciding anything, he had to talk with a council. On the council were chiefs of the clans.

Write a short answer to each question.

1. Early European kings passed their power from father to son. What sentence shows that clan chiefs in Woodland tribes did the same?

_____

2. In the 1600s European kings totally controlled their subjects. How were the chiefs of tribes different from kings?

_____

Diagram of Woodland Society

The diagram shows how Woodland tribes were organized. Write the number of each group in the correct shapes. Number 3 already has been filled in. Use the article you just read to help you.

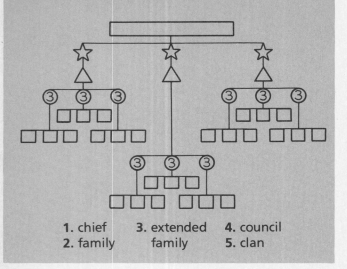

1. chief   3. extended   4. council
2. family   family   5. clan

The Pilgrims' First Year

The Pilgrims settled in the New World in November 1620, one hundred years after Cortés came. William Bradford was one of their first governors. Later he wrote about what his people went through:

"After the 14th of January, the house which they had made for general meeting fell afire, and then the sickness began to fall among them. The governor, seeing so many die and fall down sick daily, thought it no wisdom to send away the ship, till they could fix some shelter.

"[After the heart of the winter was over,] as many as were able began to plant corn. Squanto [an Indian who made friends with the settlers] showed them how to set it and tend it. Also he told them, unless they got fish and planted it in these old grounds, it would come to nothing. Some English seed they sowed [planted], peas, but it came not to good, either by the badness of the seed or lateness of the season or both."

Copy the correct answer to each question.

1. What is the main idea of the first paragraph Bradford wrote?

   a. The Pilgrims suffered hardships.

   b. The Pilgrims lived on their ship.

   _____

2. What is the main idea of the second paragraph?

   a. Peas have to be planted early.

   b. The Pilgrims had to learn new ways.

   _____

Life in a New Land

Many more settlers arrived from Europe in the early 1700s. The letters below are from two of them.

A settler from northern Ireland wrote the following letter to his sister back home:

> "It is the best country for working folk in the world. Father bought a tract of land consisting of five hundred acres. We have had a crop of oats, barley, and very good flax and hemp, corn and buckwheat. This country yields extraordinary crops of all sorts. Dear sister, I desire thee may tell my old friend Samuel Thorton he could not do better than to come here."

A German immigrant to Pennsylvania wrote the next letter:

> "Work in this new and wild land is very hard and many an old one must work very hard for his bread. However hard he may have to work in his fatherland, he will surely find it as hard, if not harder, in the new country. Besides, not only is the journey long and hard, but it costs a great deal of money. If a man has the money, then it is gone. If he does not, he must work his debt off as a slave or poor peasant. Therefore, let everyone stay in his own country. How miserably so many thousand German families have lived since they spent all their money to come here."

Answer the following questions with a few words.

1. What about the new country did the settler from northern Ireland praise the most?

_____

2. What two things did the German immigrant dislike about America?

_____

3. What do you think might explain the difference in the two men's points of view?

_____

_____

A Test-Taking Tip

Some questions on the GED Social Studies Test will ask about things people said. Make it easier to answer these questions. How? Sum up in a few words what the speaker said. Then decide how the speaker feels about this subject. Knowing these things will help you choose the correct answers to the questions.

GED Warm-up

Which of the following statements would both speakers agree with?

(1) "The New World is ideal for working people."

(2) "Everyone can find riches in the New World."

(3) "Life in the New World is not worth the cost."

(4) "Getting ahead in the New World demands work."

Recognizing Values

Picture It

Casimir finally cleared his stuff out of his parent's garage. But his apartment was not big enough to hold all his old things. So Casimir decided which things he wanted most. The rest he threw in the trash.

The picture above shows the box of things he kept and the box of things he threw away. What can you tell about Casimir based on his choices? What does he think is important? What is unimportant to him?

You could ask these same questions about people in your social studies reading. What might you tell about them based on their words and choices? What do they value, or think is important? Read on to find out.

Here's an Example

Calvin Coolidge was governor of Massachusetts in 1919. That year the Boston police, who belonged to a union, stopped working and went on strike. Coolidge became known around the country because of the following stand he took against the strike.

■ There is no right to strike against the public safety by anybody, anywhere, any time.

How does Coolidge feel about the public safety?

_____

The words clearly tell you that Coolidge valued the "public safety." To him, it was more important than labor unions or the police officers' demands.

You even might read more into the sentence than it says directly. Many voters were pleased that Coolidge spoke up for their well-being. Coolidge was a wise enough politician to know they would feel this way. So the quote also suggests that Coolidge valued the public's favor. After all, gaining public favor is the way to win votes. And winning votes is the way an office holder stays in public office. This plan certainly worked well for Coolidge! In 1920 he was elected vice-president of the United States. In 1923 he became president.

Working It Out

In 1919 the most powerful labor leader in the United States was Samuel Gompers. Of course, he thought unions were more important that Coolidge did. Decide what else Gompers valued as you read the following speech he gave.

■ To protect the workers in their inalienable rights to a higher and better life; to protect them, not only as equals before the law, but also in their health, their homes, their firesides, their liberties as men, as workers, and as citizens; . . . to secure to them . . . the right to be full sharers in the abundance which is the result of their

brain and brawn [muscle], and the civilization of which they are the founders. . . . The attainment of these is the glorious mission of the trade unions.

From the box, write down the words that describe the labor leader's values. Base your choices on the speech you have just read. Then, next to each word, copy a part of the speech that supports your choice.

> profits   equality
> high standard of living   freedom
> efficiency   upper class

_____

_____

_____

_____

Several years ago, air traffic controllers went on strike. President Reagan ordered them back to work. Those who refused to go back were fired.

1. How would Coolidge feel about the steps Reagan took?

_____

_____

2. How would Gompers feel?

_____

_____

Workers' Rights

Before You Read: Thinking About Workers' Rights

Most likely you already know what a union is. It is workers joined together to protect and promote their interests by dealing as a group with their employers. This lesson will tell you even more. Most of the articles cover highlights of union history. One article discusses a subject important to workers today—perhaps even to you.

Before you go on to the articles, however, find out what you already know. Below are paragraphs about American workers today. Finish the sentences by writing the correct word from the word box in each blank.

```
hand   services   providing   machines
```

There are two kinds of workers in the United States. There are producers of manufactured goods or farm products and providers of _____ .
                                        1
Today there are more workers _____ services than there are
                              2
producing products. Why is this so? Most goods in the United States are made by _____ . Fewer workers are
                    3
needed to produce goods this way than by _____ .
            4

Do the articles cover the workers discussed above? To find out, skim the titles and articles on the following pages. Then list the groups from the paragraphs above that are also in the articles. Also add any group from the articles that is not discussed above.

_____

_____

_____

As you read, ask the following questions about each group you have listed: What were their problems? How did they deal with them? Who helped them?

Working with Words

Some words from the articles are used in the sentences on the next page. These words may be new to you. Or you may have seen them before. Use what you already know as well as the hints in the

Workers build cars on an assembly line in the 1920s.

sentences to figure out what these words mean.

The **assembly line** at the factory turns out hundreds of cars each day.

My company offers **benefits** such as a health plan and paid sick days.

The **migrant** workers went from farm to farm.

Take apart *assembly line.* A smaller word inside *assembly* is *assemble.* This word means "put together." Now come up with a word that means the same as *line.* Hint: Try a three-letter word beginning with *r.* Read the first sentence again. Add the hints there to the ones you have just been given. Then write a meaning for *assembly line* below.

_____

_____

_____

_____

The word part *bene* means "good." Use this fact and the hints in the second sentence to come up with a meaning for *benefits.* Write the meaning below.

_____

In Lesson 9 you learned that *migrate* means "move." *Migrant* is a form of *migrate.* What words might you use to replace *migrant* in the third sentence? Write the words below.

_____

The following definitions are from the dictionary. Are they like the meanings you wrote?

Word Power

assembly line a row of workers and machines along which work is passed until the final product is made

benefits any things that are for the good of a person or thing; advantages

migrant migrating; roving

Reading On Your Own

A Factory Worker on an Assembly Line

Workers in the 1890s worked 10- to 12-hour days. Factories were dark, dirty, and dangerous. Listen to one woman who worked in a canning factory:

"Side by side in rows of tens or twenties we stand before our tables waiting for the seven o'clock whistle to blow. My first job is an easy one. Anybody could do it. I place a lid of paper in a tin jar-top, over it a cork. This I press down with both hands, tossing the cover, when done, into a pan.

Over in one corner machinery groans and roars. I move in time with the sounds of the machines filling, washing, wiping, packing. Every part of me is offering some of its energy. One hour passes, two, three hours. I fit ten, twenty, fifty dozen caps, and still my energy keeps up. . . .

My shoulders are beginning to ache. My hands are stiff. My thumbs almost blistered. I am beginning to feel tired. Oh! the monotony [sameness] of it, the never-ending supply of work to be begun and finished, begun and finished, begun and finished! Would the whistle never blow?"

Write a few words to answer each question.

1. Why did the worker dislike her job?

_____

2. What do you think was more important to the factory owners—the well-being of the workers or the number of goods produced? Why do you think as you do?

_____

Early Women Workers

Life for many American women changed with the growth of factories. Growing numbers of women took paying jobs.

Women often found discrimination, or unfair treatment. Sometimes they were not allowed to do certain kinds of work. Most of the time they were not given the same pay as men.

Beginning in the 1840s, women formed groups to gain more rights. These groups grew much larger after the Civil War, as more and more women took paying jobs. One woman, who wanted her rights as a worker, explained:

"We women did more than keep house, cook, sew, wash, spin and weave, and garden. Many of us had to earn money besides. We worked secretly, because everyone had the idea that men, not women, earned money, and that men alone supported the family. Most women accepted this as normal."

Copy a sentence from the reading that supports each statement below.

1. Early employers valued male workers more than female workers.

_____

_____

2. Early women acted as if they agreed that only men should earn money.

_____

_____

Rise of Labor Unions

After 1870, many workers grew tired of feeling they had no power to change their lives. A boss might pay little attention to one worker's complaints. But the boss could not as easily overlook the complaints of many.

To gain power, workers began to form labor unions. Union members promised to help one another when times were bad. They also worked together to get better pay, shorter hours, and better working conditions. Unions did help many workers. But not without a struggle.

Employers usually listened to workers' complaints. But they didn't always do something about them. Workers had to be willing to do more than talk.

In the 1880s and 1890s, workers tried to solve their problems by striking. The workers hoped that this would force the employer to meet their demands.

Many strikes led to violence. Employers brought in new workers to replace the strikers. Often these were immigrants, new to the country, who were happy to get a job. Strikers gathered outside factories to protest. At times, police or state armies were called in. Some workers died in the fight for the right to strike.

Circle the answer that best completes each sentence.

1. Workers who joined labor unions
   a. were happy to get a job.
   b. wanted better working conditions.
2. Workers started to strike because
   a. talk failed to produce change.
   b. employers did not listen to them.

Women Workers Die in Fire
Latest Victims of Labor Struggle

New York, 1911—One hundred forty-three women workers died yesterday in a fire at the Triangle Shirt Waist Factory. They had no chance of escape. Their bosses had locked the doors to keep out union leaders. As a result, the workers were trapped in the fire.

This story really began almost two years ago. In 1909 the women at the factory went on strike. They did not like the long hours, the low pay, and the unfair way the bosses treated them. For example, the bosses made the workers buy their own needles, thread, and sewing machines. They didn't let workers join a union. Other clothing workers wanted the same things as the Triangle factory workers. So twenty thousand workers across the country went off the job to show support for the striking Triangle factory workers.

Finally, the factory managers gave in. They signed an agreement with the workers. But the managers wanted back their power. They tried to get it by keeping workers and union leaders apart. Yesterday their efforts ended in disaster.

Write an answer to each question below.

1. Why did the factory workers strike?

_____

_____

2. How was the strike in 1909 connected to the fire in 1911?

_____

_____

Some Early Events in the History of American Labor

1768 New York tailors stage first American strike.

1869 The Knights of Labor and the National Colored Labor Union (NCLU) are formed.

1877 Railroad workers hold first nationwide strike. Federal troops break the strike.

1886 Samuel Gompers forms the American Federation of Labor (AFL).

1906 Henry Ford first uses assembly lines in his factories.

1925 The Brotherhood of Sleeping Car Porters is organized.

1935 The National Labor Relations Act (NLRA) allows workers' representatives to bargain for them. The Social Security Act is passed.

1938 The Fair Labor Standards Act limits workers to those who are sixteen years and older.

Use the time line to answer each question.

1. When did the federal government side against workers? When did it help them?

_____

_____

2. Who did workers more likely look up to—Samuel Gompers or Henry Ford? Explain.

_____

_____

A. Philip Randolph, Labor Leader

A. Philip Randolph was born in Florida in 1889. As a boy, he worked on a railroad. He found out for himself about the long hours and low pay of African American railroad workers. Later Randolph moved to New York City and went to college. While still a student, he started a union of elevator operators. However, by 1925, he was more interested in improving working conditions for sleeping car porters.

Porters worked on trains. They waited on passengers, prepared food, and cleaned up. Most sleeping car porters were African Americans.

In 1893 white railroad workers formed the American Railway Union. However, they did not allow African Americans to join. Many whites feared African Americans would take their jobs if they gained the same bargaining power.

So in 1925 Randolph organized the Brotherhood of Sleeping Car Porters. For more than ten years, Randolph fought for the right to bargain for his followers. Then in 1935 the federal government passed the National Labor Relations Act. This law required that employers bargain with the workers' representatives. Soon after, the Pullman Company—owner of the sleeping cars—accepted the porters' union.

Reread Gompers's speech on page 93. Then answer each question.

1. What part of the unions' mission did the American Railway Union ignore?

_____

2. What goals do you think Gompers and Randolph shared?

_____

_____

Unemployment Compensation

What happens when workers lose their jobs? Many apply for unemployment benefits. The way these benefits are distributed changes somewhat from state to state. The following rules hold true in Illinois.

Workers must have lost their job through no fault of their own. Then they can collect from the state about one-half of what they earned at their last job. They go in person to the state employment office to pick up weekly checks.

People who receive help from the state must look for new jobs. Before collecting their check, they list the places where they've looked. The state job counselors help them in their search.

Not everyone who is out of work can get money from the state. Suppose Ella's company did not send payments to the government in her name. Employers put in the money that keeps the system running. So Ella can't withdraw any money. A person who finds full-time work should no longer receive benefits. Some people pretend to be out of work when they aren't. If they are caught, they often pay fines and go to jail.

Should the Illinois workers below get unemployment benefits? Write yes *or* no *in each blank.*

_____ 1. Jack was fired for being late most days and working slowly.

_____ 2. Ruby has found full-time work that pays less than her last job.

_____ 3. Pedro was doing a good job. But the boss let him go because the company's sales were down.

Migrant Workers in the 1930s

In the 1930s migrant workers traveled from place to place in search of jobs. Farmers needed extra help when the crop was ready to pick. Migrant workers filled that need. They picked potatoes, cotton, berries, grapes, apples, and lettuce. They picked all day. They traveled all night. When the crop was picked, the job was over. So the picker moved on.

A writer tells what it was like.

"Top pay for potato digging was five dollars a week. That was top. Still the worker owed the boss twenty-five or thirty dollars for transportation. And more for rent on his shack. You could just about break even if you earned top pay. But most workers didn't. Most workers earned two or three dollars a week. And there were lots who earned only one. What counted was how fast your hands and arms could go. No wonder mothers took little toddlers, still too young to talk, and showed them how to put potatoes in bushels. And how to put cotton in sacks. And how to put berries in baskets.
No wonder."

Write a few words to answer each question.

1. How did the migrant workers' bosses show that they valued money more than they valued the workers?

_____

_____

2. Why did the migrant workers' children have little hope of earning a better living than their parents?

_____

_____

A Test-Taking Tip

On the GED Social Studies Test, it's a good idea to read the questions before you read each passage. Then you will have a purpose for reading. Right now, go over the second question after the passage below. Then look for hints about Cesar Chavez's values as you read.

The Migrant Workers' Grape Strike

California the 1960s—In the autumn of 1965, some of the workers in the vineyards of San Joaquin Valley in California went out on strike. "Huelga!" they shouted. "Strike!" This was the beginning of the

Cesar Chavez

famous grape strike. Farm workers had tried organizing unions before. But none had ever been really successful. The bosses had been too powerful. The workers had been too poor and too frightened to make the strike last. Sooner or later, the leaders were gotten rid of. The union was broken up. But the United Farm Workers Organizing Committee has a remarkable leader. His name is Cesar Chavez. Describing Chavez for an article in *The New Yorker,* Peter Matthiessen said he "has an Indian's bow nose and lank black hair, with sad eyes and an open smile that is both shy and friendly. . . ." Matthiessen also described Chavez as one of the

most modest men he had ever met. He is also probably one of the strongest. He is totally committed to ending the vicious "bracero" system that California grape growers thrive on. "Bracero" means "arm" in Spanish. And that is exactly what the men in the fields mean to the growers. They are not people. They are simply arms for picking crops. As Cesar Chavez keeps telling them, "Without a union, the people are always cheated. And they are so innocent."

GED Warm-up

1. Why had past farm workers' unions failed?
   (1) The bosses were innocent.
   (2) The workers feared lost wages.
   (3) The press sided with the growers.
   (4) The union leaders were too strong.
   (5) The growers could not pay any more.

   ① ② ③ ④ ⑤

2. Which of the following items does Cesar Chavez probably value most?
   (1) fame
   (2) power
   (3) friends
   (4) justice
   (5) innocence

   ① ② ③ ④ ⑤

3. Who benefits most from the bracero system?
   (1) the Spanish
   (2) Cesar Chavez
   (3) Peter Matthiessen
   (4) United Farm Workers
   (5) California grape growers

   ① ② ③ ④ ⑤

The Active Reader

Drawing Conclusions

Picture It

Miranda loves crime shows on TV. She tries to figure out the killer before the police do. She watches for clues and then puts them together. This helps her decide who the guilty party is.

Just like Miranda, you can play detective. But you don't have to wait for your favorite crime show. Every time you read, you gather facts or clues. You can put these facts together to answer your questions about what you have read. This is called **drawing conclusions.** A conclusion is a decision or opinion reached by reasoning.

Here's an Example

Walter wants to know why so many people choose to live in cities. To find out, he reads the sentences below. Notice how he decides on an answer to his question.

■ Many companies build offices and factories in cities. So cities offer many jobs. You'll find hundreds of restaurants, nightclubs, and movie theaters in a city. There are plenty of stores to shop in. And you can always go to a museum or park. You'll never be far from transportation. Many people who live in cities don't own a car. They can use subways and buses to get around. Cities also have major highways and airports close by.

Walter has picked up several facts about cities from the reading. (1) Cities have jobs. (2) Cities have interesting places to go. (3) Cities are centers of transportation. Walter reasons that people need jobs to live. People also like to do different things for fun. To hold jobs and to do different things, people need to go from one place to another. So Walter decides that jobs, fun, and transportation are reasons people choose city life.

Working It Out

Suppose you have just watched a travel show about Seattle, Washington. It looks interesting, with ocean and mountain recreation both so close. You think it might be a great place to live. The following reading can help you decide whether or not this is true. Read the passage. Then draw your conclusions the way Walter did.

■ The Seattle region is one of the fastest growing metropolitan areas in the country. Two reasons are its nearby outdoor recreation opportunities and its growing reputation as a center for small high-tech companies. The largest employer in the Seattle area is Boeing, the aircraft company that first introduced the giant commercial airliners that are so common today.

Inventiveness is a big part of Seattle's history. Color television was invented here. Rumor has it that two of the city's earliest white settlers used a horseshoe hung on a clothesline to test the depth of Puget Sound, the large body of water by which Seattle is located. Seattle's location, just a half hour by car from the Cascade Mountains and a two-hour drive from the Pacific Ocean, makes it a popular destination for people who enjoy being close to outdoor recreation. Lumbering is important to Washington's economy, and Seattle is a center of trade and shipping to countries on the Pacific rim, such as Japan and Taiwan.

Answer the following questions. They will help you look at the facts in the reading. Use your answers to decide whether or not you would enjoy living in Seattle. Copy sentences or phrases from the reading to support your answer.

1. What kinds of workers would have an easy time finding jobs in Seattle?

_____

_____

What sentences or phrases in the reading support your conclusion?

_____

_____

_____

2. Based on clues in the reading, what do people in Seattle probably do for fun?

_____

_____

What sentences or phrases in the reading support your conclusion?

_____

_____

_____

3. Now decide. Would you enjoy living in Seattle? Give reasons for your answer.

_____

_____

_____

_____

Modern Life and Cities

Before You Read: Thinking About Modern Life and Cities

The articles in this lesson are about life today, especially city life today. As you read this lesson, you'll find answers to these questions: How does your life differ from your great-grandparents' lives? What do you worry about today that they never dreamed about? How have the machines that make your life easier also caused problems?

Most likely you know plenty about modern life. Newspapers and television tell you about problems from around the world. But many problems lie as close as your own home. Is the air safe to breathe? Is the water safe to drink? Are you safe from street gangs? These questions come up every day as you listen to the news.

See how closely you follow what's happening. Finish these headlines. Fill in each blank with a word from the box.

Subway Water Computer Lead Noise

Paint-toting Gang Strikes

in _____
     1

_____ Levels Are Up in
     2
City Air

Neighbors Complain of

_____ from Freeway Traffic
     3

Sewer Runoff Pollutes

_____ Supply
     4

_____ Thief Makes Off
     5
with Millions

Are you unsure about how to finish any headline? Then look ahead at the readings. Match words in the readings with those in the headlines above. This will help you decide which word from the box fits in each blank.

Choose one headline. Write several questions you have about it. Start the questions with *who, what, where, why,* or *how.*

_____

_____

Find answers to the questions as you read.

Working with Words

Some words from the articles are used in the sentences below. These words may be new to you. Or you may have seen them before. Add what you already know to the hints in the sentences. Then figure out what the words mean.

Factories pour **pollutants** into the air.
Gangs often paint **graffiti** on city walls.
To turn off the **electronic** game, flip the switch.

Pollutants is a form of the verb *pollute.* *Pollute* means "to make dirty or impure." The ending -*ants* turns *pollute* into a noun. So what would the meaning of *pollutants* be? Write it below.

_____

Gangs in the second sentence hints at the meaning of *graffiti.* What would gangs

paint on city walls? Your answer should be close to the meaning of *graffiti.*

_____

The meaning of *electronic* is somehow tied to *electricity.* Figure out how the two words are connected. Use the third sentence to help you. Then write a meaning for *electronic* on the line below.

_____

The following definitions are from the dictionary. Are they like the meanings you wrote?

Word Power

pollutant something that makes dirty or impure

graffiti drawings or writings painted, scratched, or scribbled on a wall or other surface to be seen by the public

electronic working by electricity

Writing to Improve Your Reading

Has this ever happened to you? You read a news story. Then you can't recall the major points. For example, you may have read that certain loud sounds cause hearing loss. But you forget which ones.

Try this trick. With a yellow marker, highlight important words as you read the newspaper. Do not mark whole sentences. After you finish the story, go over what you have highlighted. Write notes in the margin or on a separate sheet of paper. Write down only the key words. This will help the facts stick in your mind.

Reading On Your Own

Pollution in Early Cities

City people always have had problems. About 1900 they thought their worst problem was pollution. But it wasn't the kind that poured out of smoke stacks. No, it was the kind that came from horses.

A horse could leave up to twenty-five pounds of manure daily on city streets. In a city such as New York, manure caused more than eye and nose pollution. When rain fell, carriages and people had to wade through a sea of manure. When it dried, the manure turned into a fine dust that crept onto and into everything.

What was the answer? "The car!" said many people thankfully. In 1900 cars began to replace horses. Now, people thought, cities would become quieter, cleaner, and healthier places to live.

Copy a sentence from the reading that supports each statement below.

1. "The good old days were not always so good."

_____

2. "In 1900 many people did not know cars could be harmful to their health."

_____

_____

Here's another conclusion you could draw.

3. "Solutions lead to new problems." What is a different example of this idea?

_____

What's on City Streets?

What dangers lurk on city streets? A study of the streets in Milwaukee, Wisconsin, came up with surprising answers. There the roads are coated with 5,400 pounds of lead, 7,600 pounds of zinc, 2,100 pounds of copper, 170 pounds of chromium, and 12 pounds of chemicals called PCBs. These pollutants are common in most cities.

Salt also covers our roads. Most cities in the northern United States salt roads to make driving safer. Nine million tons of salt are used to melt snow and ice every winter.

Many of these pollutants hurt plant life. They also eat away at underground wires and pipes. If taken in large amounts, all of the substances can make people sick. In fact, PCBs cause cancer.

Why should people worry about these chemicals? After all, people don't eat off the streets. But, believe it or not, people often drink these poisons. How does this happen? Rain washes the pollutants into sewers. From there they run off into the water supply.

Write a few words to answer each question.

1. How has the use of cars helped add to the salt pollution on city streets?

_____

2. Based on the reading, what can be done to make cities healthier places to live?

_____

Lead Poisoning and City Children

Since the early Greeks, people have known that lead is a poison. Large amounts damage the brain. Smaller amounts harm other body parts such as nerves. The greatest danger is to children.

Most lead in the air comes from gasoline. Many cities and states have passed laws to deal with this problem. These laws limit the amount of lead in gasoline. They also demand that new cars use lead-free fuel.

However, even the low amounts of lead these laws allow can be harmful. A study of 3,000 school children near Boston bears this out. The study has shown that minute amounts of lead in children's bodies cause learning problems. Studies in other cities agree with these findings.

Write the letter of the correct cause in the blank before each effect.

Effects

_____ 1. Cities have high levels of lead

_____ 2. The amounts of lead in city air have decreased

_____ 3. Some city children have learning problems

Causes

a. because of pollution control laws.
b. because of the many cars there.
c. because of lead poisoning.

Art or Vandalism?

Ali is sixteen years old. He is the leader of 50 gang members. They spend most of their time together painting graffiti.

Today Ali lies in the hospital. Burn scars crisscross his face. Bandages cover his ankles and hands. Though Ali is in pain, he tries to tell his story.

The time was 5 A.M. The place was a subway tunnel. Ali and another gang member were painting the wall of a subway car. Suddenly the train started. A spark shot out from under its wheels. The spark set fire to the 25 cans of paint they had stolen. Then Ali's clothes caught fire. He ran through the tunnel screaming. Somehow Ali made it to the street. A passing cab stopped and took him to the hospital.

"We thought we were so great," Ali said.

"We had business cards printed and had meetings every Friday. We had a waiting list of about a hundred and fifty kids who wanted to join our group. We wanted to have an art show. . . ."

Finish the sentences below.

1. Besides painting train cars, Ali also was guilty of _____.

2. Ali and his group painted graffiti because

_____.

Computer Crime

Big city thieves are using a new tool. To their lock picks and crow bars they have added computers. How do thieves steal with computers? Before finding out, you should know about a new way companies do business.

At one time companies paid their bills with checks. Now many use electronic money. Electronic money works this way: Baker Inc. sends a computer message to its bank. The message says to take $20,000 from Baker's account to deposit in Colder Corp's account. The bank's computer sends another message. It tells Colder's bank to deposit the $20,000 in Colder's account. Without receiving any checks or paper money, Colder is $20,000 richer.

Workers can easily steal their company's money. First they have to learn the company's account numbers. They also have to learn how to use its computers. Then they open a fake account in another company's name. Next, they use the computer to ask their company's bank for money. The bank deposits the company's money in the fake account. Some thieves have stolen millions this way before being found out.

Write a few words to answer each question.

1. Stealing from an employer is risky. Why do you think workers steal from companies?

_____

2. How do you think companies can stop computer theft?

_____

Measuring Sounds of the City

Sound is measured in **decibels.** Decibels measure the intensity of the sound. The more intense a sound is, the louder it is. The softest sound a human can hear has a rating of 0 decibels. Sounds over 120 decibels are painful to the ear.

A normal conversation measures about 55 decibels. If a truck passes by, your conversation may be drowned out. This is because the noise of the truck is much louder. It may measure 90 decibels.

Any sound above 85 decibels can harm your hearing. The longer you're exposed to a noise, the more hearing you can lose. Today, most Americans over 30 have some hearing loss.

Noise also causes stress. A sudden, loud sound will make you jump. A constant sound, such as a siren or dripping water, may make you feel angry or tense. Studies show that people who live near airports are more likely to enter mental hospitals. Workers in noisy environments tend to be more aggressive and irritable.

Write a few words to answer each question.

1. Why could living next to a trucking company be bad for you?

_____

_____

2. How might a decibel scale help employers make the workplace better for their workers?

_____

_____

Noise Exposure Limits

The table below lists some noises. To the left is the loudness, or decibel level, of each noise. To the right is the stretch of time someone can listen to the noise before suffering hearing loss.

Approximate decibels	Sound Source	Time Limit
115	Loud Stereo Chain Saw Live Band	$1\frac{7}{8}$ minutes
110	Slammed Door Screaming Child Air Compressor	$3\frac{3}{4}$ minutes
105	Pile Driver Garbage Truck Jackhammer	$7\frac{1}{2}$ minutes
100	Cocktail Party Farm Tractor	15 minutes
95	Dirt Bike Snowmobile Power Lawn Mower Inside Subway Train	30 minutes
90	City Traffic Heavy Truck Food Blender	1 hour
85	Home Shop Tools Construction Site	2 hours
80	Alarm Clock Hair Dryer	4 hours
75	Dishwasher Washing Machine Noisy Restaurant	8 hours
70	Freeway Traffic Inside Passenger Car Television	16–24 hours

In each space below, write **yes** *if the worker probably would suffer hearing loss. Write* **no** *if he or she probably would not. Then, on the lines that follow, explain your answer. Base what you write on facts from the table.*

_____ 1. a carpenter

_____

_____

_____ 2. a traffic officer

_____

_____

_____ 3. a waitress

_____

_____

Now do the same thing with this list of common activities. Write **yes, no,** *or* **depends** *in the blank. Give a reason for your answer.*

_____ 4. going to a rock concert

_____

_____ 5. watching a child

_____

_____ 6. riding on the subway

_____

_____ 7. drying your hair

_____

_____ 8. mowing the lawn

_____

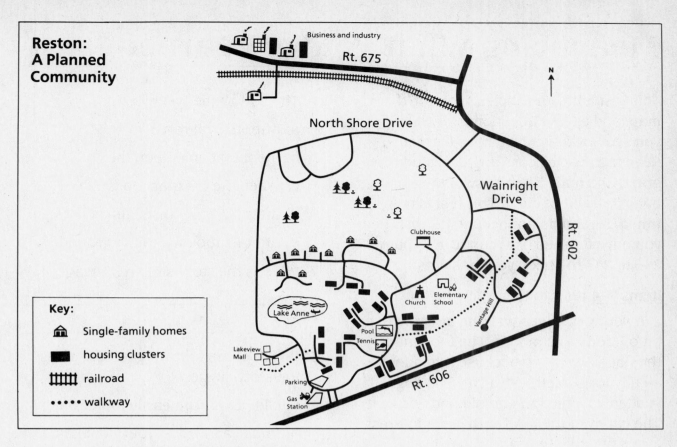

Reston: A Planned Community

Business and industry

Rt. 675

North Shore Drive

Wainright Drive

Rt. 602

Clubhouse

Church

Elementary School

Vantage Hill

Lake Anne

Pool Tennis

Lakeview Mall

Parking

Gas Station

Rt. 606

Key:

🏠 Single-family homes

▪ housing clusters

|||||| railroad

••••• walkway

One answer to city crime and pollution is to plan a community. The map above shows Reston, a planned community in Virginia. As in older cities, the people in Reston work at all kinds of jobs. Low-income housing is mixed in with middle- and high-income housing. The town's sports centers are for everyone. Use the map to help you answer the questions that follow.

1. Why is traffic light in Reston's neighborhoods?

   a. People take the train to work.

   b. The major streets bypass the homes.

   c. The neighborhoods can be reached only by walkways.

   d. People in Reston travel by water.

A Test-Taking Tip

Some tests have questions about a map. Ask yourself: Are the places in the answer choices on the map? If so, where are they? A second look at the map will help you find clues to the answers.

GED Warm-up

How did city planners try to protect the people of Reston from pollution?

(1) Factories are built along a lake.

(2) The school is close to the church.

(3) The railroad runs south of town.

(4) Factories are separate from homes.

(5) Housing is built near Rt. 606.

Measuring What You've Learned

This test has four articles, a graph, a map, and twenty questions. It will help you see how much you have learned. Read the articles carefully, and study the graph and map. Then answer the questions about each. This test is not timed. So you do not need to hurry. When you have finished, you can turn to pages 246 to 247 to check your answers.

Items 1–4 refer to the article below.

A young dog was walking along with a bit of food in its mouth. The food made the dog very happy because it had looked all day for something to eat. The dog suddenly came upon an old and wise cat. The cat eyed the food with great interest.

''I say,'' said the cat. ''You certainly have beautiful white teeth. They are the prettiest teeth I have ever seen.''

The dog, feeling very proud, opened its mouth wide so that the cat could get a better look. When the dog opened its mouth, the food fell out onto the ground. The cat quickly grabbed the food with its mouth and ran off, leaving the dog with nothing but an empty, opened mouth.

1. The dog opened its mouth
   a. after the cat ran off
   b. before it came upon the cat
   c. when the cat grabbed the food
   d. after the cat praised its teeth
   e. after its food fell to the ground

2. What is the story's main message?

   _____

   _____

3. Which of the following lessons does the story suggest?
   a. Old people are easily fooled.
   b. Pride can lead to your downfall.
   c. Young people have little to learn.
   d. Good-looking people are usually bright.
   e. Hard work is the only way to success.

4. Which of the following words best describes the cat's personality?
   a. rude
   b. proud
   c. well-read
   d. farsighted
   e. street-smart

Items 5–8 refer to the article below.

Nine and a half million people came to America between 1865 and 1890. Most were from northern and western Europe—England, Ireland, Germany, Norway, and Sweden. People from China also came during this time. Large numbers of Chinese settled in one state—California.

At the time, America needed workers, especially factory workers. Many immigrants from England and Germany knew how to run the new factory machines.

America also needed railroads built. Many Irish and Chinese became America's great railroad builders. They were used to hard, outdoor work in their homelands.

Many immigrants from Norway and Sweden had farmed for their living. They settled on America's plains, where the land was good for farming.

5. Why did immigrants from Norway and Sweden settle America's plains?

   a. They wanted to continue farming as they had done in Europe.

   b. They helped to build railroads on the plains.

   c. The plains were the first place they came to in America.

   d. The Chinese had taken all the jobs in California.

   e. They knew how to run the machines in the factories there.

6. What is the main idea of the article?

   a. Between 1865 and 1890, America needed all kinds of workers.

   b. Immigrants settled in different areas for different reasons.

   c. Irish and Chinese immigrants built the great American railroads.

   d. Millions of immigrants came to the United States in the late 1800s.

   e. Most immigrants from western and northern Europe settled in cities.

7. Based on the article, where do you think most Chinese Americans probably live today?

   a. in Puerto Rico

   b. in the Northeast

   c. in the South

   d. in the Midwest

   e. in the West

8. Why are the people in the article called "immigrants"?

   a. They farmed for a living.

   b. They worked for low wages.

   c. They could not speak English.

   d. They came from other countries.

   e. They helped build the railroads.

Items 9–11 refer to the graph below.

Value of Trade Between U.S. and Selected Countries

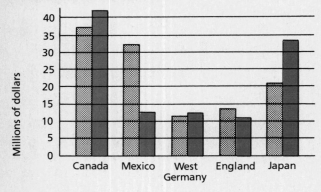

U.S. goods sold to other countries

Goods bought by U.S. from other countries

9. Which country listed on the graph sends the most dollars worth of goods to the U.S.?

_____

10. Which country listed on the graph sells the U.S. about $10 million more goods than it buys from us?

_____

11. What is the difference in value between the goods Mexico sells to the U.S. and those it buys from the U.S.?

    a. $1 million

    b. $2.5 million

    c. $5 million

    d. $20 million

    e. $40 million

Items 12–15 refer to the article below.

Until 1822, Spain ruled about half of North America. New Spain, as it was called, included California and Mexico. But in 1822, the people of New Spain fought against Spain. In this War for Independence, they won the right to rule their own country. They named the country Mexico. California was part of Mexico.

The War for Independence meant changes in California. One important change was in trade. Before 1822, Californians were allowed to trade only with Spain. The new government of Mexico decided to trade with Russia, England, the United States, and other countries.

A California girl named Prudencia wrote this account of trading with people from the United States.

"My brother had traded some deerskins for four toothbrushes, the first ones I had ever seen. I remember that we children rubbed them on our teeth until the blood came. Then we decided that, after all, we liked best the bits of willow root we had used for brushes before.

After the ship sailed, my mother and sisters began to cut out new dresses. On one of mine mother put some big brass buttons about an inch across, with eagles on them. How proud I was! I used to rub them hard every day to make them shine. One girl offered me a beautiful black colt she owned for six of the buttons. But for a long time I loved those buttons more than anything else I owned."

12. Which of the following goods did early U.S. traders view as most valuable?
   a. buttons
   b. willow root
   c. toothbrushes
   d. animal hides
   e. cotton cloth

13. Why did Prudencia value her brass buttons so highly?
   a. Everyone she knew had some.
   b. They were on her favorite dress.
   c. They were more useful than a colt.
   d. They were hard to come by in early California.
   e. She could trade them for four deerskins.

14. Based on the article, what conclusion can you draw about life in early California?
   a. Californians enjoyed Spanish rule.
   b. The leaders there were afraid of outsiders.
   c. The people there worked mostly in factories.
   d. Early California had large cities with many shops.
   e. The people there filled many needs with natural resources.

15. The War for Independence was between
   a. Spain and Mexico
   b. Mexico and California
   c. Spain and the United States
   d. Mexico and the United States
   e. California and the United States

Items 16–18 refer to the map below.

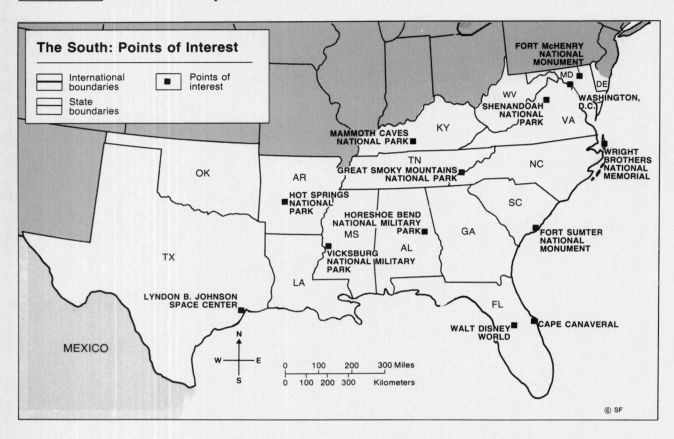

16. Which of the following states shares a boundary with Georgia?

   a. Texas

   b. Florida

   c. Kentucky

   d. Maryland

   e. Mississippi

17. Which point of interest is farthest west?

   a. Cape Canaveral

   b. Walt Disney World

   c. Fort Sumter National Monument

   d. Lyndon B. Johnson Space Center

   e. Wright Brothers National Memorial

18. Which of the following parks lies about 300 miles from Mammoth Caves National Park?

   a. Vicksburg

   b. Shenandoah

   c. Hot Springs

   d. Horseshoe Bend

   e. Great Smoky Mountains

Items 19–20 refer to the article below.

During the middle 1800s, an important change took place in Indiana. The United States government wanted all Indians to move west of the Mississippi River. Sometimes the government gave large pieces of land in Indiana to certain chiefs. In return, the chiefs persuaded their people to sell the land and move west.

One chief, Menominee of the Potawatomi tribe, refused to give up his people's land. Father Petit, a priest from France, helped Menominee write letters to Washington, D.C. The letters asked the President to let the Potawatomi stay in Indiana. But nothing helped.

Soldiers made the Potawatomi march 900 miles to a Kansas valley west of the Mississippi. One-fifth of the Indians died during the journey. Father Petit later called the trip the "Trail of Death." Even more Potawatomi died during the cold Kansas winter.

In 1840 the Miami Indians sold the rest of their land to the United States. Six years later, the last of the Miami left Indiana in boats. Their journey took them through lands that once were theirs. The Miami settled in a Kansas valley that looked much like the Wabash Valley, their old home. The last Indians had left Indiana.

19. What is the main idea of the passage? Sum it up in a couple of sentences.

_____

_____

20. Should the government have forced the Indians off their land? Why or why not? Use parts of the reading to support your ideas. Answer below in two or three sentences.

_____

_____

_____

You can check your answers to this test on pages 246–247.

Your Results

The table below is like the one for Measuring What You Know. This table shows you three things: (1) the number of each test question, (2) the main skill each question tests, and (3) the lesson in Part A that teaches that skill or gives practice in it.

Question	Skill	Lesson
1	Seeing patterns	1
2	Stating the main idea	1,2
3	Using inference	2,3,5
4	Understanding vocabulary	all*
5	Cause and effect	4
6	Stating the main idea	1,2
7	Predicting outcomes	5
8	Understanding vocabulary	all*
9	Reading a graph	6, 7
10	Reading a graph	6, 7
11	Reading a graph	6, 7
12	Recognizing point of view	9
13	Recognizing values	10
14	Drawing conclusions	11
15	Understanding vocabulary	all*
16	Reading a map	8, 11
17	Reading a map	8, 11
18	Reading a map	8, 11
19	Stating the main idea	1,2
20	Critical thinking	2,3,5,7,9

*To review vocabulary skills, study the Working with Words section in each lesson.

Which skills did you do well on? Which skills do you still need to practice? You can use the table to plan which lessons to review. If you missed fewer than five questions, you are ready to go on to Part B. If you missed five or more questions, be sure to review the lessons listed in the table before you go on.

Part **B**
Reading Skills for Science

In **Part B**, you will build skills in reading science. In **Unit 1**, you'll read about human life. Most of the articles are on your health. You'll learn about food, diet, exercise, and drugs that can help you or hurt you. As you read, you'll find diagrams, tables, and graphs. The Active Reader lessons will give you help in reading these.

In **Unit 2**, you'll read about the animal and plant world. You'll learn how animals behave. And you'll read about ecology, the ways in which plants, animals, and humans live together.

Unit 3 has articles from the physical sciences. You'll learn about the inner makeup of all matter. You'll learn about weather and climate conditions that affect your life. You'll read about planets in space and pollution here on earth. In this last unit, you'll also read articles on past discoveries and recent discoveries made by scientists.

Measuring What You Know

This test will help you find out how much you already know about science.

- In the test are four short articles. Read the articles and then answer the questions that follow.

- Many times you may find that you already know the answer to the question. With other questions, you will be able to find the answer by reading the article again.

- Take your time to read and answer questions. When you finish, check your answers on page 248.

Items 1–4 are based on the article below.

Why People Get Headaches

If you are like most people, you get headaches. Americans take more than 80 million aspirin a day. That's enough to cure about 15 billion headaches a year. What causes all those headaches?

By far the most common cause of headache is stress, or tension. Sometimes a person feels tired or under strain. The muscles in the head and neck become tense. This tension produces a headache.

Sometimes blood vessels in the head throb. This throbbing produces a headache. Sicknesses such as the flu can affect the blood vessels this way. So can drinking too much alcohol and breathing certain chemicals.

When blood vessels shrink and swell and throb a lot, a migraine headache may occur. A migraine is one of the most painful headaches a person can have. Scientists are not sure what causes migraines.

Ear and eye problems can also cause headaches. Almost everyone has had a headache due to eye strain.

It's not surprising that a blow to the head can cause a headache. But very few headaches are due to a brain disorder such as a tumor or disease.

1. What does this article tell you about? Circle the letter of your answer.

    a. how headaches compare with other illnesses

    b. the effects of aspirin on headaches

    c. the causes of headaches

2. Write the main idea of the entire article in your own words.

_____

_____

3. What would happen if people were better able to stay calm and relaxed?

_____

4. What does the word *disorder* mean in the last sentence of the article?

    a. Something is wrong with the brain.

    b. The brain isn't fully grown yet.

    c. The brain is working as usual.

Items 5–7 are based on the diagram below.

Calories Used in Walking

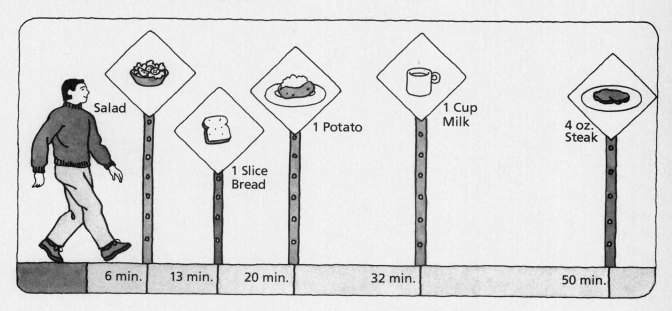

The diagram above shows how long it would take to burn off the calories of certain foods. Look at the signs at the top of the diagram. Notice that each sign pictures a food. Then look below each food sign and note that each sign has a block below it. Each block tells the number of minutes a person would need to walk to use up the number of calories contained in the food pictured above it.

5. How long would you have to walk to burn off the calories in a baked potato?

_____

6. Which contains more calories, a cup of milk or a slice of bread?

_____

7. For lunch, Sam ate a salad and a slice of bread. How many minutes would he have to walk to burn off this meal?

_____

Items 8–11 are based on the article below.

Why Do Whales Beach?

For reasons that scientists do not know, whales sometimes beach themselves. The whales swim too close to the shore. Then from the shallow waters, they swim up onto the beach. There they get stuck.

Whales cannot live out of water. Like all mammals, whales breast-feed their young and breathe air. However, whales spend their lives in water.

Whales are very large and heavy. Outside of the water, a whale's weight crushes its lungs. The whale cannot breathe.

Many whales that beach are dying even before they get out of the water. Some scientists think sick whales beach in order to keep from drowning.

Other scientists think that the whale's sonar, or sound, system fails. Then the whale loses its way and ends up on the beach.

For whatever reason, whales that beach seem to want to stay beached. Scientists have rescued whales only to find them later, beached again.

Perhaps the whales have a reason for coming onto the beach. But for now, they are not telling.

8. Which of the statements below best states the main idea of this article? Circle the letter of your answer.
   a. Whales that beach want to die.
   b. Scientists are not sure why whales beach.
   c. Whales are mammals that breathe air.

9. At low tide the water near the beach is less deep than at other times. Why would whales be more likely to beach themselves at low tide?

_____

10. Dolphins belong to the same group of mammals that whales do. Name one way that dolphins and whales are different from other mammals.

_____

11. What does the word "beach" mean in this sentence?
    "For whatever reason, whales that *beach* seem to want to stay beached."

_____

Items 12–15 are based on the article below.

Testing Ground for Rainfall

How much rain will there be next season? Test your soil and find out.

Scientists have found that soil temperatures can forecast the amount of rain to come in the next few months. But the scientists had to dig deep to find the answer—about forty inches under the ground.

Warmer deep soil temperatures mean more rain. A higher-than-normal soil temperature in winter predicts a wet spring.

Some scientists believe that this correlation between soil temperature and rainfall comes from the fact that warm soil gives off heat. The warmer the soil, the more heat it gives off.

This heat rises and adds to the flow of warm air in the atmosphere. More showers and thunderstorms result. Colder air has the opposite effect and results in less rain.

With this method, rainfall can best be predicted over small areas, scientists say. One or two soil testing stations can give good predictions for a county-wide area.

12. Which of the following best sums up the main ideas of the passage? Circle the letter of your answer.

    a. Scientists use many methods to predict weather. One method they use is testing the temperature of the soil. They dig about forty inches under the ground to test the soil.

    b. Scientists test deep soil temperatures. These temperatures predict the amount of rain that will fall in coming months. Warmer soil temperatures mean more rain.

13. Suppose this winter the temperature of the deep soil in your area is warmer than normal. Scientists then predict your area will have more rainfall in the spring. What other thing is needed for their prediction to come true? Circle the letter of your answer.

    a. There must be moisture in the air.

    b. There must be cold nights in the spring.

14. Suppose soil testing in your area shows colder than normal temperatures. What kind of weather can you expect over the next few months?

_____

15. The article talks about the "correlation between soil temperature and rainfall." Circle the letter of the meaning of "correlation" in the article.

    a. difference

    b. sum

    c. relationship

The table below will help you. It lists the numbers of the questions on the pretest. It lists the skills you need to answer those questions. To the right of the table you will also see lesson numbers. The lesson numbers show you which lessons can help you with each skill. Read those lessons in Part B especially carefully to practice the skills you need help with.

Question	Skill	Lesson
1	Seeing patterns	1
2	Stating the main idea	9
3	Drawing conclusions	4
4	Understanding vocabulary	1–11
5	Interpreting a diagram	2
6	Drawing conclusions	4
7	Applying ideas	5
8	Stating the main idea	9
9	Cause and effect	7
10	Drawing conclusions	4
11	Understanding vocabulary	1–11
12	Summarizing	9
13	Using what you know	8
14	Predicting outcomes	5
15	Understanding vocabulary	1–11

Human Life

The Active Reader

Seeing Patterns of Ideas

Picture It

Which grocery store would you shop at?

Probably the store on the right. Why? Because it would be easier to find things. Shelves and signs show you where each kind of food is. The store is *organized*.

In a similar way, science writers organize their ideas. They may even use clue words as "signs." These words help show you how the ideas are organized. Ideas can be organized in different patterns. If you understand the pattern in a science article, you'll understand and remember the ideas better.

Here's an Example

Scientists try to find out *why* things happen. That is, they study **causes.** Scientists also try to find out *what happens* as a result of things. They study

effects. For that reason, much science writing talks about causes and effects. See how the following article follows this pattern of cause and effect.

■**Why** do people get hungry? A person feels hungry **when** the level of sugar in his or her blood is low. **Because** the person is hungry, he or she eats food. That food is then broken down into a simple sugar. This sugar enters the blood. **As a result,** the level of blood sugar goes up. The person no longer feels hungry.

The words in **bold** above help you see this pattern of causes and effects:

Low blood sugar ⟶ Hunger ⟶ Eat ⟶

Blood sugar goes up ⟶ No more hunger

Writers may also use other words to show you causes and effects: *since, due to, for that reason, leads to, causes, so, therefore,* and *consequently.*

Scientists also **categorize** things. They put similar things into groups. For that reason, much science writing talks about categories, like this one.

■ Food is made up of nutrients that nourish the body. Scientists have discovered hundreds of nutrients. *Because many nutrients do similar things, they can be* **grouped together.** The **six main categories** of nutrients are proteins, carbohydrates, fats, minerals, vitamins, and water.

The sentence in *italics* is a clue. So are the words in **bold.** They tell you the writer is probably going to **list** the categories of nutrients. In the next sentence he does.

It would also be a good guess that the writer will go on to tell you more about *each* category of nutrients, like this.

■ The mineral calcium is needed to build teeth and bones, help blood clot, and help nerves and muscles work.

Good readers use such sentences and words as clues to how the writer has organized the ideas. Ask yourself—
Is the writer talking about causes and effects?
Is the writer talking about categories?
Is the writer listing examples?
Try to answer questions like these as you read. Then you'll better understand what you read. You'll remember it better too, because the information will be organized in your head as well.

Working It Out

Read this article. As you read, look for words that show the pattern of the ideas.

■ "Don't eat so much red meat!" This warning is often heard. The reason is that the fat in red meat can cause heart problems and add weight. So breeding tests began using low-fat cattle from Italy. The result was beef that has fewer calories than chicken.

1. Underline the words that signal causes and effects.

2. Fill in the cause or effect below.
   a. *Cause:* Breeding tests began using low-fat cattle from Italy.

      Effect: _____

   b. *Cause:* _____

      Effect: heart and weight problems

Now read this first sentence of a science article.

■ There are two kinds of vitamins.

3. What do you think the next sentences will tell you about?

_____

Now read the rest of the paragraph to see if you were right.

■ The first kind can be stored in your body. These are vitamins A, D, E, and K. You must be careful not to take in too much of these vitamins. The second kind cannot be stored in your body. These are the B vitamins and vitamin C. You must take in these vitamins every day.

Food and Your Health

Before You Read: Thinking About Food and Health

Are you afraid you don't know anything about science? If so, think again. Science deals with everyday things—things *you* deal with every day. Take food, for example. See what you already know about food.

1. Below is a list of food pairs. For each pair, circle the one you think is better for your health.

   soda pop   *or*   fruit juice
   broiled chicken   *or*   fried chicken
   yogurt   *or*   a candy bar

2. Look over the foods you circled. Why do you think these foods are good for you?

   _____

3. Now think about the foods you did not choose. Is there something these foods have that makes you think they are not good for you?

   _____

Keep your food choices in mind as you read the articles in this lesson. Then look back over your answers to see if you would change any.

   Take the time now to *preview* the following articles about food. Here's how.

For each selection, quickly look over, or skim, the title, the article itself, and any charts and graphs. This preview will give you a good idea of what you will be reading.

   Below are the titles of the articles you've just previewed. Take a few minutes to think about the list. Then number the titles 1 through 7. Write the number 1 next to the title you think you already know the *most* about. Write the number 7 next to the title you feel you know the *least* about.

_____ Ideal weight   _____ Cholesterol

_____ Popular diets   _____ Planning a menu

_____ Obese children   _____ Anorexia

_____ The changing eating habits of Americans

Think about the two topics you felt you knew the least about (your numbers 6 and 7). For each topic, write a question you would like answered in your reading.

Question for your topic 6:

_____

_____

Question for your topic 7:

_____

_____

See if these questions are answered in your reading.

Working with Words

Diet, nutrition, and **digestion** are three important terms you'll read in the following articles. Sometimes you can figure out the meaning of a word from other information in its sentence. Sometimes you can use what you already know. For example, read these sentences.

Dairy products, meat, fruits, and vegetables are part of a good **diet.**

Eating a variety of good foods provides the proper **nutrition** for your body.

Taking a walk after a big meal can help your **digestion** because walking speeds the release of acids that break down food.

Dairy products, meat, fruits, and vegetables are examples of foods people eat. That fact should help you see that in the first sentence above *diet* means "what a person eats."

There is another definition of the word *diet.* The sentence below gives you an idea of this meaning. Read the clue sentence carefully. Then rewrite the sentence using the word *diet.*

Clue sentence: Astrid plans to eat less so she can lose weight.

_____

Did you rewrite the sentence like this? *Astrid plans to go on a diet.*

Have you ever seen the word *nutrition* before? You may have noticed the nutrition information on the side of a cereal box. This includes the amount of salt, fat, and protein and the number of calories, vitamins, and minerals. In fact, such nutrition information is given on many foods. What does this nutrition information tell you about the food?

_____

Nutrition information tells you what's in the food. Then you can judge if the food is good for you. That's what proper nutrition is: food that is good for you because it keeps you healthy.

You know your stomach feels full after a big meal. Look at the information in the third sentence. Use that information to write your own definition of *digestion.*

_____

_____

If you wrote that digestion somehow breaks down the food you eat, you're on the right track.

Now read the actual definitions of these words below.

Word Power

diet (1) the usual kind of food and drink; (2) any special selection of food eaten during sickness, or in order to lose or gain weight

nutrition food; nourishment; food value

digestion the act of changing food in the stomach and intestines, so that the body can use it

Reading on Your Own

Ideal Weights

Height	Men	Women
4'10"	–	100–131
4'11"	–	101–134
5'0"	–	103–137
5'1"	123–145	105–140
5'2"	125–148	108–144
5'3"	127–151	111–148
5'4"	129–155	114–152
5'5"	131–159	117–156
5'6"	133–163	120–160
5'7"	135–167	123–164
5'8"	137–171	126–167
5'9"	139–175	129–170
5'10"	141–179	132–173
5'11"	144–179	135–176
6'0"	147–187	–
6'1"	150–192	–
6'2"	153–197	–
6'3"	157–202	–
6'4"	–	–

"Ideal Weight" tables like the one above have been used for years. They show how much people *should* weigh. This "ideal weight" depends on their gender and height. But doctors now ask if such tables are correct.

Is a person really healthier if he or she weighs within the range on the table? Doctors do not agree with each other. Some say the weights are too high. Others say they are too low. Some doctors think it is best to be a little thin. Others believe a few extra pounds are good. Many doctors believe older people should weigh a few more pounds than the tables show.

Use the information you just read to answer these questions.

1. Florence is 5'6" tall and weighs 135 pounds. According to the table, is she overweight? Why or why not?

_____

2. Weights on the table are grouped according to a person's _____

   and _____.

3. Fill in the chart below to show the different opinions doctors have about weight. The first one is done for you.

Some doctors think . . .	Others believe . . .
a. older people should weigh within the range on the table.	*older people should be a few pounds heavier.*
b. weights on the table are too high.	
c. it's better to be a little thin.	

Popular Diets

A dieter often feels confused. The newsstands are full of books and magazines that offer "wonder diets." The most important questions to ask when choosing a diet are, Is it a healthful diet? And can I stick to this diet?

The best way to diet is to eat the same healthful foods that non-dieters should eat. But a dieter should eat less of them. To stay healthy, people need protein. An ounce or two of meat and a glass of milk each day will provide plenty. People also need a few fats. These can be found in margarine and cooking oils. Fats are also found in meat and milk. For energy, people need carbohydrates. Breads, fruits, and vegetables have many carbohydrates. More than half the food a person eats should be these energy foods.

A healthful diet is high in carbohydrates, lower in fats, and lowest in protein. A "high protein" or "low carbohydrate" diet often includes too much meat, milk, and eggs. The body can easily turn the protein of this milk and meat into fat.

What is the real secret to losing weight and keeping it off? Form new eating habits. Eat the right foods in the right amounts all the time.

Answer each of the following questions with a few words or a sentence.

1. According to the article, what is the best way to lose weight?

_____

_____

2. A "high protein diet" sounds good, but it may not help you lose weight. Why not?

_____

_____

3. Look at the second paragraph. What three kinds of foods are needed to stay healthy? Give an example of each. Use the table below for your answers.

Kinds of Foods	Example
1. _____	_____
2. _____	_____
3. _____	_____

Obese Children

Obese. The word describes people who weigh too much. Children as well as adults can be obese. In fact, today there are more obese children than ever.

Scientists don't know what causes obesity. But there are some things they know for certain about obese children. Most of these children have at least one overweight parent. And obesity is not something that children "outgrow."

Obese children do not seem to eat much more food than other children. But obese children do seem to be less active than children who are not overweight. In fact, many scientists believe TV watching helps cause obesity. Children don't get much exercise while they're watching TV. As they watch TV, they often snack. They usually eat the junk foods they see advertised on television.

Answer the following questions with a phrase or sentence.

1. Give two reasons that watching too much TV is a main cause of obesity in children.

_____

_____

2. Why do you think obese children often have obese parents?

_____

_____

The Changing Eating Habits of Americans

Since the 1950s the life-styles of Americans have changed. Eating habits have changed too.

Thirty years ago, there were few kinds of quick-cooking packaged foods. In the 1950s, meat was the main food in the diet. People ate meat at lunch and dinner and sometimes at breakfast. Breads, fresh fruits, and vegetables were served along with the meat. Most people ate butter and drank whole milk.

Since then, things have changed. We use many foods that are packaged and take little time to prepare. Packaged foods, though, are not as healthful as fresh foods. Sugar and salt are often added to foods as they are packaged. Many people don't eat enough fruits and vegetables. Many also eat too many sweets.

We now know more about nutrition—what foods are good and why. As a result, people are eating more chicken and fish and less beef than they did before. Butter isn't used as much, and most people drink low-fat or skim milk. Salads are popular. Experts say these are good signs. Thus, in some ways, Americans have formed better eating habits. But in other ways Americans still do not eat as well as they should.

Now answer the following questions about "The Changing Eating Habits of Americans."

1. What effect has better knowledge of nutrition had on eating habits?

_____

_____

2. Why do you think people eat packaged foods even though such foods are not as good for them?

_____

_____

Match each statement about an eating habit in Column 1 with its time period in Column 2. The first one is done for you.

Column 1

__b__ 3. more aware of nutrition

_____ 4. people eat more red meat, less chicken or fish

_____ 5. longer time to prepare meals

_____ 6. margarine and skim milk used often

_____ 7. fresh foods used, not prepared or frozen foods

Column 2

a. 1950s

b. now

Cholesterol

Cholesterol is often in the news. Just what is cholesterol, and how can you avoid too much of it?

Cholesterol is a kind of fat from animals. Chickens, cows, and pigs all make cholesterol. They use it to make many other important chemicals in their bodies. Any food made from part of an animal has some cholesterol. Meat, eggs, butter, and whole milk have a great deal of cholesterol. Low-fat milk and yogurt have less. The human body makes cholesterol too. People need some cholesterol, just as animals do.

But too much cholesterol can be harmful. If you have 20 percent more cholesterol than you need, you will be three times more likely to have heart disease. You can't really change how much cholesterol your body makes. But you can change how much you eat. Eat less meat. Some vegetables, such as peas, beans, and soybeans, have the same good food ingredients as meats. But these vegetables have no cholesterol. Use vegetable oils and shortening instead of butter. Eat oatmeal. Oats help the body get rid of extra cholesterol. If you eat wisely, you can lower the amount of cholesterol in your blood. You will also lower your chances of heart disease.

Use the information you just read to answer these questions.

1. Here is a list of foods.

   liver   skim milk
   oatmeal   eggs
   fried chicken pepperoni pizza

   Below are two categories of foods. Decide if each food above is high or low in cholesterol. Then list it on the table.

High in Cholesterol	Low in Cholesterol
_____	_____
_____	_____
_____	_____
_____	_____

2. Juan eats two eggs, bacon, and buttered toast each morning. Juanita has oatmeal, fruit, and skim milk. Which breakfast has less cholesterol? Explain your answer.

   _____

   _____

Planning a Menu

Americans have more foods to choose from than any other people in the world. But many Americans have poor eating habits. Many Americans do not know what foods are most important to good health. They do not plan meals that include these foods.

The body gets important chemicals from food during digestion. The table below shows three groups of foods the body needs. It also shows healthful foods in each group.

Protein	Starches and Sugar	Fats
chicken	grains	safflower oil
lean beef	(rice, breads, pasta)	soft margarine
fish	fruits	
skim milk	leafy green and yellow	
beans	vegetables	
nuts		

A few guidelines will make planning a healthful meal easy.

1. Choose one protein and one grain.
2. Serve many different fruits and vegetables.
3. Use as little fat as possible. Use vegetable oils instead of animal fats. Avoid fatty meats and foods made from whole milk.
4. Choose at least half of your foods from the starches and sugars group.

A sample meal might be spaghetti or noodles in a tomato sauce with mushrooms, onions, and a little meat; bread or rolls; a tossed green salad; broccoli; and a dessert of fresh fruit.

Plan a menu for a day—breakfast, lunch, and dinner. Use the table and guidelines to make sure your menu is healthful. Use a separate sheet of paper.

Anorexia: The Diet That Kills

Debra is twenty-two years old and 5'6" tall. She weighs 99 pounds. She exercises for nearly two hours each day. Debra looks very thin. But she says her legs are too fat and feels she must lose a few more pounds. Debra is anorexic.

In our society, looking slim is very important. For a small number of people, being thin becomes more important than anything else. Some young women especially feel this way. These women begin to diet all the time because they are afraid of becoming fat.

Like Debra, an anorexic woman often sees one part of her body as being too fat. She eats less and less. In a short time, she no longer feels hunger pains. Her fear does not go away even when she has become very thin. When she looks in a mirror, she actually sees herself as fat.

Anorexics slowly starve. Without medical care, anorexic people like Debra will die. They can recover only with help from their doctors and families.

The GED Warm-up below gives you a chance to practice answering a multiple-choice question. You will find questions like this on the GED Test. Choose the best answer. Then fill in the circle for that answer.

GED Warm-up

Debra is anorexic because she

(1) exercises two hours each day
(2) always sees herself as being fat

Interpreting Diagrams

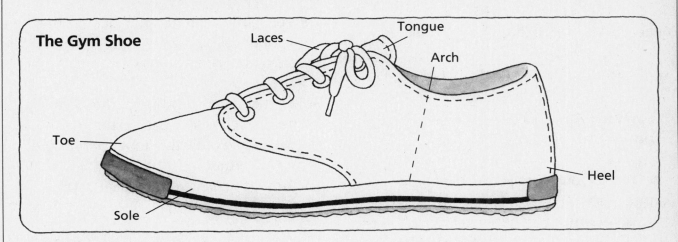

The Gym Shoe

Laces · Tongue · Arch · Toe · Sole · Heel

Picture It

Take a look at the diagram of the gym shoe above. A diagram shows how something is made or how it works. Often a diagram is easier to read than a long, complicated explanation. You might say one good diagram is worth a thousand words.

Understanding diagrams is a very important skill for reading science. It is also useful in your everyday life. You often see and use diagrams. One example is the diagram that comes with directions for putting something together. Can you think of other places where you see diagrams in daily life?

One place you may have thought of is a shopping mall. When you look at a mall map and see "You Are Here," you are using a diagram. In a restaurant, you may have noticed a poster about the Heimlich maneuver. This poster has a diagram that shows how to help someone who is choking.

You read a science diagram the way you read diagrams in everyday life.

Here's an Example

Look again at the diagram above. Like most diagrams, it has a title. It is important to look for the title first. It gives you a general idea of what the diagram is about.

The diagram is titled, "The Gym Shoe." Each part of the shoe is clearly labeled. A line is drawn from a particular part of the shoe to its name. Find the laces and the arch on the diagram. Note how the labeling lines are different. A solid line is used to label the laces. Laces are outside the shoe and can be seen. On the other hand, a broken line is used to label the arch. The arch is inside the shoe and cannot be seen. Using solid or broken lines is the usual way to label diagram parts that can or cannot be seen.

Working It Out

Look at the diagram below. It is incomplete. Try your hand at completing it. First review what you know about athletic shoes. What do you recall about the diagrams you have seen before?

Remember it is important to combine what you already know with what you have just learned about diagrams.

Next, read the following descriptions of the parts of the running shoe. Read each description carefully. Notice whether the part is located inside or outside the shoe. Use the names in **dark print** to label the parts of the shoe.

tongue—the flap under the laces at the top of the shoe

insole—the inside bottom or lining of the shoe

sole—the outside bottom of the shoe

laces—the cord that passes through the eyelets and pulls the upper part of the shoe together

toe box—the piece of material at the very front of the shoe

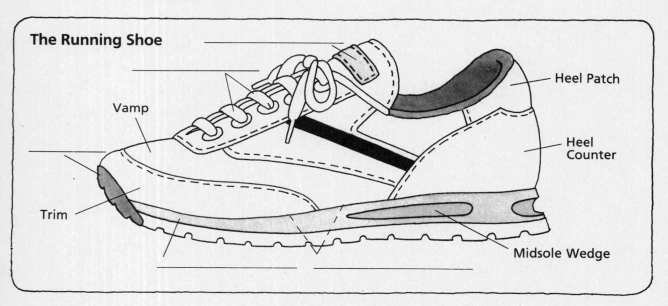

The Running Shoe

Vamp

Trim

Heel Patch

Heel Counter

Midsole Wedge

Staying Healthy

Before You Read: Thinking About Staying Healthy

Staying healthy is a popular issue today. There is a great deal of health-related information out there. Take a few minutes now to think about all the facts you already know about staying healthy. Eating low-fat foods and stopping smoking are just a few examples.

Now start brainstorming. Here's how. List every idea that comes to mind about ways to stay healthy. Spelling or the order of ideas doesn't matter. Just let your thoughts run freely. Use the space below to jot down your brainstormed ideas.

_____

_____

_____

_____

_____

_____

Now look over the articles in this lesson. Do any of the titles or diagrams make you think of more ideas about staying healthy? If so, add those new ideas to your list.

Reread your brainstorming list. Once again look over the titles you will be reading about in this lesson. Which two areas do you feel you already know the most about?

_____

_____

Which two areas do you feel you know the least about?

_____

_____

Think of at least one question you expect to have answered from your reading. Write your question(s) here.

_____

_____

_____

At the end of your reading, check back here to see if you found your answer(s).

Working with Words

Three scientific terms you'll find in the following articles are *blood pressure*, *vessels*, and *transplant*. Each one is used in a sentence in the box that follows. As you read each sentence, try to figure out the meaning of the word in dark print.

First, think about what you already know about each word. Then try to figure out its meaning from other information in the sentence. This two-step approach can help you figure out the meaning of a new word.

Blood pressure changes with activity, excitement, health, and age.

It is a difficult operation to **transplant** a kidney from one person to another.

Veins and arteries are called blood **vessels** because they carry blood throughout the body.

Think about the kinds of information you have seen or heard about blood pressure. Maybe you have had your blood pressure taken. You know then that good blood pressure is important to your health. Now look at the way *blood pressure* is used in the first sentence. You learn that blood pressure changes. You now know that blood pressure can be measured, it affects your health, and it changes. Write a sentence here using the term *blood pressure*.

_____

_____

If the word *transplant* made you think of gardening, you've got the right idea. When plants are moved from one spot to another, they are transplanted. The idea is the same when we talk about human transplants. Stories of transplants are often in the news. Think of the parts of the body you know can be transplanted.

Now write a sentence using the word *transplant*.

_____

_____

Vessel is not a very common word. But the third sentence gives you a clue to its meaning. The word "carry" is the key word. You learn that a vessel is able to carry, or move, blood. Can you think of other things that work like vessels? One example is a wire carrying electricity. Think of another example. Write it here.

_____

_____

Below are the definitions for each word. See if your idea of each word's meaning is similar.

Word Power

blood pressure the pressure of the blood against the inner walls of the arteries

transplant to transfer skin, an organ, or the like from one person, animal, or part of the body to another

vessel a tube carrying blood or other fluid

Now you're ready to read these and other terms as you read about staying healthy.

Reading on Your Own

Your Heart: Keep It Healthy

Thirty million Americans have some kind of heart disease. Many things make a person more or less likely to have heart problems. Some of these cannot be changed. For instance, heart disease seems to run in families. Women are less likely to have heart disease; older people are more likely. But heart disease does not have to happen. Here are some ways to keep your heart healthy.

Eat the right foods. Too much fat and cholesterol in foods can cause heart disease. Fish and chicken have less fat and cholesterol than beef and eggs.

Watch your weight. Heart disease is more common in overweight people. For a middle-aged man, the chance of a heart attack is three times higher if he is overweight.

Don't smoke. Heart disease is the main cause of death among cigarette smokers. A smoker who quits is less likely to die from heart disease than someone who doesn't quit. A person who has never smoked is healthiest of all.

Have your blood pressure checked. People with high blood pressure have more heart disease. High blood pressure means that the heart is working too hard to pump blood to all parts of the body. High blood pressure can be treated.

Exercise regularly. Exercise makes the blood flow faster. It strengthens the muscles of the heart. It may keep a person from gaining weight. Exercise can also lower blood pressure.

Answer each of the following questions in a few words.

1. List five ways in which you can lower your risk of heart disease.

   _____

   _____

   _____

   _____

   _____

2. Describe a person with a high risk of heart disease.

   _____

   _____

   _____

Put a check in front of your answer.

3. The force of blood as it flows from the heart through the body is a definition of

   _____ **a.** heart attack

   _____ **b.** heart disease

   _____ **c.** blood pressure

Warning Signs of a Heart Attack

Many people think a heart attack happens when a person is exercising very hard. However, scientists have studied what many people were doing when their heart attacks began. Fifty-nine percent were asleep or resting. Thirty-one percent were doing usual activity.

Rarely, heart attacks occur without warning and cause instant death. More often, there are early signs that a person is having a heart attack. Here are a few clues to watch for.

A person having a heart attack feels pressure in the center of the chest. Some people say it feels like "pain" or like "being squeezed." This pain may spread to the shoulders, arms, back, neck, or jaw. The pain will usually last more than two minutes. It may be steady, or it may come and go.

Sweating, shortness of breath, and an upset stomach are other signs of a heart attack. A person may also feel weak.

Not all heart attack victims have all these signs. The pain does not have to be sharp. The person does not have to "look sick." But if even some of the signs appear, get help immediately. Without help, most victims will die within two hours of the first signs of an attack.

Write your answers to these questions.

1. List five possible signs of a heart attack.

_____

_____

_____

_____

_____

2. The article says, "Many people think that a heart attack usually happens when a person is exercising very hard." Are these people right? Explain your answer.

_____

_____

Artificial Hearts

A healthy heart is a muscle about the size of a fist. Life depends entirely on this small organ. The diagram below shows a healthy heart and how it works.

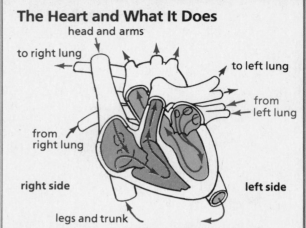

The Heart and What It Does

head and arms
to right lung
to left lung
from left lung
from right lung
right side
left side
legs and trunk

The right side of the heart receives blood from the rest of the body. This blood (grey lines) carries very little oxygen. The right side of the heart pumps it to the lungs. There the blood picks up fresh oxygen.

The left side of the heart receives blood rich in oxygen (red lines) from the lungs. This blood is pumped to the rest of the body.

What happens to a person whose heart has stopped working? Most people who have serious heart damage die very soon. A person can be saved, though, if he or she is given a *new* heart.

Very few people can receive a healthy heart from another person. There are not enough hearts for all the patients who need such heart transplants. If a human heart is not found quickly, a person may be given an artificial heart.

An artificial heart is a machine that pumps blood to the lungs and the rest of the body. It will do the work that the heart cannot do by itself. Artificial hearts cannot be used for long periods of time, though. Bleeding, strokes, and other problems may develop. Once a human heart is found, the artificial heart can be removed, and the new one put in place.

Use information from the article "Artificial Hearts" on page 138 to answer these questions.

1. Tell in your own words what the heart does.

   _____

   _____

2. An operation to replace a damaged organ, such as the heart, with a healthy one is called a _____ .

3. Look again at the diagram of the heart on page 138. Can you think of a reason that people who smoke are likely to have heart disease?

   _____

   _____

Hardening of the Arteries

One of the most common forms of heart disease is hardening of the arteries. Arteries are large blood vessels that look like rubber hoses. They carry blood from the heart to the rest of the body. The diagram below shows what happens inside an artery as it hardens.

Hardening of the Arteries

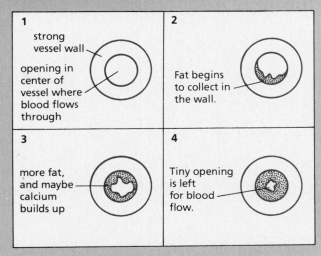

1 strong vessel wall / opening in center of vessel where blood flows through

2 Fat begins to collect in the wall.

3 more fat, and maybe calcium builds up

4 Tiny opening is left for blood flow.

An artery has walls made of muscle (picture 1). Hardening of the arteries begins when cholesterol and other fats collect inside the vessel. The vessel wall becomes thicker than it should be. The opening for the blood to pass through becomes more narrow than it should be (picture 2). Gradually, calcium and more fat gather. The artery walls become hard (picture 3). Over a long period of time, the opening may become so small that blood flow slows or stops altogether (picture 4).

The effects of this disease depend on which artery walls are hardened most. Poor blood flow in the legs may lead to cramps during exercise. A heart attack may follow if too little blood reaches the heart. If the brain doesn't get enough blood, a person may have a stroke.

Put a check in front of your answer.

1. As used in the article, "vessel" means
   _____ a. a container like a cup or bowl
   _____ b. a tube carrying something along
   _____ c. a ship or large boat

Answer with a few words.

2. What causes the walls of the blood vessels to become thick and hard?

   _____

   _____

3. On the next page are diagrams of arteries and descriptions of four people. Match the drawing of the way each person's arteries probably look with his or her description. You will use each picture once.

_____ **a.** a healthy 30-year-old man who eats fatty foods

_____ **b.** an 8-year-old girl in excellent health

_____ **c.** an elderly man who has survived two heart attacks and still smokes

_____ **d.** a woman who has poor eating habits and doesn't exercise

Smoking and Its Effects on the Lungs

"Surgeon General's Warning: Smoking Causes Lung Cancer, Heart Disease, Emphysema, and May Complicate Pregnancy."

A warning similar to this is on every pack of cigarettes sold in this country. People still smoke, even though they know smoking causes cancer and other medical problems.

The diagram below shows the human respiratory system.

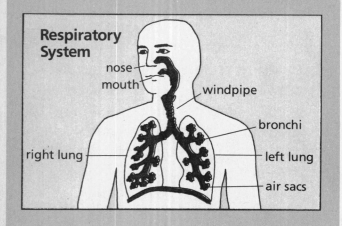

Respiratory System

nose
mouth
windpipe
bronchi
right lung
left lung
air sacs

When you breathe air in, it goes down through the windpipe and into the bronchi. Bronchi divide into smaller tubes that lead into tiny air sacs. From these air sacs, oxygen in the air passes to the blood. The blood then carries oxygen to all parts of the body.

Smoking keeps the lungs from working well in several ways. The nicotine in cigarettes does not let the bronchi open as large as they should. Air cannot move in and out easily.

Cigarette smoke also hurts the lungs. It contains a gas called carbon monoxide. Like oxygen, this gas passes easily into the bloodstream. The blood cannot carry as much oxygen as it should. During exercise, a smoker will therefore tire more easily than a nonsmoker.

After a person smokes for many years, the air sacs break down. Then the lungs cannot send enough oxygen into the blood. Taking just a few steps can be very tiring. This disease is emphysema.

Use the information you just read to answer these questions.

1. Give three ways smoking interferes with the work of the lungs.

_____

_____

_____

2. Why do smokers tire more easily than nonsmokers?

_____

3. Look at the diagram of the respiratory system. Why can you keep breathing even if your nose is blocked?

_____

Aerobics

Is aerobics just a fad? Or are there some good reasons that aerobics classes are so popular?

In aerobics classes, people jump and jog for twenty minutes or more. Such aerobic exercise makes the muscles work for a long time. The heart and lungs must work hard and fast to keep bringing oxygen to these muscles.

Experts believe that such exercise can make your heart stronger. To strengthen your heart, you must exercise without stopping for twenty to thirty minutes, three to five times a week. This exercise should be done at a comfortable speed. If you're out of breath and can't talk, you're working too hard. If you exercise regularly, your heart and lungs become stronger. These organs can then do more work with less effort.

You don't have to join a class to do aerobic exercise. Jogging and swimming are examples of aerobic exercise. Folk dancing, cross-country skiing, and handball are others. Even brisk walking can be aerobic exercise.

Answer the following questions about aerobics.

1. What two organs are strengthened through regular aerobic exercise?

_____

2. Do you think aerobics is a fad and will die out soon? Or do you think aerobics will stay popular? Give reasons for your answer.

_____

_____

_____

How Exercise Affects the Bones

As people age, bone loss can become a problem. Bones are made up mostly of calcium. Older people do not take in calcium well. They also tend to lose calcium from their bones. The bones become thinner and weaker. They become more brittle, and they break more easily. Knowing this, many older people are afraid to exercise. They are afraid that even walking may put too much stress on their bones.

Researchers compared people who exercise with people who don't. They found that people who exercise actually have *stronger* bones. Their bones are more dense. They contain more calcium. They are thus less likely to break. Exercise may actually slow down the bone loss that comes with growing old.

Use the information you just read to complete this table.

Bones of People Who Exercise	Bones of People Who Do Not Exercise
a. stronger	_____
b. _____	less dense
c. _____	less calcium
d. slower bone loss	_____

GED Warm-up

Which form of exercise is probably better for an older person?

(1) good, hard exercise, such as running, once a week

(2) regular mild exercise, such as walking

①　　②

Interpreting Tables and Graphs

Picture It

In science reading, you will often come across tables and graphs like the ones on these pages. Think how tables and graphs are used in newspapers. Some examples are TV program schedules, sports standings, news on the economy, and weather information. There's a way to read tables and graphs to get the most out of them.

Here's an Example

Effects of Alcohol (on a 160-pound person)

Number of drinks in one hour	Level of alcohol in blood (percent)	Effects on behavior
1	.02	Mild change
2	.05	Mood swings
5	.10	Legally "under the influence"
7½	.15	Drunk
15	.30	In a daze
19	.40	Unconscious

First read the title to find out the topic of a table. What do you think the table above is about?

You should have the idea that the table shows how drinking changes people.

Now read the headings at the top of each column. They tell you what specific information is given about the topic. The first column gives the number of drinks drunk in one hour. The second column lists the level of alcohol in the blood in percents. The third column shows the effects of alcohol on behavior.

Look down each column. What kind of information is given?

You know from the heading that column 1 will be numbers. The numbers are put from lowest to highest.

Notice the heading in column 2. It tells you the numbers in that column are percents. The percents get higher as you go down the column.

The third column does not deal with numbers but descriptions. Read down this column. How would you explain the order of these descriptions?

If you thought of a range of change, just like a range of numbers, your explanation was correct. The behavior ranges from bad to worse.

Here's how to find information on the

table. Suppose a person weighing 160 pounds drinks 7½ beers in one hour. You want to find the percent of alcohol in his blood and its effect. Run your finger down the first column ("Number of drinks") until you get to the number 7½. Then run your finger directly across the table to the other columns. The level of alcohol in the blood is 0.15 percent, and the person is drunk.

The very same information that was given on the table was used to make the line graph below. Now the information makes a strong picture. Line graphs show changes or trends.

Effects of Alcohol
(on a 160-pound person)

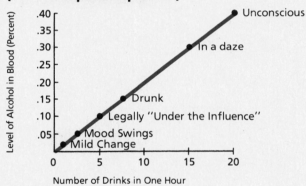

Read the parts of the graph as you read the table.

First, *read the title* to see what the topic is. Next, *read the labels* along the bottom and side. The number of drinks is shown along the bottom. The range is from 0 to 20. The level of alcohol in the blood is shown up the side. Every space is equal to 0.05 percent. The range is from 0 to 0.40 percent.

Here's how to answer a question using the line graph. *Question:* How many

drinks must a person drink to have 0.30 percent alcohol in the blood?

Begin with what you know. Run your finger up the side of the graph to 0.30. From that point, run your finger straight across. Stop at the point where you meet the line on the graph. Now run your finger down to the bottom line. You find the answer is 15 drinks.

You could also use the graph to answer the question from the opposite view. What is the level of alcohol in the blood after drinking 15 drinks in one hour? Again, begin with what you know. Use the bottom line to find 15 drinks. Go straight up to the point where your finger meets the line. Now run your finger over to the left. You find your answer: 0.30 percent.

Working It Out

1. According to the table, what is the level of alcohol in the blood and its effect on behavior for a 160-pound person drinking 2 drinks in one hour?

   _____

   _____

2. According to the graph, how many drinks must be drunk in one hour for a 160-pound person to have a 0.10 percent level of alcohol in the blood?

   _____

3. Describe how drinking changes the way a person acts.

   _____

   _____

Drug Abuse

Before You Read: Thinking About Drug Abuse

Take a few minutes to preview the articles in this lesson. They all deal with drug abuse. Think about each title. Then look over the articles. Notice the tables and graphs too. What two drugs will you be reading about the most?

_____

_____

If you said alcohol and cocaine, you're right. Did you know alcohol was considered a drug? It's a drug because it is a chemical that affects the body. You probably know the names of drinks that have alcohol in them. List a few here.

_____

_____

Some examples of alcoholic drinks are beer, wine, wine coolers, and whiskey.

Think about what you already know about drugs and drug abuse. Television, magazines, and newspapers play a big part in our awareness of drugs. You may also know someone with a drug problem. Perhaps you personally know the effects of drugs. Jot down all the things you know about drug abuse already.

_____

_____

Some things you may already know are these ideas: Drugs are harmful. They can even kill. Drugs can control one's life.

Perhaps you also already know of the "Say no to drugs" program. Do you have any ideas on how to solve the drug-abuse problem? If so, take the time to write them down.

_____

_____

_____

Are there any questions about drugs you would like answered? Write your questions here.

_____

_____

_____

As you read the articles on drug abuse, use the information you already know to understand the new ideas you read. Look for the answers to your questions too. Perhaps you'll even think of a good way to help solve the problem.

Working with Words

You already know many words about drugs and drug abuse. You hear them on

TV shows often. You hear people speak them. You may even use them yourself. But perhaps you have trouble *reading* such words.

You know you can figure out a word by looking at how it is used in a sentence. Sometimes you can also look at the parts of a word to figure it out.

Look at the word *alcoholism,* for example. You've probably heard the word many times. You know what alcohol is. The word part *-ism* can mean "a condition produced by." When you read a sentence like "Many deaths are due to alcoholism," you can tell you're reading about the disease produced by drinking too much alcohol.

Below are three sentences with words you'll read in this lesson's articles. You may already hear and speak these words. Can you read and understand the words in dark print?

Drugs affect the brain and other parts of the **nervous** system.

The nurse gave the upset patient a **tranquilizer.**

After the boxer got knocked out, he lay **unconscious** for a few minutes.

Look at *nervous.* Do you see part of the word *nerve* in it? The word part *-ous* means "having to do with." You can use that information to figure the meaning of *nervous* in the sentence above. Write your definition here.

Now look at the second sentence. The word *tranquil* means "calm." The word

part *-ize* means "to make." The word part *-er* means "something that."

Read the second sentence again. Then write what you think *tranquilizer* means.

Finally, look at *unconscious* in the third sentence. The word part *un-* means "not." *Conscious* means "aware of what's happening." You know what happens to a person who is knocked out. Write a meaning of *unconscious.*

Now check the meanings you wrote with the meanings given for the words in Word Power.

Word Power

nervous having to do with the nerves of the body

tranquilizer a drug that relaxes muscles, reduces tension, and lowers blood pressure

unconscious not able to feel or think; not aware

When you read a science word you think you don't know, you can do two things:

- Look at how the word is used in the sentence.
- See if you know any small words within the larger word.

You can use these word skills whenever you read.

Reading on Your Own

Alcoholism—Get the Facts

Eighteen million Americans have serious drinking problems. Of these, 10 million are probably alcoholics. Alcoholics are different from other problem drinkers in one important way: A problem drinker *won't* stop drinking. An alcoholic *can't* stop.

At one time alcoholism was called a weakness in a person. Less than 30 years ago, scientists started calling it an illness. There is no perfect description of "an alcoholic." Doctors cannot always say who is an alcoholic.

Here are a few facts you may not know about alcoholism and drinking problems.

- One in every four families has a member with an alcohol problem.
- Alcoholism often runs in families.
- Alcohol hurts the liver. Liver damage begins after only three to four weeks of heavy drinking.
- Alcoholism develops more quickly in women than in men. Alcohol does more damage to women's bodies in a shorter time.
- An alcoholic woman is more likely to have a baby with a birth defect.
- Alcohol is involved in nearly 100,000 deaths each year.

Many experts believe alcoholics have a chemical problem in their bodies. This keeps them from being able to stop drinking. Scientists are looking for a chemical that alcoholics have but other people do not. They could test very young people for this chemical. They could then warn anyone likely to become an alcoholic.

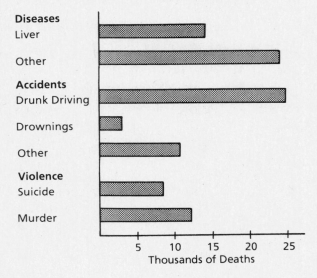

Yearly Deaths Related to Alcohol

Now answer these questions about alcoholism.

1. What do some experts believe causes alcoholism?

_____

_____

2. A problem drinker *won't* stop drinking. An alcoholic *can't* stop drinking. Explain the difference between the use of the words *won't* and *can't* in these two sentences.

_____

_____

_____

_____

_____

_____

3. Rank the reasons for deaths related to alcohol from 1 to 7. Use the number 1 for the category with the highest number of deaths, the number 2 for the category with the next highest number, and so on.

_____ liver disease
_____ other diseases
_____ drunk driving
_____ drownings
_____ other accidents
_____ suicide
_____ murder

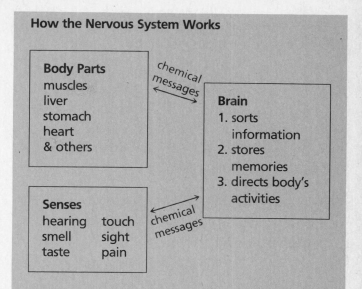

How the Nervous System Works

Body Parts
muscles
liver
stomach
heart
& others

chemical messages

Brain
1. sorts information
2. stores memories
3. directs body's activities

Senses
hearing   touch
smell   sight
taste   pain

chemical messages

Alcohol's Effect on the Brain

Maybe you've watched someone as he or she took one drink, then another, and another. Did you notice the changes in that person? Perhaps the person's face turned a bit red. Maybe he or she began to react more slowly to things. Perhaps the person laughed louder and more often, or spilled a drink. Finally, that person couldn't walk straight, and his or her words slurred together.

All these things happen when alcohol takes effect on the brain. The brain is the center of the body's nervous system. The nervous system controls all the activities in the body. A bundle of nerves called the spinal cord runs down the back from the brain. From this spinal cord, nerves reach out to all parts of the body. They carry information to and from the brain. The diagram shows how the nervous system works.

Alcohol acts like a tranquilizer. The alcohol from an alcoholic drink enters the blood. When the alcohol reaches the brain, it slows the brain down. Gradually, it numbs the nervous system.

As a person drinks more alcohol, he or she goes through several stages. This is because the alcohol slowly moves into different parts of the brain. The brain does not "sort" information in the right way. The drinker doesn't see clearly. Movements become clumsy. The brain has lost full control of the muscles. If enough alcohol gets into the brain, parts of the brain stop working for a time. They do not receive or send messages. The person becomes "unconscious."

Those are short-term effects of alcohol on the brain. Alcohol has some serious, long-lasting effects on the brain too. If too much alcohol gets into the brain very often, some brain cells are changed. Many die. New ones do not replace them. New memories are not stamped in the brain. Old memories are lost. Blackouts happen often. Senses become dulled because the brain no longer understands the messages sent to it.

Use the article on page 147, *Alcohol's Effect on the Brain*, to answer these questions.

1. List at least two short-term and two long-term effects of alcohol on the brain.

   Short-term:

   a. _____

   b. _____

   Long-term:

   a. _____

   b. _____

2. Look at the diagram on page 147 of how the nervous system works. Why do the arrows that show the path of the chemical messages point in *both* directions on the diagram?

   _____

   _____

   _____

   _____

Cocaine

The Spanish explorers of South America were amazed by the coca plant. When hungry, tired natives chewed the leaves of this plant, their strength returned.

About 1860 a chemist found the chemical in coca leaves that had this effect. He called it cocaine. Cocaine in wine became a popular drink. So did a cola drink that contained cocaine.

Soon, however, harmful effects of the drug were reported. The amount of cocaine in a coca leaf was small, and its effect was mild. But pure cocaine had a stronger effect. Cocaine could cause illness and even death. In 1905 cocaine was taken out of cola drinks. In 1906 sale and use of the drug were limited. By the time of World War I, few people were using cocaine.

But in the 1970s and 1980s, many people again began to use cocaine. The drug has the same effects it has always had. Within minutes of taking the drug, a person feels strong and self-confident. Hunger and tiredness disappear.

How does cocaine produce these effects? Once cocaine is in the blood, it moves to the nervous system. Somehow, cocaine changes certain chemicals in the body. These chemicals carry messages to the "pleasure center" of the brain. The brain thinks something good has happened to the body. So it produces a feeling of pleasure, or a "high." This high usually lasts less than an hour. Then the chemicals drop off, and the cocaine user feels "down."

For some people, however, this short feeling of pleasure becomes more important than anything else in their lives. These people become cocaine addicts.

Use the information you just read to answer these questions.

1. How does cocaine affect the brain?

   _____

   _____

   _____

2. Why does the feeling of pleasure from cocaine last just a short time?

   _____

   _____

   _____

3. Why do you think people began to use cocaine again even though it can hurt them?

   _____

   _____

   _____

Effects of Drug Abuse

Harry grew up on a farm in Montana. He was a big kid—6′3″, 185 pounds. He studied farming at college. Then he went home to help his father run the farm. But Harry was looking for something new. He moved a few times and finally ended up in Dallas. He found a job, friends, and excitement there. His new friends showed him something he'd only heard of before. They showed him cocaine.

Harry was found unconscious on a street in Dallas five years later. After hospital care, he was taken to a drug treatment center. He weighed 123 pounds. He had no money. His clothes were rags. He couldn't name one friend.

Harry told a worker at the treatment center how drugs had changed his life. At first, he used them for fun on the weekends with his friends. As his interest in cocaine grew, he lost interest in other things. He saw his friends less. He never wrote home. He felt depressed, irritable, and often frightened. He spent more and more of his money for drugs. But he couldn't keep his mind on his work and finally lost his job. He began to steal money to buy "coke."

Harry couldn't remember some parts of the past five years. He often had blackouts. He said he was tired. He had felt very tired for a long time. Yet he had trouble sleeping. For the last weeks before he was found, he had lived on—and for—cocaine. When he wasn't using it, he was looking for it. Cocaine abuse had ruined his health, but he told himself that the drug was his pleasure in life.

Not all drug abusers have all of Harry's problems. But all abusers do share some of them, no matter what drug they abuse.

Now do the following activity.

Below is a list of areas in Harry's life. Each one was changed because he used cocaine. Write a brief description of the way each area was affected.

1. friends _____

   _____

2. job _____

   _____

3. feelings _____

   _____

4. money _____

   _____

Drug Abuse Cases in Emergency Rooms

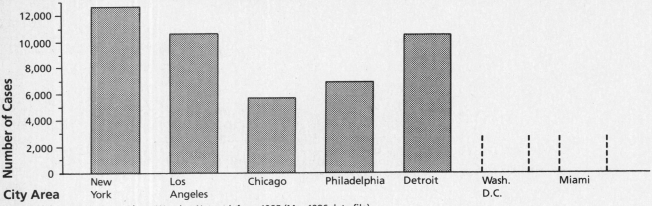

Source of data: NIDA, Drug Abuse Warning Network from 1985 (May 1986 data file)

Drug Abuse Cases

The graph above shows the number of drug abuse cases in hospital emergency rooms in the year 1985. The city areas are listed in order of their overall population, from largest to smallest.

Use the graph to answer these questions.

1. Which city had the most drug abuse cases in emergency rooms?

_____

2. About how many drug abuse cases happened in Chicago?

_____

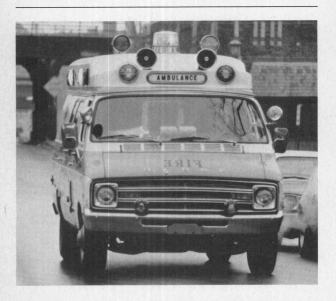

3. Here are the number of drug abuse cases for two other cities.

Washington, D.C.	5,344
Miami	4,599

Make bars for these two cities on the graph.

A Test-Taking Tip

For a multiple-choice question, it's often best to answer the question in your own words. *Then* look at the answer choices and pick the one that is most like your answer.

GED Warm-up

Detroit has a much smaller population than Los Angeles. It seems to have a much more serious drug problem than Los Angeles because

(1) it has fewer emergency rooms than Los Angeles

(2) it has just as many drug abuse cases as Los Angeles has

 ① ②

The Animal and Plant World

Recognizing and Drawing Conclusions

Picture It

Monday	Tuesday	Wednesday	Thursday	Friday

JUDY

It's too cool near the window.

Wow! A bud.

JODY

Great story!

Z Z Z Z

I love this show.

On Monday two sisters went to the plant shop. Each brought home a healthy lily plant. By Friday Judy's plant was growing a new bud. Jody's plant was brown and drooping. What happened? Study the cartoon above before you decide on your answer.

Judy took good care of her plant. Jody never paid attention to hers. As a result, Judy's plant stayed healthy, and Jody's plant slowly died.

Did you come to the same decision after looking at the cartoon? When you make a decision after thinking about the facts, you draw a conclusion. You draw conclusions all the time.

Here's An Example

Suppose you switch on the radio. The weather forecast is cool and rainy. You decide to dress warmly and to take your raincoat and umbrella.

Then you stop at the grocery store to buy paper towels. One brand is 89¢ per roll. A similar brand is priced at two rolls for $1.50. You realize the two rolls of paper towels cost 75¢ each. So you buy the two rolls. You have concluded that they are the better value.

Both of those decisions were made by using facts and common sense. In other words, you were drawing conclusions. It's the same when you read. You draw conclusions by putting together your common sense with the information you read.

Sometimes you read conclusions that the author is making. Words or phrases often let you know that a conclusion is being made. Examples of these signals are *therefore, so, determined that, concluded,* and *it follows that.* Look for signal words and phrases like those when you read. They will help you spot conclusions.

Working It Out

Now read the following passage. You'll be asked to draw some conclusions from it.

■ It's spring and they're here again—weeds! No matter how often you yank weeds out of the ground, they fight their way back. Weeds are very stubborn and tough—yet beautiful in their own way. Did you ever stop to think how good a dandelion can look poking up between a broken beer bottle and a pile of bricks?

City weeds are uncared for and ignored. Yet they grow and even spread. How is it possible? A large part of the answer can be found by looking at their seeds.

Many weeds have seeds that can travel. They are shaped like wings or parachutes. These seeds catch the wind and fly very far. Other seeds have barbs or hooks. They attach to animals and hitch a ride to a new home. Many weeds also give off thousands, even millions of seeds. The large numbers give many chances for the seeds to take hold and grow.

Also, many city weeds do not need a very rich, fertile soil. A few minerals in city earth are enough to keep some weeds growing.

Therefore, city weeds are made for survival. They make a great number of seeds, ready for faraway travel. They can live and grow in poor soil. That makes them very special. Keep that in mind the next time you pass an empty lot filled with ugly garbage . . . and dotted with dandelions.

Now use the information you just read to draw some conclusions.

1. Picture a large rooftop of a very old apartment building. Dirt has collected in the corners. Do you think weeds could grow there? Explain.

   _____

   _____

2. What sentence in the article above is a conclusion? Write the sentence here, and circle the signal word.

   _____

   _____

3. How would the author describe the weeds growing in an empty city lot?

   _____

Animal Behavior

Before You Read: Thinking About Animal Behavior

In this lesson, you will read about animals and different things they do. In other words, you'll read about animal behavior. Most people like animals. You've probably watched animals in a number of places. List as many of these places as you can think of here.

_____

_____

_____

Some places you may have thought of are a park, a zoo, a farm, a pet shop, on TV, in the movies, and outside in general.

You probably know many facts about animals already. For example, which of these animals live in large groups? Circle the three that do.

> bears   geese
>
> buffalo   ants

Which of these animals hunt? Circle the three that do.

> tigers   snakes
>
> cows   wolves

Which of these animals build homes? Circle the three that do.

> robins   bees
>
> beavers   lions

Did you know that buffalo, geese, and ants live in groups? Tigers, snakes, and wolves hunt. And robins, beavers, and bees build nests, lodges, and hives as homes.

Now look over the articles in this lesson. Pay close attention to the titles. Look at the diagrams and graph. Write down the title of the article you think will be the most interesting to read.

_____

What do you hope to learn from this passage?

_____

Have any questions about animal behavior come to mind? If so, write them here.

_____

_____

After finishing this lesson, check back here to see if your questions have been answered.

Working with Words

Sometimes you'll read a scientific word that's new to you. But the writer may also give you examples of what the word means. You can use those examples to understand the word. Here's how.

Read the following sentences. The three words in dark print are scientific words in this lesson.

A spider weaves its web, a bird builds its nest, and a moth moves toward light—all by **instinct.**

To train a dog, offer such **reinforcement** as a dog biscuit, praise, or a pat on the head.

Primates such as gorillas, chimps, and monkeys have thumbs that can touch the other fingers on the hand.

Look again at the first sentence. The word *instinct* may be new to you. But look at the examples of instinct: A spider weaves a web. A bird builds a nest. A moth moves toward light. What do these examples have in common? They are things animals do. Use that idea to figure that instinct deals with animal behavior. Write a sentence with the word *instinct*.

_____

_____

Now read the second sentence. The word *reinforcement* has a special scientific meaning. Fill in the examples of reinforcement for a dog: a biscuit,

_____, and _____ .
Those examples are all rewards. And that's what reinforcement is: a way to reward behavior. Can you write a

sentence with the word *reinforcement*?

_____

_____

What could be reinforcement for a child's good behavior?

_____

Did you mention rewards like a hug, a word of praise, and a piece of fruit? Those would be good ways to reinforce a child's behavior.

Finally, look again at the third sentence. Examples of primates are

gorillas, _____ , and _____ .
You can tell that a primate is a kind of animal. Write a sentence with *primate*.

_____

_____

Here are the meanings of the three words you've worked with.

Word Power

instinct a way of acting that is inborn in an animal, not learned

reinforcement something that strengthens, as a reward strengthens behavior

primate one of a group of mammals that have advanced brains and hands with thumbs that can be used to hold things

---

When you read a new word, look for examples. These words can be clues to examples: *such as, examples include,* and *like.* Ask yourself what the examples have in common. You can use the common idea to understand the general word.

Reading on Your Own

Help from Pets

Some animals help other kinds of animals. For example, certain birds eat insects from the hide of cattle. Certain fish swim with sharks and use them for protection. And pets help their human owners in a number of ways.

Studies show that having a pet can help a person's mental health. Pets are a big help for lonely people. A pet gives a person someone to love and care for. The person feels needed. Just petting an animal can make a person feel calmer and less sad or depressed.

Petting an animal can help a person's physical health too. Petting actually can lower a person's blood pressure. Lower blood pressure lessens the chance of heart disease.

Doctors now know the good that pets can do in some cases, doctors prescribe a pet instead of a drug.

Now use the information above to answer these questions.

1. The writer categorizes the kind of help pets give. Pets help both the _____ health and the _____ health of their owners.

2. The writer tells how pets help their owners. In what ways do owners help their pets?

_____

_____

_____

Social Order

Some animals are considered "social." Social animals live together by very strict rules. The rules keep order and divide the work in the group.

Each animal knows its place in a group. In every group, one animal is in charge, at the top of the social order. Sometimes this dominant animal is the strongest one. But that is not always the case.

Ants and bees are social. Males do no work. Their only job is to mate. There is one female queen. She spends her life laying eggs. The queen is at the top of the social order. The worker ants and bees are females that do not mate. They are at the bottom of the social order. They build the nests and look for food.

Other social orders have ways to show power. Hens have a pecking order. They peck to show who is dominant. Hens can peck the hens that are below them in social order, but not the ones above them.

The diagram shows that hen 1 can peck hens 2, 3, and 4. Hen 2 can peck hens 3 and 4. Hen 3 can peck hen 4. Hen 4 can peck no one.

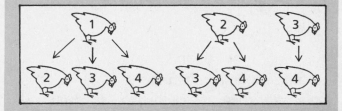

Monkeys and many other animals groom, or clean, one another. The animal lower in the social order grooms the one higher in the order.

Write a few words to answer these questions.

1. What is the queen's role in the social order of ants and bees?

   _____

   _____

2. Have you ever heard the phrase "lower in the pecking order"? Use the diagram to explain what the phrase means.

   _____

   _____

3. One monkey is groomed by all the other monkeys in a group. Where does this monkey stand in the social order of its group? Explain your conclusion.

   _____

   _____

Animal Instincts

Have you ever noticed a dog turn around a few times before it lies down? Have you ever seen a cat rub its head against a person's legs? Why do these animals act this way?

The dog and cat are showing instincts, or inborn behavior. Dogs in the wild walk around a spot before they lie down. It makes the spot flat, and it gets rid of bugs. A cat rubs against a person to mark that person with its scent. The scent shows the cat "owns" the person.

All animals do some things by instinct. When they are born, animals already "know" what to do at certain times.

Animals will follow their instincts even when there is no real need.

Instinct helps animals stay alive. It makes them move away from danger. It helps them find food and shelter. It tells them when and how to mate.

Newly born robins open their mouths for food when the parent comes back to the nest. The babies feel the nest move. Then they know the parent is there. The moving of the nest is a "sign" for them to open their mouths. Scientists call such signs "triggers." Later the young robins open their mouths for food at new triggers, such as the call of the parent.

Write a few words to answer these questions.

A newborn baby turns his or her face when something brushes against it. The baby then begins to suck.

1. What action is the "trigger" in this case?

   _____

   _____

2. What action is the instinct?

   _____

   _____

3. Why do you think a baby has this instinct? Write your conclusion here.

   _____

   _____

   _____

How Animals Learn

All animals are born with some instincts. But many animals can also *learn* to do things.

One way some baby animals learn is by watching a parent or other adult animal. The babies then do what the adult does. In other words, the young animals imitate.

In one experiment, some baby ducks were taken away from the mother soon after birth. Other baby ducks were left with their mothers. The ducks that watched the mother could swim right away. But the ducks that had no mother to model, or imitate, could not swim till much later.

In other experiments, animals were taught to do certain tasks. A rat was taught to press a bar to get food. At first the rat pressed the bar by accident. Each time it pressed the bar, it received food. After many tries, the rat learned that food came after it pressed the bar. It pressed the bar whenever it wanted food. This way of learning is by reward, or reinforcement, as scientists call it.

A few animals seem to be able to think and get ideas. They can learn from their own ideas and actions. In one experiment, a bunch of bananas was put up high so that chimpanzees could not get to it. One chimp took boxes and put one on top of the other. Then it climbed up to the bananas. Another chimp put one pole inside another to make a long pole. Then it knocked the bananas down.

Use the information you just read to do these activities.

1. Complete this chart to show the three ways in which animals can learn.

   Animal Learning

   a. _____

   b. _____

   c. _____

2. How could you use what scientists call reinforcement to teach a dog to sit on command?

   _____

   _____

   _____

A Gorilla Who "Speaks"

Koko, a gorilla, was taught how to "speak" in sign language.

Scientist Penny Patterson worked with the one-year-old gorilla. Patterson showed Koko how to make signs with her paws. A gorilla, like a human, is a primate. Primates have five fingers that can move well and grasp objects. Koko's fingers were able to make the signs that stand for ideas and things.

After six years, Koko knew 375 signs. She could "talk" to her teacher and understand what Patterson signed back to her.

Koko can ask for a banana or an apple to eat. She also has made signs for "happy," "sad," and "mad." She has lied to keep out of trouble. She signs "hug" when she wants a hug. She even asked for a new kitten as a pet when her cat was hit by a car.

Now do these exercises.

1. Below are some of the signs Koko has made. Classify them. Write the name of the general category that the specific signs belong to. Choose from these categories.

Emotions	Food	Action	Animal

_____ _____

banana   happy
apple   sad
                    mad

_____ _____

hug   kitten

2. Why did Patterson probably choose a gorilla to teach sign language to?

_____

_____

3. Tell what you know about primates from the information in this article.

_____

_____

How Bees Communicate

Bees get their food from flowers. A scout bee finds the food. Then it returns to the hive. The bee "dances" up the side of the hive to tell the other bees the location of the food. The dance is a series of figure eights. The direction of the dance tells the direction of the food. The bee shows where the food is in relation to the sun.

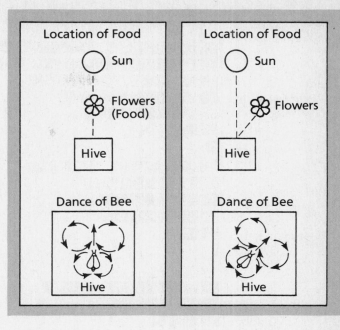

Now answer these questions about bees.

1. Why do bees dance?

_____

2. Why can't a bee show where food is at night?

_____

_____

3. Below is a diagram of a bee dance. Which of the following pictures show where the food is located? _____

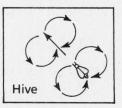

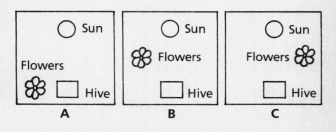

Speeds of Animals

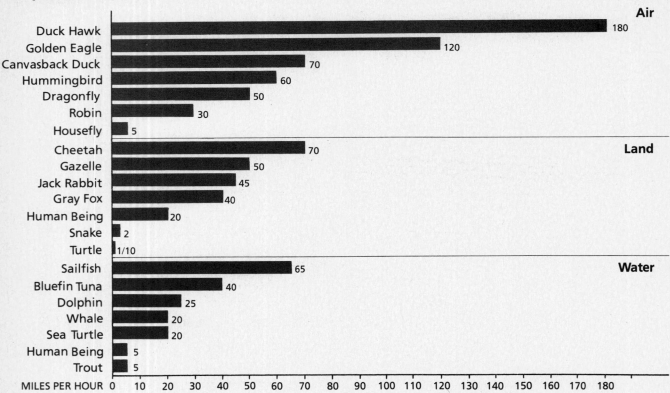

Air
- Duck Hawk: 180
- Golden Eagle: 120
- Canvasback Duck: 70
- Hummingbird: 60
- Dragonfly: 50
- Robin: 30
- Housefly: 5

Land
- Cheetah: 70
- Gazelle: 50
- Jack Rabbit: 45
- Gray Fox: 40
- Human Being: 20
- Snake: 2
- Turtle: 1/10

Water
- Sailfish: 65
- Bluefin Tuna: 40
- Dolphin: 25
- Whale: 20
- Sea Turtle: 20
- Human Being: 5
- Trout: 5

MILES PER HOUR 0 10 20 30 40 50 60 70 80 90 100 110 120 130 140 150 160 170 180

Animals on the Move

Most animals move. They move to find food and water. They move to escape other animals. They may move to find a cooler or a warmer spot.

The graph above shows the fastest speeds that can be reached by certain animals.

Now do the following graph activities.

1. What is the fastest animal on land?

_____

2. How much faster can a human being move on land than in water?

_____

3. What kind of animal can move faster in the water than on land?

_____

GED Warm-up

Based on information on the graph, you could conclude that it is easiest for animals to move

(1) in the air
(2) on the land
(3) in the water

The Active Reader

Applying Ideas

Picture It

A small child went to her father. She told him, "I don't feel well." She was holding an empty bottle of aspirin.

The father asked his little girl, "Did you eat the pills in the bottle?"

"Yes, Daddy. I ate this candy."

The father knew the situation was serious. He reached in the closet for the first aid kit. He found these directions for poison treatment (see box).

The father read the information. He knew how to apply it to his problem. First he called the poison center. This is how the conversation went.

Father: "My daughter ate a lot of aspirin."

Poison Treatment

FIRST Call the nearest poison center. Use one of the two treatments as directed. Then get medical care immediately.

Ipecac syrup will produce vomiting in about 20 minutes. It should be given when the poison must be removed from the victim's system.

Activated charcoal will absorb a poison. It soaks up the poison before it can be absorbed into the body. It should be given when it is dangerous for the victim to vomit.

Warning. Do not give treatment to an unconscious person.

Poison Center: "How much has she taken?"

Father: "It was half full this morning— about 20 pills."

Poison Center: "You need to make her vomit. Then bring her to the emergency room of the hospital."

Father: "I have ipecac. How much should I give her?"

The father applied the directions for poison treatment. Applying ideas is the ability to take information and use it. You can apply ideas in different ways.

Here's an Example

One way to apply ideas is to predict. You try to predict what *will* happen based on your knowledge of what *has* happened. For example, you know John feels strongly about protecting the environment. His employer asks him to cover up a business activity that will pollute. You could predict that John would rather quit.

A second way to apply ideas is to give an example of a general idea. For example, it takes less energy to move up an incline than to move straight up. That is a general rule of science. You *apply* that general idea when you push a heavy box up a ramp rather than lift it straight up to put it into a truck.

A third way to apply ideas is to take a rule in one situation and use it in a similar situation. For example, at work you may wear goggles. The goggles protect your eyes from flying bits of dirt and dust. You could apply that safety rule at home. You might wear goggles while you are sanding a plaster wall.

Working It Out

Read the directions for poison treatment on page 161 again. Decide what treatment to use in each of these situations.

1. A person has swallowed paint thinner. Vomiting could cause serious lung and throat damage.

_____

_____

2. A child has swallowed a large bottle of vitamins. Vomiting is not dangerous.

_____

_____

3. A person is unconscious on a bed with an empty bottle of sleeping pills at her side.

_____

_____

Now try to predict. First study this graph. It shows the estimated number of bluegill fish in a lake. The number of fish was estimated each season for two years.

The Bluegill Population in North Lake

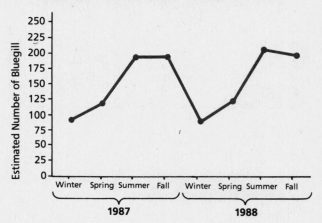

4. What do you think happened to the number of bluegill in the lake in the winter of 1989? Why?

_____

_____

_____

Ecology

Before You Read: Thinking About Ecology

In this lesson, you will be reading about ecology. Ecology is the study of the relationship between living things and their surroundings.

Picture a park in your mind. In the park are living things such as grass, trees, squirrels, and people. What other living things could be in the park?

_____

_____

Perhaps you pictured these living things in the park: bugs, bushes, flowers, rabbits, and other kinds of animals.

Nonliving things are also part of the park. Air, sunlight, and park benches are three examples. What other examples of nonliving things can you add?

_____

_____

You may have thought of water, soil, wastebaskets, playgrounds, sidewalks, and so on.

All these living and nonliving things are related to each other. Without certain nonliving things, the plants and animals could not exist. For example, what would happen in the park if there was no rain for two months?

_____

_____

Water is a very important part of the surroundings. Without rainwater, many plants in the park would die. Insects and animals need plants for food and protection. Since there would be fewer plants, fewer animals and insects would survive in the park.

This is a good example of how living things and their surroundings are related.

Now preview the articles you will be reading in this lesson. Be sure to notice the diagrams and graphs too. What two articles do you think will be the most interesting? Write the titles here.

_____

_____

Write one question for each article that you would like answered when you read.

_____

_____

_____

After you have finished reading, check back to see if your questions were answered.

Working with Words

Below are three sentences with words from this lesson. You may already know the words in dark print. If not, you can use the sentences to figure out their meanings.

Exhaust from automobiles can **pollute** the air.

An animal is affected by all the living and nonliving things in its **environment.**

There are no longer any dodos because the bird became **extinct** in the 1600s.

Look at the first sentence. If you don't already know the meaning of *pollute,* think of cars in a traffic jam. The exhaust fumes enter the air. The air becomes dirty and hard to breathe. Use that idea. Write a definition of *pollute* here.

_____

_____

Now look at the second sentence. Picture "all the living and nonliving things" that could affect an animal. Write a definition of *environment.*

_____

_____

Look at the third sentence. Can you spot the clue to the meaning of *extinct*? It's "There are no longer any." Write a definition of *extinct.*

_____

_____

Compare your definitions with these.

Word Power

pollute to make dirty or impure
environment all the surroundings that influence the growth of a living thing
extinct no longer existing

Now you know the meanings of *pollute, environment,* and *extinct.* Use your knowledge. Write a meaning for the word in dark print in each of these sentences.

Pollutants such as smoke, ashes, and dust enter the air.

A *pollutant* is _____

_____ .

Oil spills and acid rain cause **environmental** damage.

Environmental damage is _____

_____ .

The **extinction** of the rhino is possible unless this animal is protected.

Extinction means _____

_____ .

A pollutant is anything that pollutes, or dirties, the air. Environmental damage is harm to the living and nonliving things in the environment, or surroundings. And extinction is the dying out of an entire kind of animal.

When you read a word you don't know, look at how it is used. Also look at the word itself. You may know what part of the word means. Your knowledge can help you understand the whole word.

Reading on Your Own

Pollution Problem for Fish

Freshwater fish such as trout may be in short supply someday, scientists warn. These fish are dying out in many places. Pollution in the water is the cause.

Many people think pollution means poisons or dirt. But pollution comes in many forms. One kind of pollution is thermal, or heat, pollution. Often factories take cold water from streams. They use it to cool off hot metal and other products. Then the heated water is emptied back into the stream. This hot water raises the temperature of the stream.

Some fish, like carp and catfish, can live in an environment of warm or cool water. But trout and many other fish can live only in cool water. They die if the water gets too warm.

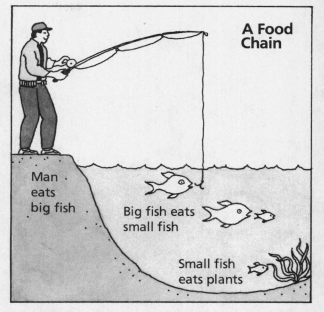

A Food Chain

Man eats big fish

Big fish eats small fish

Small fish eats plants

Use the diagram above to answer these questions.

1. What happens first in this food chain? What happens next? What happens last?

_____

_____

_____

2. What would change for the man in this food chain if the plants in the pond died?

_____

3. Describe another example of a food chain.

_____

_____

Answer these questions in a few words.

1. What is thermal pollution?

_____

2. A garfish is much like a catfish. Many garfish live in a stream near a factory. The factory begins to dump hot water into the stream. Are the garfish likely to live? Explain your answer.

_____

_____

3. Why do you think factories keep on using water from streams to cool their products?

_____

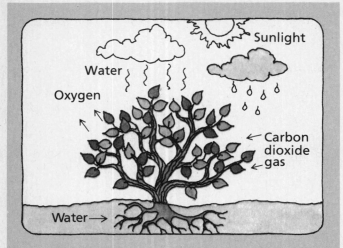

Photosynthesis— How Plants Make Food

Roots of a plant take in water from the soil. Leaves take in sunlight and carbon dioxide gas from the air. The plant uses the energy of the sun to change the carbon dioxide gas and water into food. The plant uses the food for energy and for growth. Oxygen and a little water are put back into the air.

Use the diagram and explanation to help you answer the questions below.

1. What three things does a plant use to make food?

   _____

2. How could a long dry spell affect photosynthesis in plants?

   _____

3. How does photosynthesis help make the air better for humans?

   _____

4. What bad effect for humans and other animals could come from cutting too many forests?

   _____

Algae as Food

More and more people are living on the earth. Scientists are looking for new ways to feed people. Some things that are not often thought of as food may someday be used to feed people. Algae, tiny plants that grow in water, could be one of these.

Most algae are so small that a single plant cannot be seen with the naked eye. But algae are very good at photosynthesis. Photosynthesis takes place when plants use sunlight and water to make food. Algae have no roots, flowers, or fruit. All of the plant is used to make food. There is no waste of energy. When the need for food is great, plants that do not waste energy are important. And because algae are small, they can provide more food in less space than other plants.

Someday scientists may find a way to make good food from algae. They may find a way to make the plants taste good so that people will want to eat algae. Already some people eat seaweed, a form of algae.

Now use the information above to answer these questions about algae.

1. Name two reasons that algae might be useful during a long trip in a spaceship.

   _____

   _____

2. Where would algae be more likely to become an important food, in Africa or in North America? Why?

   _____

   _____

The People Problem

Every five days, about one million more people are born worldwide. By the year 2000, there will be about $6\frac{1}{2}$ billion people on earth. These people will need food and houses. Yet some scientists think that by the year 2000 about one-third of the land that grows food may be gone. The world's forests could be cut in half. The graph below shows what these scientists think may happen. The wheat stands for farmland, the tree for forests, and the man for population.

Write a short answer to each question.

1. What is happening to the population?

_____

2. What is happening to the farmland and forests of the world?

_____

3. How may the change in farmland and forest affect people living in 2020?

_____

Plants That Save Lives

The National Cancer Institute is taking a close look at plants these days.

About 3,000 plants may be useful in treating sicknesses. Many life-saving drugs have already been made from parts of plants. A drug made from the foxglove plant helps millions of people lower their blood pressure. A sponge plant can help victims of a brain disease and certain viruses.

Leukemia is treated with a drug from a tropical plant. This drug has given leukemia patients a much better chance of surviving.

Plants have been used to make other drugs as well. The birth control pill is made from parts of a forest yam. Plants also provide a product that is used to help people stop smoking.

The use of some plants may be cut short, however. Many kinds of plants have become extinct. They have died out. Other plants may soon become extinct. Some scientists say we lose one kind of plant each day. Once these plants die out, they never come back.

Now answer these questions.

1. What does the word *extinct* mean?

_____

2. Some native people in Africa do not use medicine as we know it. They treat the sick with plants and herbs. How could these people help us and our doctors?

_____

3. If the foxglove plant becomes extinct, how would some people be affected?

An Island Laboratory

Isle Royale is a national park in Lake Superior. It has also become an outdoor lab for ecologists.

During the 1800s humans destroyed most of the large animals on Isle Royale. There were no deer, no moose, no wolves. About 1912 the food supply for animals on the nearby Canada shore shrank. There weren't enough plants for moose and other large animals to eat. A group of half-starved moose swam 20 miles over to the island.

By 1930, the moose on Isle Royale numbered about 3,000. The moose population then began to decrease. Once again, there weren't enough plants to feed all the moose.

Then in 1948, a pack of wolves crossed over the ice in winter to the island. The wolves began to feed on the moose. Since then, ecologists have been studying the moose, wolf, and plant populations. They keep track of the numbers of moose and wolves. The following graphs show that these numbers have become fairly stable. The ecologists are waiting to see what, if anything, will change the situation.

Moose Population

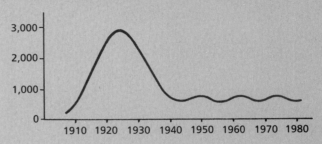

Wolf Population

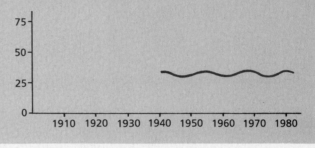

Use the article and the graphs to answer the following questions.

1. Why did the moose population decrease after 1930?

   _____

   _____

2. What appears to happen when there is a slight dip in the wolf population?

   _____

   _____

3. What would most likely happen to the moose if a drought killed many plants on the island? Why?

   _____

   _____

4. What would then likely happen to the wolves? Why?

   _____

   _____

   _____

Disappearing Animals

The giant panda is one of about 1,000 animals that are in danger of becoming extinct. In the last 200 years, more than 50 kinds of birds have become extinct. Over 75 kinds of mammals and perhaps hundreds of other kinds of animals have died out. Human beings have caused most of these extinctions.

The extinction of animals can upset the balance of nature. Each kind of animal is part of a food chain. When a certain kind of animal dies out, a link in the food chain is broken. Animals that feed on that animal will have problems finding food. If an animal's food is gone, it too will die. The food chain can turn into a chain of extinctions.

Many times animals die out because they lose their homes as well as their food supply. The earth's tropical forests cover only 7 percent of the land, but they hold almost one-half of all the earth's animals. Many of these animals can live only in a very warm and wet environment. As people cut down more of the forest, many animals will die. They will lose the trees that make their homes.

When animals are protected, they can sometimes come back. The cheetah, the polar bear, and the whooping crane are starting to grow in numbers. But while a few animals like these are saved, thousands of others still die out.

Now write your answers to the following questions.

1. What can happen when one kind of animal in a food chain dies out?

_____

2. What do you think would happen if about *half* of one kind of animal in a food chain died?

_____

_____

3. How can human beings cause the extinction of animals even without actually killing the animals?

_____

_____

A Test-Taking Tip

Sometimes a multiple-choice question will ask for the meaning of a word or phrase. You know you can understand the meaning of a word by the way it is used in its sentence. Pay attention also to the sentences *before* and *after* the phrase. These sentences may also help explain the meaning to you.

GED Warm-up

What is meant by the balance of nature?

(1) Animals depend on one another to stay alive.

(2) Large animals usually eat smaller animals.

(3) The number and kind of living things in an area tend to stay the same.

Land, Water, Air, and Space

The Active Reader

Asking Questions

Picture It

Antarctica is a continent. It lies farther south than any other continent. It also is the coldest place on earth.

Many people have gone to Antarctica to explore. They take tools to help them survive. They bring ice axes to break the ice. They also bring special shoes. The soles of the shoes have spikes to help the explorers climb the ice-covered mountains. These tools make moving across Antarctica easier.

Reading also can be easier if you use tools. The tools are questions that you ask yourself as you read.

Here's an Example

Helga found an article about Antarctica. She read the first few sentences.

■ On January 27, 1820, a Russian sea captain sighted a stretch of ice-covered hills. For several weeks his ship sailed along the edge of the ice. Finally, the captain realized that he had found an "icy continent."

Before Helga went on reading, she asked herself, "What questions about Antarctica will this story most likely answer?" Then she listed the following questions:

Who came to Antarctica next?
What did they find there?
How did the cold affect them?
Who lives there now?

Next Helga read the rest of the story.

■ In the next hundred years, people from many countries sailed to Antarctica. Some went to hunt seals and whales. Others went to find out about the life and the land of the coldest place on earth. The following words, written by a sailor, show what the cold was like: "I raised my head to look round and found I couldn't move it back. My clothing had frozen solid as I stood."

After finishing the story, Helga looked over her list of questions. Which ones had been answered?

The answer to the first question is "people from many countries."

An answer to the second question is seals and whales. However, people most likely found more than seals and whales in Antarctica. So the story answered this question only in part.

The third question also was answered only in part. The sailor's report says that Antarctica was so cold it froze his clothing. But what else did the cold do?

"What question is not answered at all?" Helga asked herself. The last one was not. The story says nothing about who lives in Antarctica today.

Helga's questions begin with *who, what,* and *how.* Those words ask for general facts. *When, where,* and *why* also ask for general facts. Use them to begin questions *you* ask about *your* reading.

Helga asked the first four questions as she read. But she also asked these questions after she finished reading:

What questions were answered?

What questions were only partly answered?

What questions were not answered?

Be sure to ask yourself these questions after you finish reading.

Working It Out

Read the next part of the article.

■ In 1911 several men from Norway led by Roald Amundsen built a base on Antarctica's coast. So did several men from England led by Robert Scott. Both groups planned to be first to reach the South Pole.

1. Write two or three questions you think the article will answer.

_____

_____

Now read the rest of the article.

■ During this race to the South Pole, Scott and his men battled high winds. They crossed dangerous cracks in the ice. And they endured "snow like heavy wet sleet."

On January 17, 1912, Scott's party reached the South Pole. But the Norwegians had reached the Pole earlier—on December 14, 1911.

Scott and his men died on the trip back to their base. Before Scott died, he wrote: ". . . feet frozen, no fuel, and a long way from food. . . . We are very near the end, but have not and will not lose our good cheer."

2. Underline the sentences in the article that answer your questions.

3. Put a check next to any of your questions that were not answered or answered only in part.

4. Circle the letter of the question below that the article did *not* answer.

   a. What is the South Pole?

   b. Who reached the South Pole first?

5. Copy the sentence from the article that tells when the first people to reach the South Pole arrived.

_____

_____

Changes in Matter

Before You Read: Thinking About Changes in Matter

The articles in this lesson are about changes in matter. Matter changes when you boil or freeze it. Much of what you read will sound familiar. After all, you boil and freeze things every day.

The following foods and drinks are examples. Before each one, write *B* if you have ever seen it boiled or boiled it yourself. Write *F* if you have ever seen it frozen or frozen it yourself. Write *BF* if both are true.

_____ 1. orange juice

_____ 2. chicken

_____ 3. eggs

_____ 4. beef

_____ 5. soup

_____ 6. water

_____ 7. carrots

_____ 8. shrimp

_____ 9. TV dinners

_____ 10. bananas

Food or drink that is being boiled or frozen goes through changes. What are these changes? How do they happen? The articles in this lesson will help you find out.

Look ahead at the titles of the articles. On the lines below, write the titles that are about cold or freezing. Then write the titles that talk about heat or boiling. Some titles don't tell whether the article is about cold or heat.

Cold and Freezing

_____

_____

_____

Heat and Boiling

_____

_____

_____

You might have written these titles under "Cold": "How Does a Pond Freeze?" "Inside a Refrigerator," and "Super Cool Science." And these titles should be under "Heat": "Heat on the Move," "How a Pressure Cooker Works," and "A Watched Pot."

What questions do you think the articles will answer?

_____

_____

Look for answers to your questions when you read the articles. Jot down the answers on your own paper or underline them on the pages.

If you ask and answer questions as you read, you'll understand more. You'll also remember better. That's why active readers are successful readers.

Working with Words

Some words from the lesson are used in the following sentences. These words may be new to you. Try to figure out their meanings. Use the following sentences and hints to help you. Also use what you already know.

The steam inside the pot continued to build until the **pressure** blew the lid off.

The water will slowly **evaporate** and, in time, completely disappear.

The glass vase is **brittle,** so it can be very easily broken.

The word *pressure* has the word *press* in it. One meaning for *press* is "to use force." Another key to the meaning of *pressure* is the word *continued.* The sentence also gives an example of how pressure works. Combine these hints. Then write what you think *pressure* means.

What happens to the water in the second sentence may sound like magic. But the explanation is scientific—it evaporates.

The word *evaporate* has the word *vapor* in it. *Vapor* means "gas." The word *evaporate* in the sentence tells of

something that happens. What will happen to the water?

The meaning of *brittle* is right in the third sentence. Which part of the sentence do you think it is? Copy that part on the following line.

The meanings below are from the dictionary. Do they match the ones you came up with?

Word Power

pressure the continued action of a force

evaporate to turn into a gas

brittle very easily broken

Look for the words *pressure, evaporate,* and *brittle* as you read the following articles.

Reading on Your Own

Solids, Liquids, and Gases

Solid		In solids particles are packed tightly together.
Liquid		In liquids particles are not as close together.
Gas		In gases particles have large amounts of space between them.

Solids, Liquids, and Gases

All things are made of matter. Matter comes in one of three forms—solid, liquid, or gas. Water is liquid matter. But it can change. Sometimes water changes to steam—a gas. Other times water changes to ice—a solid.

How can water change its form? It changes because of the way its molecules move. Molecules are small particles that make up matter.

Particles such as molecules are always on the move. As they move, they can be made to come closer together. The molecules in a liquid are closer together than the molecules in steam, or vapor. The molecules in a solid are even more tightly packed together than the molecules in a liquid.

Use the diagram and the article to help you answer the following questions.

1. Are the particles more tightly packed together in hot liquid steel or in a steel building? Why?

   _____

   _____

   _____

2. In your own words, explain what happens when you melt margarine in a pan.

   _____

   _____

   _____

Heat on the Move

What makes ice melt? Heat transfers, or moves, from the air to the ice.

The particles that make up matter are always moving. Some particles move faster than others. When particles are heated, they speed up. The faster particles transfer their energy to the slower ones. This transfer of heat goes on until all the particles are moving at the same speed. Warm objects always move their energy to cooler objects until both are the same temperature.

In a solid, the particles are packed very closely together. But if a solid is heated, the particles move about more. They hit one other. This makes the particles move even farther apart.

As the particles get farther apart, they can move about easily. When this happens, the solid has changed to a new state. The new state is the liquid state.

Write a short answer to each question.

1. How does the temperature of an object affect the speed of its particles?

_____

_____

2. Explain what happens to particles when a transfer of heat takes place.

_____

_____

_____

3. Explain what happens when you add cold milk to a cup of hot coffee.

_____

_____

_____

How Does a Pond Freeze?

Hot air rises. Cool air sinks. That's why the top floor of a house is warmer than the bottom floor.

Why does hot air rise? Because air gets lighter and spreads out when it gets warmer. Most matter spreads out, or expands, this way when it is heated.

But not all matter follows this rule. Water is one thing that does not. When it is cold, water shrinks. When it freezes, however, water expands. A pond of water will start to freeze from the top. Here's why.

As water in a pond cools, it loses heat to the air. At first, the cooling water shrinks and becomes heavier. This heavier water sinks to the bottom of the pond. The water at the top keeps cooling and sinking until all the water reaches 39° Fahrenheit. At this point water is heaviest. Above or below this point, water is lighter.

Once all the water is 39°, any further cooling makes the water lighter. It does not sink. It stays at the surface till it freezes completely, from the top down.

Write a few words to answer these questions.

1. You see a pond covered with ice. Is it safe to walk on? How can you tell?

_____

_____

2. Ice cubes sometimes rise up higher than the top of the ice tray. How does this happen?

_____

_____

Don't Catch Cold!

"Button your coat, or you'll catch cold."
You may have heard that often. Can a
temperature change really make you sick?
Scientists have studied this question.
They've found that a temperature change
does *not* make you sick.

What does cause colds? You catch a cold
from germs. Germs are tiny living things.
Some germs cause disease. Cold germs are
usually spread by human contact.

Germs can live and grow only when the
temperature is right. They prefer warm,
moist places. Human hands and mouths
are perfect for germs. A cold spreads
quickly when people live or work closely
together.

Write a short answer to each question.

1. If you swim in a cold lake, will you
   catch cold? Why or why not?

_____

2. Most germs can't live in very hot or
   very cold temperatures. In what ways
   do people use this knowledge to keep
   food free of germs?

_____

How a Pressure Cooker Works

If you are in a hurry, you know you can
cook food faster in a pressure cooker. A
pressure cooker uses energy from steam to
cook food. In normal cooking, most of the
steam escapes. In pressure cooking, very
little steam escapes.

The lid of a pressure cooker fits very
tightly. Steam builds up inside the pot. As
the steam expands, the molecules of steam
bump against the sides of the pot. This is
called pressure. It makes the particles move

even faster, giving off more heat. The extra
heat cooks the food faster.

A Pressure Cooker

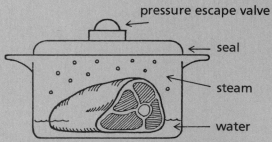

Start of cooking—water starts to boil.

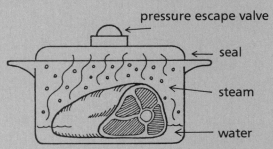

During cooking—steam and pressure
build up inside cooker.

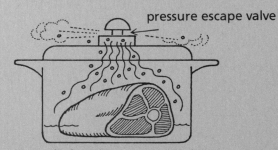

End of cooking—steam is let out
through pressure escape valve.
Then pot can be opened.

Now answer the following questions.

1. Why does a pressure cooker need a
   steam escape valve on its lid?

_____

2. A car's radiator acts much like a
   pressure cooker. If your radiator
   overheats, should you remove the lid
   and look inside? Explain your answer.

Inside a Refrigerator

The refrigerator may be the busiest appliance in any house. Unlike a stove, a dishwasher, or an oven, a refrigerator is "on duty" twenty-four hours a day.

How does a refrigerator work? What keeps the inside of a refrigerator cool?

A refrigerator works by taking heat away. A liquid called a refrigerant does the cooling. A refrigerant is a liquid that evaporates easily. When a liquid evaporates, it loses heat to the air and gets cooler. The cooler liquid can then pick up more heat.

In a refrigerator, the refrigerant picks up warm air from the inside of the refrigerator. As the refrigerant begins to evaporate, it cools. Then it picks up more heat. This continues until the inside of the refrigerator and the refrigerant are both the same temperature.

The vapor that is made from the evaporation of the refrigerant goes through pipes to a compressor. The vapor is squeezed back into liquid form. The heat escapes through pipes in the back of the refrigerator.

Now write a few words to answer these questions.

1. What happens to the temperature of a liquid as it evaporates?

   _____

2. Why does a refrigerator run more if you open the door a lot?

   _____

   _____

A Watched Pot

A watched pot never boils . . . or so the saying goes. But of course it's not being watched that determines if a pot will boil. It's temperature.

Each liquid has its own boiling point. For example, water boils at 100° Celsius or 212° Fahrenheit.

Once a liquid has reached its boiling point, it changes into a gas. Boiling water becomes water vapor, or steam.

Boiling points differ at different heights, or altitudes. Water boils at a lower temperature in the mountains than it does at sea level.

Use the information above to answer these questions.

1. Define the term *boiling point* in your own words.

   _____

   _____

2. Would it take less time to heat a pot of tea to boiling in the mountains or at sea level? Why?

   _____

   _____

Super Cool Science

Some scientists are out in the cold these days. But they don't mind because they have made hot news.

Cryogenics is a new science that studies the effects of very low temperatures on matter. Already cryogenics is being used in many ways. Foods are quick-frozen. Medical uses of cryogenics include freezing cells to control bleeding. Cryogenics may also be used to preserve organs for donors.

Now scientists are excited about the strange results they get when materials are *super*-cooled. The temperature "absolute zero" is the point at which all motion of molecules would stop. Near absolute zero, matter acts differently.

At very low temperatures, many solids become brittle. Super-cooled steel shatters like glass. Most gases turn into solids. Oxygen becomes a solid. It also becomes a magnet at super-low temperatures.

Even computer scientists can use cryogenics. Scientists have found that many materials conduct, or pass on, electricity more easily when they are super-cool. This effect is called superconductivity. Superconductivity allows scientists to build computers that can hold more information than ever before. And the new computers work faster and cost less money to use. Superconductivity will also help make electric power cheaper for homes and factories. There will be many new areas of research and many new useful products in the coming years.

A Test-Taking Tip

Some multiple-choice questions try to see if you understood what you read. Others ask you to apply information to new facts. Ask yourself if these new facts use the information you have already been given.

GED Warm-up

1. What is the physical law that makes it possible for superconductors to work?

   (1) Molecules act differently at very cold temperatures.
   (2) At very low temperatures, molecules stop moving.
   (3) At very cold temperatures, molecules break apart.

   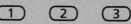

2. *Cryogenics has changed people's lives in many ways.* Which of the following examples does <u>not</u> support that statement?

   (1) Frozen foods can be thawed quickly.
   (2) Body organs can be saved.
   (3) Computers can work faster.

Now go back to page 174. See if all your questions were answered.

The Active Reader

Identifying Cause-and-Effect Relationships

Picture It

Weather Conditions

1. _____

2. _____

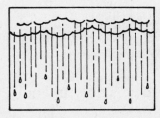

3. _____

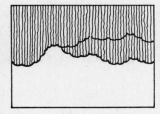

4. _____

Activities

Delay a baseball game
Decide to cook outside on the grill
Shovel the sidewalk
Cancel a day at the beach and stay home

Each picture above shows a different kind of weather. Each activity took place as a result of the weather. Under each picture, write the activity that happened as a result of the weather.

You've just made a connection between weather and an activity. In other words, you've been working with cause-and-effect relationships.

Here's an Example

Look at the first picture. Under the picture of the snow, you probably wrote, "Shovel the sidewalk." You could write the cause-and-effect relationship this way.

■ Since it snowed all morning, I had to shovel the sidewalk.

To find the effect, ask yourself, "*What* happened?" The effect is having to shovel the sidewalk. To find the cause, ask, "*Why* did it happen?" The cause is the snow.

A clue to the cause-and-effect relationship is the word *since*. Often you will read clue words that can help you see causes and effects. Helpful clue words are *because, reason, cause, since, as a result of,* and *on account of.*

Clue words that help you find an effect are words such as *so, thus, as a result, consequently,* and *therefore.*

You can also draw a picture to help you see causes and effects when you read. Here is a picture for the sentence above.

Ⓒ   ⟶   Ⓔ

(snow)   (shovel the sidewalk)

The second picture shows sunny, warm weather. What activity would result from such weather? You probably chose, "Decide to cook outside on the grill." Both the sunshine and the warmth *caused* something to happen. Cooking outside is what happened. It is the *effect*.

Here's a sentence for this cause-and-effect relationship.

■ The sunshine and warm weather felt good, so we decided to cook outside on the grill.

The clue word in this sentence is *so.* A picture for this sentence would look like this.

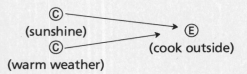

Look at the third picture. It shows rain. The activity that took place because of this weather is "delay a baseball game." A sentence for this cause-and-effect relationship could be this one.

■ The baseball game was delayed on account of rain.

Delaying the baseball game is what happened, or the effect. Why was the game delayed? Write the cause here.

_____

If you wrote *rain,* you found the cause.
On account of is the clue in this sentence. Here's how you could draw a picture of this cause-and-effect relationship.

Ⓔ   ←———   Ⓒ
(delay of game)   (rain)

The fourth picture shows dark storm clouds. Under this picture, you probably wrote, "Cancel a day at the beach and stay home." You could write the sentence like this.

■ We canceled our plans to go to the beach and just stayed home because the sky was filled with dark storm clouds.

Canceling plans and staying home are *what* happened. They are the effects. The dark clouds in the sky are *why* the plans were canceled. They are the cause.

What is the signal word in this sentence? If you thought of the word *because,* you were right. Here is how you would draw the cause-and-effect relationship.

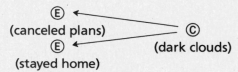

Working It Out

■ For ten days, there was no rain and the temperatures were over 90°. The result was a dangerous water shortage.

1. What is the cause in this example?

_____

_____

2. What is the effect?

_____

3. Draw a picture of the cause-and-effect relationship on your own paper.

4. Circle the signal words in the sentences.

Weather and Climate

Before You Read: Thinking About Weather and Climate

You already know a lot about weather because you *live* in it every day. Weather often influences everyday activities. For this reason, people usually take the trouble to find out the weather forecast for the coming day.

What are some ways you find out about the weather?

_____

_____

You may listen to weather reports on TV or the radio. Perhaps you read the forecast in the newspaper. You may also go outside and draw your *own* conclusions about the weather from what you feel and see.

Why is it helpful to know what the weather will be like?

_____

_____

You may have written something like this: Changes in the weather can affect what you wear and what you do.

Here's a good way to understand the effects the weather has on you. Imagine you are planning a weekend vacation trip. You find the following forecast in the newspaper.

Weekend Weather Forecast

Friday	**Saturday**	**Sunday**
Sunny	Afternoon showers	Partly sunny
High 78°/		Much cooler
Low 55"	Clearing at night	High 60°/
	High 80°/	Low 46°
	Low 55°	

Notice the different weather symbols and descriptions. The forecast changes for each day of your trip. As a result, you must plan different things to do.

Write a few sentences describing each day of your trip. Pretend you have *lots* of money to spend.

Friday: _____

_____

Saturday: _____

_____

Sunday: _____

_____

Now look over the articles you will read in this lesson. Be sure to preview the table and diagrams too. What two articles do you think will be the most interesting? Write one question you hope to have answered by each of these articles.

_____

_____

Working with Words

Here are sentences with two words you will read in this lesson.

> People and animals suffer when there is not enough **precipitation** (the rain, snow, or other forms of water that fall from the sky.)
>
> Changes in weather take place because of changes in the earth's **atmosphere,** or the air around the earth.

Sometimes the meaning of a word is given right in the sentence. That's true of the sentences above.

You may already know *precipitation.* The word is used very often in weather reports. Look again at the first sentence. Write the part of the sentence that tells you the meaning of *precipitation.*

_____

_____

What kind of punctuation mark sets the meaning off? _____

The parentheses ( ) are used to tell you the meaning of *precipitation.* Now write your own sentence with *precipitation* here.

_____

_____

Look at the second sentence. The comma and the word *or* tell you a definition for *atmosphere* will follow. Write that definition here.

_____

Sometimes only a comma is used to set off a word's meaning. The word *or* is not used, as in this sentence: The earth is special because of its atmosphere, the air around it.

Now write a sentence with *atmosphere.*

_____

_____

Here again are the meanings of the two words you've worked with.

Word Power

precipitation the water that falls to the earth in the form of rain, snow, sleet, or hail

atmosphere the air that surrounds the earth

As you read, look for punctuation that tells you that the meaning of a word may follow.

Reading on Your Own

Weather and Climate

What's the weather going to be like today? That's a good question. People need to know if it's going to be cold or hot, wet or dry, windy or calm. Changes in the weather can change one's plans. And the weather can change quite often—from day to day, even from hour to hour.

But what about climate? Does climate change from day to day the way weather does? No. Climate is the kind of weather a place has in general over a very long period of time.

Many things affect the climate that a place has. The tilt of the earth is one major cause of different climates. Places near the equator get more of the sun's heat. The sun's rays strike these places directly most of the time. Such places generally have warm climates.

Places near the North and South Poles receive the sun's rays at a slant. These places have cold climates.

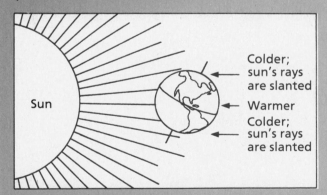

Sun

Colder; sun's rays are slanted

Warmer

Colder; sun's rays are slanted

Large bodies of water, such as oceans, also affect climate. Water does not heat up or cool off as fast as land. Places near oceans have milder climates than places inland. There is less difference in temperatures from summer to winter.

For instance, the temperature in Hawaii is about the same all year round. On the other hand, the climate of Kansas has great differences in temperatures. In summer it is hot there. In winter it is cold.

Use the diagram and article to help you answer the following questions.

1. What is the difference between weather and climate?

   _____

   _____

2. Why is the earth warmer at the equator?

   _____

   _____

3. Why is the earth colder at the poles?

   _____

   _____

4. The Gulf Stream is a warm part of the Atlantic Ocean. Air over the Gulf Stream flows to England. What effect would you expect this to have on England's climate?

   _____

   _____

5. Would you expect more difference in winter and summer temperatures on a Caribbean island or in Idaho? Why?

   _____

   _____

Weather Forecasting

If you're like many people, you watch the weather report on TV. Weather people use radar, satellites, and weather balloons to help them forecast the weather. Radar can spot storm clouds. Satellites take pictures from above the earth. The pictures show clouds and clear places. Weather balloons give information on temperature, wind, and other conditions. By studying all this information, weather people try to predict the weather.

In the next column are some of the symbols weather people use to tell about their weather forecasts.

Use the symbols and the map below to answer the questions that follow.

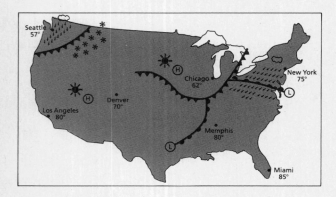

70   Temperature

Sunny

Rain

Snow

Warm Front
A warm front is the front edge of a large mass of warm air.

Cold Front
A cold front is the front edge of a large mass of cold air.

H   **High**
A high is a mass of air that has high pressure. A high-pressure area is often cool and clear.

L   **Low**
A low is a mass of air that has low pressure. A low-pressure area is often warm and cloudy.

1. What kind of front will move past Seattle?

_____

2. What kind of weather is forecast for New York City?

_____

3. Why would a low-pressure area often be found near a warm front?

_____

Rain, Snow, Sleet, and Hail

Have you ever wished for a white Christmas or wished away a rainy day? People look for different kinds of precipitation—the water that falls from the sky.

Water moves back and forth between the earth and the sky. Water evaporates into the air from oceans, rivers, and moist land. The amount of water vapor the air can hold depends on its temperature. Warm air can hold more water than cool air.

The water eventually falls back to earth. This precipitation happens when the air can't hold the water anymore. Sometimes warm, moist air rises and cools off. Or it may meet a mass of cold air. The cold air forces the warm air up, and it cools off. The cooler air can't hold all the water. The water vapor turns into the water drops that make up clouds. If the water drops get too heavy, the water falls as precipitation.

Will the precipitation be rain, snow, sleet, or hail? That, too, depends on temperature. This table shows which precipitation is likely to reach the earth at a particular temperature.

Temperature of clouds	Temperature at ground	Precipitation
below 32°	up to 37°	snow
below 32°	37°–39°	sleet
below 32°	above 39°	hail
any temp.	above 39°	rain

Use the information you just read to answer the following questions.

1. Precipitation is the result of a series of causes and effects. Below is a list of events that lead to precipitation. Number these events 1–6 in the order in which they happen. The first one is numbered for you.

   __1__ Water evaporates into warm air.

   _____ Warm, moist air rises.

   _____ Water vapor turns to drops and forms clouds.

   _____ Water drops become too heavy for air to hold.

   _____ The air cools.

   _____ Precipitation falls.

2. One day the temperature in the clouds is 30°F. Yet on the ground it's 33°F. If precipitation falls, what kind will it probably be?

   _____

3. In a summer thunderstorm, hailstones fall. The air at the ground is 75°F. How is it possible for the precipitation to be balls of ice on such a warm day?

   _____

   _____

Hurricanes

Hurricanes are among nature's most violent storms. Wild winds and pouring rain are the mark of a hurricane. Hurricanes start over warm ocean waters. Cities on or near the ocean's shore are often hit by hurricanes. High waves, along with severe rains, can cause flooding.

Hurricanes travel at a speed of 12 to 20 miles per hour. They can last a few hours or up to two weeks. Winds in a hurricane often reach 100 miles per hour or more. Such winds can tear apart buildings and uproot trees. In one hurricane, a wooden stake was driven all the way through a tree.

Hurricanes start when air comes together with very warm ocean water. In late summer, the surface of parts of the ocean can reach 80 degrees or higher. Water evaporates from the surface. So the air above the ocean's surface warms up and gets moist.

This warm, moist air soon begins to rise. The surrounding air is drawn into the area. It flows in and swirls around the rising column of moist air. This swirling movement of air creates a spiral wind.

The moist column of air grows for days. The water vapor forms clouds. Rain and thunderstorms begin. The spiral winds get stronger. Once they reach 75 miles per hour, a hurricane has formed.

The pressure inside the warm inner column of air drops very low. It becomes quiet at the center of the hurricane. In fact the center, called the eye, has calm, clear skies. But all around it are heavy rain and howling winds.

Hurricanes die when they run out of warm, moist air. This can happen after the hurricane blows over a cooler area of the ocean.

A satellite photograph of a hurricane off the coast of Florida. Notice the swirling movement of the clouds.

Use the article to help you answer the following questions.

1. What causes the damage to property during a hurricane?

   _____

   _____

2. Why do hurricanes most often occur in late summer or early fall?

   _____

   _____

3. What happens once the pressure inside the inner column of air drops low?

   _____

   _____

4. What two things can happen to cause the death of a hurricane?

   _____

   _____

Is the Earth Getting Warmer?

Some scientists believe the earth is getting warmer. That may seem like good news to people who live in cold climates. But it may be bad news for everyone someday.

The warm-up may be due to the greenhouse effect. Heat from the sun gets trapped in the atmosphere, the air around the earth. Carbon dioxide gas and water vapor in the atmosphere hold in the heat.

The greenhouse effect is not new. The greenhouse effect is the reason that the earth does not get too cold at night. In the day, light and heat from the sun reach the earth. But after the sun's rays hit the earth, some bounce back into the atmosphere. Carbon dioxide and water vapor in the atmosphere make a "seal" of sorts. They hold this heat near the earth.

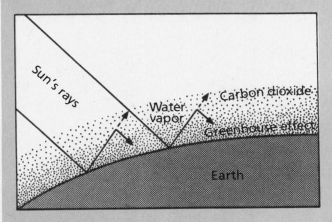

This seal around the earth may be getting too thick, however. When carbon dioxide gas is added to the air, it becomes part of the seal. More heat is sealed in. Because factories and cars put carbon dioxide into the air, more of the greenhouse effect is felt on the earth.

There may come a time when the earth gets too warm. It does not take a big change in temperature to make a change in rainfall. A rise in temperature of only 2 or 3 degrees would make a big difference.

Some places that now get little rain would get more. Other places would get less. Changes would have to be made in the way people grow food. If the earth warmed up too much, the ice caps of the North and South Poles would start to melt.

Answer these questions about the greenhouse effect with a few words.

1. What two substances produce the greenhouse effect?

_____

_____

2. How do cars help increase the greenhouse effect?

_____

_____

_____

_____

GED Warm-up

If the greenhouse effect melts the polar ice caps, the level of the ocean will rise. Which of the following events could result from this rise?

(1) The ocean will not be able to support as much animal life.

(2) The ocean will become much warmer than it is now.

(3) Cities along the ocean shore may be flooded.

(4) More islands will be created in the middle of the ocean.

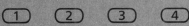

The Active Reader

Using What You Know

Picture It

Tim's fourth-grade son wanted to be an astronaut for Halloween. Tim had to help him make his costume. Tim wasn't an astronaut himself. But he already had some ideas about what an astronaut looks like. He knew astronauts wear helmets with air hoses so that they can breathe while they are in space. He put some platforms on the soles of his son's boots to help weigh his son down.

How did Tim know what the costume should look like? Tim had seen astronauts on the news. He had also watched a TV show and movies about astronauts. He had this information about astronauts stored in his mind. In short, he used what he already knew about space and astronauts.

You also have a great deal of information in your mind. It comes from what you have seen, read, and done all your life. What you already know can help you every time you read. You link what you are reading with what you have stored in your mind. In this way, you understand better. Your knowledge grows.

Sometimes it helps to stop and think a bit *before* you begin to read an article. Try to remember what you already know about the topic of the article. You may find the article easier to understand.

Here's an Example

Read the following paragraph. Use the lines to show that you are familiar with some of the words and ideas. Look at the word in dark print just before each blank line. On the line, write an explanation of that word or idea.

■In September, 1992, NASA sent an **unmanned spacecraft**

(_____) to **Mars.** A **space**

shuttle (_____)
carried the craft out of the earth's

atmosphere. (_____)
From there, the spacecraft headed toward Mars. It reached its target in about a year. Then it circled Mars many times. The spacecraft told us

about the **seasons** (_____)
and atmosphere on Mars.

How did you do? Did you find that you had something to say for each line?

How about *unmanned spacecraft*? You might know that astronauts have gone on some rocket ships into space. You could say that this rocket ship will have no people aboard.

What about *Mars*? You might know it as a planet. Or you might know it as a place where monsters in very old movies came from. You may even have used this name to mean someplace far out in space.

Were you able to write information for *space shuttle, atmosphere,* and *seasons*?

For all the information you wrote down, you used your knowledge. You got the knowledge from news reports you've heard, from TV shows and films, and from just talking and listening to others. By using that knowledge as you read, you can better understand new information.

Working It Out

Now read this article about the sun. (You can already be asking yourself, "What do I know about the sun?") Answer the questions as you read. They will show you how your knowledge helps you understand new information.

■ How "old" is the sun? Do we need to care how old it is? Scientists say the sun is about 4.5 billion years old. That makes it "middle-aged."

1. The article says the sun is "middle-aged." You know what it means for a *person* to be middle-aged. If the sun is middle-aged now, about how much longer do you think it will live?

_____

_____

■ Scientists guess that the whole life of the sun is about 10 billion years. They say that about 5 billion years from now the sun will have used up almost all its nuclear fuel. For a time, it will slowly shrink in size. During this time, it will glow with great heat. Oceans on the earth will boil. All forms of life will burn up. Then the sun's nuclear fuel will burn out.

2. You know what happens when the fuel for a fire or a car runs out. What will happen to the sun when its fuel runs out?

_____

_____

■ The sun will slowly cool off. As it does, the earth will pass into an ice age that will last forever.

Use what you already know to help you read the articles in the next lesson. Take time to ask yourself, "How is this like something else I've heard of? What have I read or experienced before that helps me understand this?"

The Planets in Space

Before You Read:
Thinking About the Planets

On the following pages, you'll read some interesting articles about space. Your reading will take you into an exciting area of earth science.

You may already know more about space than you think. Think of times you have looked up at the starlit sky on a clear night. Think of TV shows and movies about space that you've seen.

Now try filling in the blanks in the paragraph below. You'll probably find that you know some basic facts about space already. You are familiar with many of the words used by scientists to talk about space. Your knowledge will help you as you read.

| moon | sun | Earth |
| telescopes | rockets | weightless |

Space and the objects in it make up the universe. To get a closer look at objects in space, people invented _____. In this century, scientists also have sent powerful, tube-shaped _____ into space. Cameras aboard them have given us even closer views of the

mysteries of space. Some U.S. astronauts even landed and walked on the _____. Astronauts have to wear special gear because in space they are _____ and could float off into space. Besides the moon and stars, there are also planets in space. _____ is the planet we live on. The star that warms our planet and brings us daylight is the _____.

Did you already know many words that have to do with space and the planets?

Now see how many ideas and facts you know. Read each statement below. Put a check next to each statement you think is true.

_____ 1. Earth travels around the sun.

_____ 2. Earth travels around the moon.

_____ 3. Other planets also have moons.

_____ 4. All the planets rotate, creating days and nights.

_____ 5. At one time, there may have been water on Mars.

Read through the statements above one more time. Were there any that you were not sure about? If so, put a question mark next to those statements.

You'll learn the answers to all the true-false questions above as you read the articles in this lesson. But before you go on, give some more thought to what you already know and what you might like to know. Write some questions you would like to have answered about space or the planets.

_____

_____

Working with Words

Some words you'll read in this lesson are used in the sentences below. You may already be familiar with these words. You will certainly want to use your knowledge to help you define each word. But you'll also want to use clues each sentence gives. The clues will help you figure out how scientists use the terms.

Mars is one of the most fascinating planets in our **solar system.**

Earth is in **orbit** around the sun, but the moon is in **orbit** around Earth.

Objects on the moon weigh less than they do on Earth because the moon's force of **gravity** is much weaker.

Here's how the sentences help you understand the words. The first sentence refers to Mars as a planet in our solar system. You were right if you guessed that planets are part of the solar system. You might think of "solar energy" or "solar heating" when you hear the word

solar. Do you know what the word *solar* means? If you do, write it here.

_____

You're on the right track if you think that the *sun* must be part of the solar system too. Try to picture a "system" with sun and planets. Can you write a sentence of your own using the words *solar system*? Write it below.

_____

_____

Now look at the second sentence in the box. It uses the word *orbit* twice. The words "around the sun" and "around Earth" tell you that *orbit* deals with traveling around another object. Try writing a sentence using the word *orbit.*

_____

_____

The word *force* in the last sentence is your best clue to the meaning of *gravity.* It tells you that gravity involves power or energy. If you know anything more about gravity, write it here.

_____

Now look at the definitions below. See if you figured out the meanings of the words.

Word Power

solar system the sun and all the heavenly bodies that travel around it

orbit the path of any heavenly body around another heavenly body

gravity the natural force that attracts or pulls one object toward another

Reading on Your Own

The Solar System

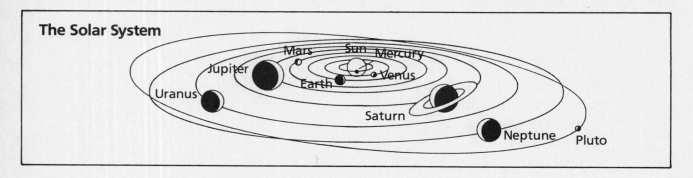

The Solar System
The solar system contains the sun, the nine planets, many moons, and thousands of other smaller objects. The huge sun is the center of the solar system. It gives off heat and light.

The planets travel around the sun. Each planet has its own orbit, or path. Each planet also takes a different amount of time to orbit the sun. A planet that is farther away from the sun takes longer to orbit the sun than a closer planet. Earth makes one full trip around the sun every 365 days, or one year.

Because Mercury is close to the sun, it is blazing hot during the day. Pluto is the farthest planet we know. It is a frozen world.

Use the article and the diagram above to answer these questions.

1. Which planet do you think is colder, Venus or Saturn? Why?

_____

_____

2. Which has the larger orbit, Mars or Mercury? How do you know?

_____

_____

Gravity and Orbits
What keeps the planets in orbit around the sun? The force of gravity keeps the planets from flying out of the solar system. Gravity is a pull, or attraction, between two objects. Gravity draws objects toward each other.

Without gravity, a planet would move in a straight line away from the sun. A planet has more force to move in a straight line.

But gravity from the sun pulls the planet toward the sun. The planet is caught between its forward movement and the sun's gravity. This balance creates the planet's orbit.

When a planet is close to the sun, it travels faster. It moves in a straight line. As the planet moves away from the sun, it slows down. Then gravity pulls it back toward the sun. This change in speed makes the planet's orbit oval. It is not a true circle.

Why a Planet Stays in an Oval Orbit

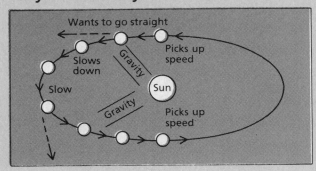

The force of gravity acts between *all* objects in space. Gravity keeps the moon in orbit around Earth. It keeps Jupiter's 16 moons in orbit around that planet.

The amount of pull between objects depends on two things: the size of the objects and the amount of space between them. A large object has more gravity, or pull, than a small one. And the closer the objects are to one another, the more pull there is between them.

Answer these questions in your own words.

1. What keeps any object in orbit around another?

_____

2. If a planet did not get pulled toward the sun, what would happen to it?

_____

_____

3. If two moons orbit a planet, the one closer to the planet will move faster. Why?

_____

_____

Sun and Earth, Day and Night

Through history, many people thought the sun and planets moved around Earth. In 1543 a man named Copernicus helped change that thinking. Copernicus showed that Earth and other planets circle the sun. When people thought the sun was moving, it was really Earth moving.

Earth not only moves around the sun every year. It also rotates, or turns itself around, every 24 hours. First one side of Earth faces the sun. It is daytime. Then that side of Earth turns away from the sun. It becomes night. When people on one side of Earth have daytime, people on the other side have night.

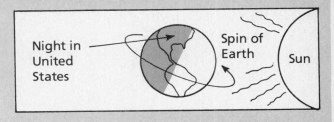

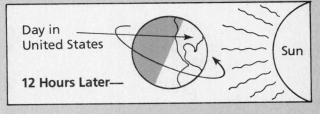

Now answer the following questions.

1. Why do you think people thought the sun moved around Earth?

_____

_____

2. What is really happening when you see the sun rise in the east and set in the west?

_____

_____

Phases of the Moon

The moon has no light. Moonlight is really sunlight. Light from the sun is reflected by the moon.

As the moon orbits Earth, different parts of the moon face the sun. We see different shapes on Earth when different parts of the moon are lit. These different shapes are called the phases of the moon.

Sometimes there is no moon in the night sky. This "new moon" is dark because the moon is between the sun and Earth. Its "backside" is lit, not the side that faces Earth.

Two or three nights later, however, a crescent moon appears. The moon has moved in its orbit. A small part of the moon is in light. A few nights later, half of the lighted side can be seen from Earth. The moon has made one fourth of its orbit around Earth.

A gibbous moon comes next. Most of the side of the moon facing Earth is in sunlight. When the moon is full, the whole side is in the sun. The moon looks like a full, glowing circle.

After a full moon, the sun lights less and less of the moon. After $29\frac{1}{2}$ days, there is another new moon. The moon has made a full orbit.

Use the article and the diagram to help you answer the following questions.

1. What does the sun have to do with moonlight?

_____

2. The moon has made one-half of its orbit around the earth. Which phase is the moon in? What shape does it have?

_____

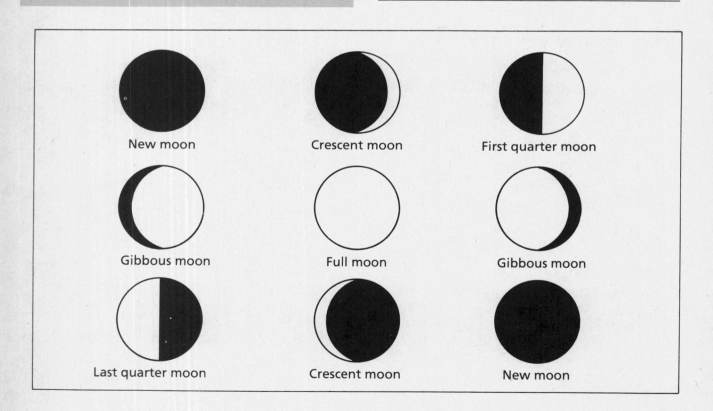

New moon	Crescent moon	First quarter moon
Gibbous moon	Full moon	Gibbous moon
Last quarter moon	Crescent moon	New moon

The Making of a Moon

Earth's moon may have been made by a crash, some scientists say. These scientists think Earth hit some other object in space $4\frac{1}{2}$ billion years ago.

This idea was tested by computer. It showed how the crash might have happened. An object about the size of Mars crashed with Earth. Pieces of both were thrown out into space. The heavy material fell back to Earth. Light gases and bits of matter stayed in space. After a while, gravity began to pull the small pieces together. The result was the moon.

Circle the letter of the answer you think is best for each question below. Use the article to help you.

1. If this theory is right, what part did gravity play in the making of the moon?

   a. It drew together small bits of matter.

   b. It pulled large bits of matter away from Earth.

   c. It caused a crash between Earth and Mars.

2. Suppose the idea of the scientists is true. Which of the following statements would also have to be true?

   a. Jupiter's moons were made by a crash of two objects in space.

   b. It was the moon of Mars that crashed into Earth.

   c. Earth is at least $4\frac{1}{2}$ billion years old.

What Is Mars Really Like?

Mars may not have always been the cold, dry planet it is today. Many scientists think that Mars had rivers billions of years ago. Areas on the surface of Mars look like dry riverbeds. Canyons and deep gorges also lead scientists to think water once flowed on Mars.

Today the only water we know of is in the air in *very* small amounts. But Mars also has white "caps" at its north and south poles. These may be ice caps of frozen water. Earth has similar ice caps at its poles.

If there *is* more water on Mars, could there be life? Some scientists think not. The air on Mars does not seem right for life. The atmosphere is made up mostly of carbon dioxide gas. Earth's atmosphere has oxygen and nitrogen. Other scientists feel there *is* a chance that some kind of Martian life exists, perhaps plant life.

Even without life, Mars is full of wonders. On the surface is rusty red sand. Dust storms blow over the planet for weeks or months at a time.

Mars has many dead volcanoes too. One is more than twice as high as Mount Everest, the highest mountain on Earth.

Write a short answer to each question.

1. Why would the canyons and gorges on Mars make scientists think Mars once had rivers?

   _____

   _____

2. Name one reason some scientists think there may *not* be life on Mars.

   _____

   _____

Discoveries from Space

In 1977 the United States launched two space probes, *Voyager I* and *Voyager II.* These spacecraft were launched to study Saturn, Uranus, and other planets.

It took three years for the space probes to reach Saturn. *Voyager I* flew within 78,000 miles of the planet. *Voyager II* came within 63,000 miles. Photos from *Voyager II* showed a seventh ring around Saturn. Scientists also learned from *Voyager II* that Saturn's rings are actually made up of many narrow rings. They are called "ringlets."

Voyager II found ten small moons around Uranus in 1986. Now the count is fifteen moons orbiting this planet. Scientists think these small moons are made up of the same material as the rings around Uranus. These rings weren't discovered until 1977.

The rings and small moons of Uranus have ice and some kind of very black material. The rings are not solid. They are made of small chunks of this unknown black material. It looks as if thousands of lumps of coal are spinning around the planet.

Write true *or* false *before each statement.*

_____ 1. Saturn has large numbers of small rings that blend together to look like bands when seen from Earth.

_____ 2. The black material that makes up the moons and rings of Uranus is ice.

The Asteroid Belt

Scientists have discovered thousands of asteroids in orbit around the sun. Asteroids are small, rocky objects. They are in the area between Mars and Jupiter. These asteroids are like small planets, but they are not round like planets. Most asteroids have irregular shapes.

Scientists want to find out where asteroids came from. Because of the unusual shapes of asteroids, scientists think they may be part of a planet that exploded long ago. This planet would have orbited the sun between Mars and Jupiter.

Other scientists believe that asteroids may be bits of matter left over from the forming of the planets. Still others say the asteroids are the remains of an explosion of one of Jupiter's moons.

GED Warm-up

1. In what way are asteroids like planets?
   (1) They orbit the sun.
   (2) They are made of rock.
   (3) They have irregular shapes.
   (4) They lie between Mars and Jupiter.

   ① ② ③ ④

2. Which of the following is one possible explanation for the asteroids?
   (1) a crash between Mars and Jupiter
   (2) a crash between Jupiter and one of its moons
   (3) the explosion of a planet
   (4) the explosion of a moon of Mars

   ① ② ③ ④

The Active Reader

Writing a Summary

Picture It

You know that a baseball game takes hours to play. Yet a newsperson can tell all about the game in a minute. He or she gives a summary. The reporter summarizes the game telling only the important things. The reporter tells you the final score and who made runs. But the reporter does not talk about unimportant things. For example, he or she does not explain how every out was made.

Like a reporter who sums up a game, you can write a summary of what you read. A summary is a few sentences that give the main idea. Writing a summary helps you figure out which parts of an article are important. It is a way to make sure you understand what you read.

Here's an Example

Inez was reading the article below about plastic and pollution. She wanted to make sure she understood what she was reading. She decided to write a summary.

■ Almost one-tenth of all the garbage in the United States is made of plastic. Plastic bags, boxes, and food wrap fill the garbage dumps.

Plastic garbage is hard to get rid of. Some cities take care of garbage by burying it. When wood and paper are buried, they rot. But plastic does not rot when it is buried. A plastic bag can last for 100 years!

Burning plastic is not a good idea either. When burned, plastic gives off black smoke that poisons the air.

First, Inez decided on the most important idea of the story. This main idea is stated in the third sentence: "Plastic garbage is hard to get rid of." Second, Inez looked for facts or ideas that explain *why* plastic is hard to get rid of.

Here is the summary that Inez wrote.

■Plastic garbage is hard to get rid of because it does not rot and it is dangerous to burn.

Notice that Inez left out several facts. To make her summary short, she did not name the different kinds of plastic garbage. She did not write that a plastic bag can last 100 years. She did not need these facts to explain the main idea. In one sentence, Inez summed up what the story said.

Working It Out

The following article tells how spray cans can poison the air. As you read, think how you would write a summary of it.

■ Since the 1950s, Americans have used spray cans to clean their homes. They have used them to kill bugs, shine their furniture, and make the air smell fresh.

Spray cans are handy for cleaning, but they are not good for the air. Certain gases inside the cans make them work. Once the gases come out of the can, they do not go away. There are now eleven million tons of these gases in the air.

These gases are breaking down the ozone. The ozone is a ring of gas around the earth that blocks the harmful rays of the sun. Without this ring of ozone, the sun would burn people badly.

1. Like Inez, first decide on the main idea of this article. Ask yourself, "What is this about?" Then read the following sentences. Decide which sentence states the main idea. Underline it.

   a. People have used spray cans since the 1950s.

   b. Spray cans are used for cleaning furniture.

   c. Spray-can gas is not good for the air.

2. What other facts will you put in your summary? Read the following sentences. Pick out *two* that help explain the main idea. Underline them.

   a. There are eleven million tons of spray-can gas in the air.

   b. Spray-can gas harms the earth's ozone.

   c. People should not use spray to kill bugs.

   d. Without the ozone, the sun would burn people badly.

3. Now sum up the reading in two or three sentences. State the main idea. Then add important facts that help explain the main idea.

   _____

   _____

   _____

Pollution

Before You Read: Thinking About Pollution

The articles in this lesson are about the problems of pollution and waste. Waste from factories can poison the air. Waste from people's homes is dumped on the land. You hear about these things on news shows. But you also see signs of pollution all around you.

See how much you already know about pollution. Finish these sentences. Fill in each blank with a word from the box.

rain   poison   wildlife   smog   landfill

1. Burying garbage in a _____ uses up too much land.

2. People in cities sometimes have trouble breathing because of _____ .

3. Lead is a _____ found in the drinking water of many Americans.

4. When acid _____ falls on lakes, the fish begin to die.

5. The wind carries waste to faraway forests, poisoning _____ .

Are any of the ideas in those sentences new to you? If so, you will learn more about the ideas in the articles ahead. Pollution is a big problem these days. Learning about pollution is the first step in solving the problem.

Think about the ideas in sentences 1–5. Choose two or three that interest you. For each idea you choose, think of a question. Begin each question with the word *how*. Write the questions on the following lines.

_____

_____

_____

_____

Try to find the answers to your questions as you read. That way, you will learn *how* pollution starts and *how* people can fight it.

Working with Words

Some words from the articles in the previous lesson are used in the sentences below. These words may be new to you. Or you may have seen them before. Add what you already know to the hints in the sentences. Then decide what the words mean.

The farmer covered his fields with **fertilizer.**

Plant and animal **fossils** in this rock pit are a million years old.

The amount of noise in a subway is about 100 **decibels.**

The word *fertilizer* contains the word *fertile.* When something is *fertile,* it can produce lots of things. You know a farmer wants fields to produce lots of plants. The ending *-izer* turns *fertile* into the name of something. So what is the meaning of *fertilizer*? Write it below.

_____

_____

The second sentence tells you that fossils are found in rock pits. It tells you that they can be very old. It also tells you that they can be part of a plant or animal. Put these three facts together. Then write what you think a fossil is.

_____

_____

The word *amount* in the third sentence is a hint that something is being measured. This sentence has the same form as "The amount of sugar is two cups." So you can tell that *decibel* is a unit of measure just as *cup* is. What do decibels measure? Write your answer below.

_____

_____

The following definitions are from the dictionary. Are they like the meanings you wrote?

Word Power

fertilizer a substance put into or on the soil to make it produce more

fossil the hardened remains or traces of something that lived in a past age

decibel a unit for measuring the loudness of sounds

Writing to Improve Your Reading

Writing notes is a good way to remember what you read. Notes will help you write summaries too. But you need to keep your notes short. Sum up what you read in just a few words.

Suppose you read, "The man bought pears, apples, bananas, and grapes." Don't write down everything the man bought. Just write, "The man bought fruit." When you read, "She put a stamp on the letter and dropped it in the mailbox," you can just write, "She mailed the letter." When you read a list of things, try to sum them up with one general word.

Reading on Your Own

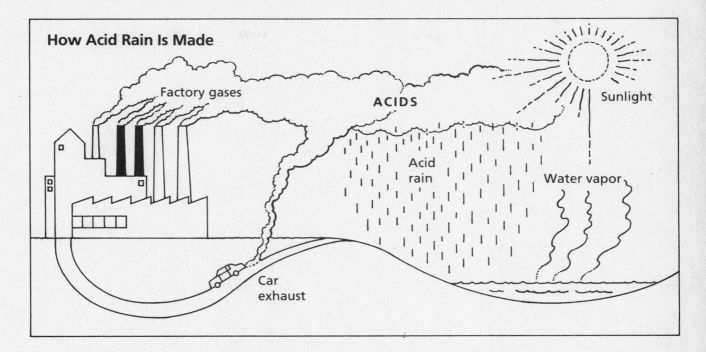

How Acid Rain Is Made

Factory gases

ACIDS

Sunlight

Acid rain

Water vapor

Car exhaust

Acid Rain

Would you be surprised to learn that rain can hurt living things? Acid rain—or rain that has acid in it—can hurt plants and animals. It can even destroy buildings.

Normal rain has just a little acid in it. But some of the rains that are falling around the world hold up to 1,000 times more acid than they should. In the northeastern United States and Canada, acid in the rain is five to thirty times more than normal. Because of this acid, fish and plants have died in many lakes in New York state.

Acid rain can kill fish by killing the plants they eat. It also lets some chemicals from the soil get into the water. These chemicals hurt the fish. Plants and trees do not grow well if the soil has too much acid in it. Acid rain also makes buildings and bridges fall apart too fast. It eats away at the stone and cement.

Acid rain is made when certain chemicals in the air mix with water vapor. Fertilizers for farm crops and gases from cars and factories get into the air. With water and sunlight, they change to acid. Then the acid falls to earth with the rain.

Some lakes are now being treated with lime. Lime changes the acid so that it will no longer be harmful. People are trying to find other ways to cut down on acid rain. But for now, every time it rains, there is trouble in the air.

Answer the questions below.

1. What things might people do to cut down on acid rain?

_____

2. Write a summary of the article "Acid Rain."

_____

_____

Getting the Lead Out

Studies show that many people may be slowly getting poisoned. And it is children who are most at risk, especially inner-city children.

Inner-city homes often have peeling paint with lead in it. Newer paint does not have lead. But many people in the inner city do not have money to repaint. Small children sometimes eat the lead paint.

Lead poisoning can cause hearing problems and other medical problems. Almost one out of ten preschool children who were studied had lead poisoning. Almost one-fourth of the African American children in one study had been poisoned by lead.

It is not just old peeling paint that has lead in it. One place that most people don't think to check for lead is in their drinking water. One out of five Americans may have dangerous lead in their water. Backyards near roads or highways often have lead in them. Fertilizers have lead too. Some cars still use gas that puts lead into the air.

Doctors say a diet high in protein and low in fat will help cut down the poisonings. But getting rid of the lead is the most important step.

Write a few words to answer the questions below.

1. Explain why inner-city children are at risk for getting lead poisoning.

_____

_____

2. What step have carmakers taken that lowers the amount of lead in the air?

_____

Fossils in the Dump

A garbage dump in western Germany is causing a big stink. But it's not the smell of garbage that has people up in arms. It is what's *under* the garbage that concerns people.

At the bottom of a large hole in the ground is a fossil-lover's find. A fossil is some kind of remains of life long ago. Many fossils that are hard to find in other places can be found here. There are hundreds of plant, animal, and insect fossils. But the fossils are in danger of being destroyed.

The hole used to be a mine. It now belongs to a garbage company. The garbage company plans to use it as a dump. After garbage fills up the hole, the hole will be covered with dirt and grass. Then the fossils will be lost forever.

Some scientists are very upset. They have tried to save the fossils. For a time, a hold was put on dumping garbage here. But now the time limit is up. Scientists are trying again to stop the dumping of garbage on this important fossil find.

Now answer the questions below.

1. Why is this particular fossil find so important to scientists?

_____

_____

2. Write a short summary of the article ''Fossils in the Dump.''

_____

_____

_____

"No Waste" Waste

New ways have been found to solve an old problem—what to do with waste. Americans are making more garbage every day. Today people make twice as much trash per person as their parents did. This waste has to go somewhere.

Old ways of getting rid of trash are not good enough any more. Open dumps take up land and can cause disease. Landfills, which cover the trash with dirt and grass, are better. But landfills also use up too much land. And groundwater can be polluted by garbage in dumps and landfills. Burning trash puts smoke and chemical pollutants into the air.

Recycling is a newer, better way to deal with garbage. Today there are many places that will reuse paper, glass, steel, and aluminum. Even rubber can be recycled.

Other new ideas help the trash problem. Some people use garbage to make "bricks" for buildings. Burning trash can be used to make steam. Then the steam becomes a kind of energy to run factories.

Use the information in the article to answer the question below.

1. The article categorizes ways to deal with trash as old ways and new ways. Complete these lists with examples from the articles.

Old Ways

Dumps _____

_____

New Ways

_____

Using garbage (to build, to produce energy)

Noise Pollution

Mrs. Delgado lives near an airport. Each time a plane takes off, she stops talking. The noise of the jet drowns out her words.

Mr. Russo worked in a factory most of his life. Now he's losing his hearing. The doctor says factory noise hurt his ears.

Noise pollution is a growing problem. Bigger airplanes mean extra noise. More factories also mean more noise. The sounds on a city street can reach high levels. There is a point where noise is painful. Loud noise can make people lose their hearing.

The graph below shows how much noise is created in different situations. A decibel is a unit of sound energy. The higher the decibel number, the louder the noise.

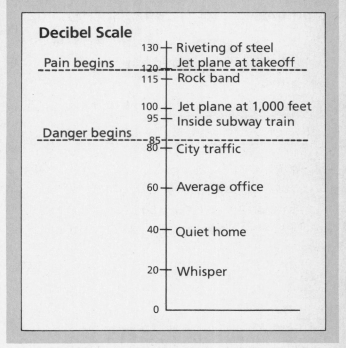

Decibel Scale

130	Riveting of steel
120	Jet plane at takeoff — Pain begins
115	Rock band
100	Jet plane at 1,000 feet
95	Inside subway train
85	Danger begins
80	City traffic
60	Average office
40	Quiet home
20	Whisper
0	

Answer the following questions.

1. How loud is a subway train? Can you harm your hearing on the subway?

_____

2. Summarize the article and graph on your own paper.

Pollution Fallout

Something strange is happening to wildlife in an isolated place. Scientists have been alerted to a deadly problem.

On a small island in Lake Superior, many animals have birth defects. Scientists found that deadly chemicals were being carried to the island by the wind. The chemicals came from farms in the Midwest and South.

This kind of pollution "fallout" is worse than other air pollution. These chemicals are very toxic to begin with. Sometimes the chemicals combine to make new chemicals. Scientists do not even know what harm the new chemicals might do.

Now answer these questions.

1. Why do many of the animals on the Lake Superior island have birth defects?

_____

_____

2. Wind can carry pollution fallout from place to place around the whole earth. How might this fact cause problems between people of different countries?

_____

_____

_____

_____

Ozone Alert

Ozone is a gas in the upper atmosphere. Twenty to thirty miles above the earth, ozone shields us from harmful rays from the sun.

Sometimes, however, ozone gets produced much closer to the earth's surface. Exhaust from cars and factories can react with sunlight to make ozone close to the ground.

Ozone is helpful when it is high above us in the upper atmosphere. But it is harmful when we come into contact with it. It makes people's eyes burn. It can harm their lungs. People with lung disease are especially at risk.

Big cities can have a problem with ozone. Too much ozone can build up in the air over the city. At such times, health officials put out an ozone alert. They tell people with breathing problems to stay inside. They ask people to drive their cars less. They ask factory managers to put less pollution into the air.

Use the article to help you answer the questions below.

1. Why would there be more ozone near the ground in a large city than in the country?

_____

_____

2. When is ozone helpful to people? Why?

_____

_____

Air Pollution in Cities

People who live in or near a big city can feel the effects of air pollution. It burns their eyes and noses and gives some people headaches. Air pollution is a big problem in cities.

Much of the air pollution in cities comes from cars. Burning fuel makes smoke and gases that escape into the air. Sometimes this kind of air pollution is called smog. Smoke and gases from factories and dust also get into the air.

Air pollution has many bad effects. It eats away at nylon and rubber. It makes statues and buildings crumble. Air pollution even makes it hard for sunlight to get through.

Air pollution hurts people as well. Scientists know that people in cities with lots of pollution have more colds. They have more lung disease too. Lung cancer seems to happen more often in people who live in cities with a lot of smog.

Today cars are being built in a way that cuts down on air pollution. Laws tell factory owners how much pollution they can put into the air. But these changes cost money. Since the bad effects of pollution take place over a long time, some people do not see the problem as being as serious as it really is.

Now write your answers to these questions.

1. Name two causes of air pollution.

_____

_____

2. Name two effects of air pollution.

_____

_____

3. Write a summary of "Air Pollution in Cities."

_____

_____

_____

_____

A Test-Taking Tip

Sometimes you have strong views on a topic. A multiple-choice question may include an answer choice that you agree with. But if it doesn't actually answer the question, it's the *wrong* answer. Use information from the article to answer questions. Don't let your opinions get in the way.

GED Warm-up

According to the article, why are some people slow to deal with air pollution?

(1) They do not see that air pollution hurts them.

(2) There is nothing people can do to solve the problem.

(3) The air pollution will go away by itself.

(4) Air pollution is not really a serious problem.

Assessing Supporting Data

Picture It

Did you ever bring a gold ring to a jewel shop to see what it was worth? You had the ring *assessed.* To assess something is to judge its value. To judge the ring's value, a jeweler must answer several questions. How much does the ring weigh? Is it well made? How pure is the gold?

Like a jeweler, you must do assessing when you read scientific subjects. You must judge the data, or facts, you read. You must ask yourself, "Are the facts good enough to support what the author says?"

When you assess the facts, you must answer three questions:

1. Do the facts lead to the conclusion made?

2. Have enough facts been gathered?

3. Were the facts gathered in a scientific way?

Here's an Example

The following story shows how important judging facts is.

■ Aristotle [ar'ə stot' l], a great thinker, lived 2,300 years ago in Greece. One day Aristotle wondered, "What makes some things float on water? What makes other things sink?" He saw that boats with flat bottoms floated. He saw that round rocks would sink. So he decided a thing's shape was the reason it floated or sank.

For many years, people accepted what Aristotle said. It seemed to make sense. And Aristotle was known to be wise.

But 1,900 years later in Italy, a man named Galileo [gal' ə lē' ō] asked, "Was Aristotle right?" Galileo believed that ideas must be based on facts. Facts are statements that have been tested. They have been proved true. If Aristotle were right, it had to be proved that everything flat floats and everything round sinks.

So Galileo tried floating all sorts of

things on water. He found that flat things, if they were heavy enough, would sink. If round things were light enough, they would float. Finally, he decided that weight, not shape, determines whether something floats.

Galileo assessed the facts behind Aristotle's idea. It was true that flat boats floated and round rocks sank. These facts did lead to Aristotle's conclusion.

However, Galileo saw that Aristotle had not gathered enough facts. Aristotle had not looked at enough floating things to make such a general statement.

Galileo proved his own idea right by gathering facts in a scientific way. First, he carefully studied things in the real world. Galileo did not accept Aristotle's idea just because most other people accepted it. Scientific facts are gathered by observing the real world, not by accepting what somebody says.

Second, Galileo gathered facts through testing. He did tests that other people could repeat. If Galileo said, "A one-inch flat gold coin will sink," people did not have to take his word for it. They could try floating such a coin for themselves.

When assessing the facts that support an idea, be sure the facts were gathered in a scientific way. This means—

1. The facts were gathered by looking at the real world.

2. The facts can be tested again and again.

Working It Out

Suppose you read the following ad in a magazine.

■ You can be slim again! Try Fat-Off, the new diet aid. Fat-Off is made from dried snake livers. As everybody knows, all snakes are slim and firm. Tracy L. of Cleveland, Ohio, says, "With Fat-Off, I lost 20 pounds in 20 days!"

Answer the following questions. They will help you assess the facts in the ad.

1. The ad says Fat-Off has snake livers in it. It also says all snakes are thin. Suppose these two statements are facts. Do they lead to the conclusion that Fat-Off makes you thin? Explain your answer.

_____

_____

_____

2. Tracy L. says Fat-Off helped her lose weight. Is this enough to support the idea that Fat-Off makes you thin? Explain your answer.

_____

_____

_____

3. The ad claims "everybody knows" snakes are thin. Do you think this is a fact that was gathered in a scientific way? Why or why not?

_____

_____

_____

The Structure of Matter: Scientists at Work

Before You Read: Thinking About Scientists at Work

The articles in this lesson are about the way scientists work. By reading about great scientists, you will also learn the answers to these important questions: What is everything in the world made of? How do we make electricity? Where does atomic power come from?

As you will see, early scientists greatly improved our understanding of the world. They could do this because they used the scientific method:

- They looked closely at the way the world worked.

- They thought of questions they wanted answered.

- They gathered facts to answer their questions.

- They thought of ideas to explain the facts they gathered.

- They did many experiments to test their ideas.

- Often their experiments did not turn out as they expected. But they learned from failure as well as success.

Take time now to think of what you already know about this topic. What do you know about scientists? What do you know about matter in the world? What have you heard on the news or seen on TV shows? Read this list. Put a check next to each thing you know a little about.

_____ atoms

_____ Einstein

_____ electricity

_____ nuclear energy

_____ quarks

_____ atomic bomb

_____ radiation

All those things have something to do with the structure of matter in the world. One — Albert Einstein — was a very famous scientist. His work helped us understand matter.

Now play the part of a scientist yourself. Scientists gather facts in an organized way. They think of the questions they want answered. These questions guide their fact gathering.

Make a plan before you start reading. Think of questions you have about atoms, electricity, or atomic energy. Write your questions on the following lines.

_____

_____

_____

_____

See if you can find answers to your questions as you read.

Working with Words

Some words from the articles are used in the sentences that follow. Add what you already know to the hints in the sentences. Then figure out what the words mean.

Light is **radiation** from the sun.

When atoms undergo **fission,** they split and give off energy.

The earth's movement around the sun is **perpetual.** If it stopped, there would be no day and night.

The word *radiation* contains the word *radiate. Radiate* means "to give off rays." The ending *-ion* turns *radiate* into the name of a thing. Write what you think *radiation* means.

_____

_____

The second sentence gives you a clue to the meaning of *fission.* It tells you atoms "split" during fission. The ending *-ion* tells you *fission* is the name of an action.

See if you can write a definition for fission.

_____

_____

Think about the last two sentences. If the earth's movement stopped, there would be no day and night. You know night always follows day. So what does this say about the earth's movement? Your answer should be close to the meaning of *perpetual.*

_____

_____

The following definitions are from the dictionary. Are they like the meanings you wrote?

Word Power

radiation rays, such as those of light or heat, that are given off

fission the splitting apart of atoms to produce tremendous amounts of energy

perpetual lasting forever

A nuclear power plant produces electricity by using fission.

Reading on Your Own

Using the Scientific Method

Scientists have a special way of finding out things. They use the scientific method to test ideas they think may be true.

A scientist makes use of both thinking and experimenting. A scientists starts with an idea or a question about something he or she sees. Then the scientist thinks of an experiment that may help test the idea or answer the question.

The scientist tests the idea carefully. He or she keeps a record of what happens at all times. Records and measurements must be exact.

The results of the experiment may prove that the scientist's idea was right. Other scientists may then try the same experiment to check it.

The results of the experiment may show that the scientist's idea was wrong. But some of the information from the experiment may lead the scientist to a new idea and a new experiment.

Now answer these questions.

1. Check each activity that is part of the scientific method.

    _____ **a.** getting exact information

    _____ **b.** keeping track of what happens in an experiment

    _____ **c.** thinking of ways to test an idea

2. Suppose you think the temperature outside is below freezing. You don't have a thermometer. How might you test your idea?

Alchemists—Mad Scientists

Alchemists were some of the first people to do experiments on matter. Hundreds of years ago, alchemists tried to make gold and silver from other metals. They thought metals were living things. They thought most metals were "sick." Only gold and silver were "well." Alchemists wanted to change the sick metals into healthy ones.

Alchemists thought all matter was made from three or four basic building blocks. They thought they could separate matter into its basic parts. Then they could move the parts around to make something new.

Alchemists never made gold or silver from other metals. Even so, they made some important discoveries. They put chemicals together and made alcohol and acids. They separated zinc from other particles in order to study it.

Write whether each of the following statements is true or false.

_____ 1. The experiments of alchemists failed because the idea they set out to prove was false.

_____ 2. An experiment based on a false idea may still be valuable because the scientist may learn something else.

_____ 3. The work of alchemists led to other discoveries.

Getting Down to Basics

Everything is made of atoms. Atoms are the building blocks of matter. Atoms are so small that you cannot see them. In fact, atoms are so small that the period at the end of this sentence contains more atoms than there are people in the world.

Scientists have found that most of the mass of the atom is in its center. This central part of the atom is called the **nucleus.** The nucleus is made of small particles. One of the particles that makes up the nucleus is the **proton.** A proton has a small charge of positive electricity. The other kind of particle that makes up the nucleus is the **neutron.** The neutron has no charge of electricity. Atoms of different substances have different numbers of protons.

The **electron** is the third kind of particle that makes up an atom. An electron has a small negative charge of electricity. In an atom the number of electrons is the same as the number of protons. Their electrical charges balance, so the atom is neutral—or has no charge.

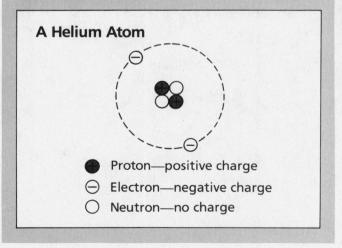

A Helium Atom

● Proton—positive charge
⊖ Electron—negative charge
○ Neutron—no charge

Now use the diagram and the article to help you answer these questions.

1. Describe the two parts that make up the nucleus of an atom.

_____

_____

2. What is an electron?

_____

_____

3. A neutral atom of iron has 26 protons and, usually, 30 neutrons. How many electrons does it have?

_____

Atoms in Combination

Different atoms combine to make all the things in the world. In fact, most atoms are found in combination with other atoms. When atoms of different elements combine, a new substance is created.

For example, two atoms of hydrogen combine with one atom of oxygen to make one molecule, or particle, of water. When atoms of hydrogen and oxygen come together with a third element, carbon, sugar is made. Atoms of sodium and chloride combine to bring you salt.

Mark each statement below true or false.

_____ 1. When atoms of different elements come together, new forms of matter are made.

_____ 2. The atoms of different elements rarely combine on earth.

Power from Atoms

Nuclear energy. It is our most modern source of power. Nuclear energy is used to make bombs that can destroy entire cities. The same energy, in nuclear power plants, can produce electricity to light and heat an entire city. Most people find nuclear power plants mysterious and a little frightening. How do they work?

Nuclear plants use **fission,** the splitting of the nucleus of an atom, to make energy. This energy is changed to electricity.

Many nuclear power plants use uranium for fission. The nucleus of a uranium atom is hit with neutrons. A huge amount of energy is released. In addition, the nucleus "splits" and releases other neutrons. They hit other atoms. These atoms release neutrons, and still other atoms are hit. The chain reaction keeps going. Meanwhile, a great deal of energy is produced.

Nuclear power plants control the chain reaction so an atomic explosion doesn't happen. Yet many people worry that fission at power plants may get out of control. They also worry about the waste that is produced. It is radioactive and can be harmful to human life.

Fission at a Nuclear Power Plant

Neutron shot at nucleus of uranium atom

Neutrons from nucleus freed to hit other atoms

High–energy radiation

Use the diagram and the article to answer these questions.

1. How is our knowledge of the nucleus of the atoms put to use in nuclear power plants?

_____

_____

_____

2. Try to explain in your own words what a chain reaction is.

_____

_____

_____

3. According to the article, what two things about nuclear power worry people?

_____

_____

A worker checks the controls inside a nuclear power plant.

Radioactivity and the Curies

Scientist Marie Curie gave her life to her work—in more ways than one.

Marie and her husband, Pierre, studied radioactivity. Radioactivity is the breaking down of the nucleus of certain atoms. An element such as uranium is unstable. The nucleus of an unstable element decays, or breaks down, into smaller particles over time. As it breaks down, radiation is released. The radiation is rays of energy and small bits of matter.

Marie Curie worked with a substance that had been stripped of its radioactive uranium. Without uranium, she expected the substance to no longer be radioactive. Still, she found radioactivity. Puzzled by her results, Marie did more experiments. These experiments led Marie to discover radium, another radioactive element.

Marie Curie died from being exposed to radiation. Scientists now know that large amounts of nuclear radiation can cause death.

Use the article to answer the questions.

1. Marie Curie was not looking for radium when she found it. After coming across some unexpected findings, what was Marie's next step?

_____

_____

2. Plutonium is a radioactive element. Circle the letter of the answer that supports this statement.

   a. Plutonium has a nucleus that always has 94 protons.

   b. Plutonium has a nucleus that breaks down, or decays.

Magnetism and Michael Faraday

When scientists ask "What if?", exciting things can happen. An English scientist, Michael Faraday, studied the work of another scientist. From this work, he learned that magnetism could be made from electricity. Then Faraday asked, "What if I try the experiment another way?" He decided to see if *electricity* could be made from *magnetism.*

Faraday put a magnet inside a copper coil. The coil was connected to a machine that measured electric current. Faraday found that when the magnet was inside the coil there was no current. But if he moved the magnet in or out, current was made. It was the *moving* of the magnet that made the difference. As long as he moved the magnet, electricity flowed.

Faraday's experiment proved that electricity could be made from magnetism. The results also showed that large amounts of electricity could be made. Before Faraday's experiment, people had been able to make only small amounts of electricity in batteries.

Now answer these questions.

1. Use information from the article to support this statement: *The work of an earlier scientist helped Michael Faraday to discover that electricity could be made from magnetism.*

_____

_____

2. What was a result of Michael Faraday's discovery that electricity could be made from magnetism?

_____

_____

A Perpetual Motion Machine?

The dream of making a perpetual motion machine has been around a long time. A perpetual motion machine is one that would never stop. It would run on the same energy that it makes. It would never need any extra energy to run. One kind of perpetual motion machine was supposed to make more energy than it used. Such a machine could solve a lot of problems.

Over 100 years ago a scientist in Philadelphia told the world that he had made a perpetual motion machine. But after his death, an air pump was found under the floor of his lab. His machine had been a fake.

More recently, another machine that some people called a perpetual motion machine was invented. Its owner, Westley Newman, said he had made an "energy machine." He said his machine ran on a new kind of energy that he had discovered. This energy could do more work than any other known energy.

But few scientists believed Newman. They were not able to repeat Newman's experiment and find this "new" energy.

A Test-Taking Tip

Sometimes a multiple-choice question will ask you to choose an answer that supports a statement or that helps show a statement is true. You can best do this by thinking about each answer choice in turn. Look for the answer choice that leads you to believe in the truth of the statement. The answer that helps you believe in the statement is the correct one.

1. Why did most scientists not believe in Newman's "new" energy?
   (1) Perpetual motion machines can't be made.
   (2) Newman was not a scientist.
   (3) All the known energy sources have been found.
   (4) Newman's experiment could not be repeated with the same results.
   (5) Newman was just trying to become famous.

2. *A machine always needs more energy than it puts out.*

   Which of the following statements best supports the statement above?
   (1) A machine uses more energy when it is new.
   (2) Some machines can produce more work than others.
   (3) In any machine, parts rub or push against each other and use up energy.
   (4) Oiling a machine makes it need more energy to run.
   (5) Some machines do not need energy to run.

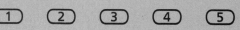

The Active Reader

Identifying Facts

Picture It

Builders know that a house is only as good as its base. The house may seem strong. But if it is built on sand, it will blow away with the first big wind.

In a way, ideas are like houses. To see if they will "hold up," you look at what they're built on. Are they based on facts? Or are they based on opinions and hypotheses?

Facts are the strongest base. **Facts** are statements that have been proved true. Opinions and hypotheses are less strong. A **hypothesis** is something that could be true but hasn't been proved. An **opinion** is just something a person believes. It can't be proved true or false.

When you read, you must sort out the facts from the opinions and hypotheses. Then you'll know if an author's idea has a strong base.

Here's an Example

Vanessa was thinking of buying a microwave oven. She wanted to know more about it before she shopped. She read the following article in a magazine.

■Microwave ovens are the worst thing to happen to American kitchens. Microwaves are waves that move up and down very fast. The oven passes these waves through food. The waves "shake up" the food's molecules. When the molecules rub together, they get hot. This inside heat cooks the food. Clearly, waves that can do this must be dangerous to people. Tests show that these waves damage the nerves of small animals.

Vanessa looked for the facts. Are microwave ovens really the worst thing to happen to the American kitchen? This could not be proved one way or the other.

It was just what the author believed—an opinion.

Vanessa knew that the description of how the ovens work was most likely fact. She could check it in a science book. Facts in science books have been proved by scientists.

Then Vanessa studied the last two sentences. Are microwaves really dangerous? She looked at the author's reasons for saying this: First, if the waves cook food, they can hurt people. Second, the waves damage animal nerves.

Vanessa knew the first reason did not hold up. "Fire cooks food too. But people can use fire safely," she thought.

The second reason sounded strong. It was most likely a fact that the waves harm animals. Vanessa could look this up. But she noticed the author said nothing about tests proving the waves harmed *people.* So the danger of the waves to people is a hypothesis. It *could* be true. But not enough facts have been gathered to prove it.

Vanessa put off buying her oven. The magazine piece did not prove that microwave ovens harmed people. But it

made her want to read more about their safety.

Working It Out

Suppose you receive this newsletter from your local school board. As you read it, sort out the facts from the opinions and hypotheses.

■ Smith School proudly invites all in our community to see the new gym. The walls are padded with cork. Sounds do not bounce off these walls. Noises make no echoes. This makes the gym quieter. With less noise, students will play better basketball. You'll find this new gym is well worth your tax money.

1. The note says sounds do not bounce off the padded walls. Is this probably a fact? Why or why not?

_____

_____

_____

2. "With less noise, students will play better basketball." Tell whether this is a fact, an opinion, or a hypothesis. Give your reason.

_____

_____

_____

3. "You'll find this new gym is well worth your tax money." Is this fact, opinion, or hypothesis? Give your reason.

_____

Advances in Science

Before You Read: Thinking About Advances in Science

In this lesson, you will read about some of the wonders of our age, including lasers and computers. These things came about because of advances in the science called physics.

Physics is the study of how things move. Have you ever heard the saying, "What goes up must come down?" Physics tells you why this is so.

Physics is also the study of forms of energy: light, heat, sound, electricity, and radio waves, among others.

Many people think physics is hard to understand. But most likely you know more about it than you think.

Try finishing the following facts. Fill in the blanks with words from the box.

laser	iron	radio	chip

1. A magnet is made of steel or

   _____.

2. You can see light, but you can't see

   _____ waves.

3. Light from a _____ can cut a

   diamond.

4. A _____ is a tiny part of a

   computer.

Did you have trouble finishing the sentences this way: iron, radio, laser, chip? Even if you did, don't worry. This lesson will give you a better understanding of magnets, radios, lasers, and much more.

Look ahead at the titles of the articles. "Super Train." "Bits, Bytes, and Chips." Do they make you wonder? What do you think makes a train super? What could a byte be? Think of questions about the titles that interest you. Write your questions on the following lines.

_____

_____

_____

_____

_____

Look for the answers as you read the articles.

Working with Words

Three words from the articles in this lesson are used in the sentences below. These words may be new to you. Or you may have seen them before. Add what you already know to the hints in the sentences. Then figure out what the words in dark print mean.

The **frequency** of radio waves from a radio station is more than 535,000 per second.

Because the element **silicon** is so easy to find in the earth, it is a cheap material for making computer chips.

Some telephone calls are carried by light beams through **optical fibers.**

You may already know one meaning of frequency. *Frequency* can mean "number of times." "He visited with great frequency" is the same as saying, "He visited many times."

From the sentence, you know that *frequency* here describes something radio waves do many times per second. What do radio waves do? Radio waves are like water waves. They go up and down. Can you figure out the meaning of *frequency?* Write it down.

The second sentence tells you that silicon is an element that's easy to find in the earth. It is also used to make computer chips. Write down what silicon is.

Do you know what *optical* means? The words *light beams* in the third sentence are a clue. You might think of optical

illusions or a doctor called an optometrist. *Optical* means "having to do with

_____ ."

You probably have an idea that fibers look like long, thin cords. Think of a fiber that is optical, having to do with sight or light. Look at the clues in the boxed sentences. What is an optical fiber?

These definitions are from the dictionary. Are they like the meanings you wrote?

Word Power

frequency the number of vibrations per second of a radio wave

silicon a very common chemical element

optical fiber a glass or plastic tube through which light can be sent

---

Writing to Improve Your Reading

When you read, you need to remember how ideas are connected. Suppose you wanted to remember a chain of steps. To describe how a microwave oven works, you might draw this diagram.

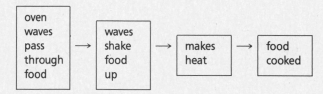

This picture is a kind of flowchart. It reminds you of the order of the steps. It also tells you which event caused another. This kind of note-taking makes things clear. It is also quicker than writing the steps out in complete sentences.

Reading on Your Own

Power from Magnets

Magnets seem almost to have magic powers. They use no outside source of energy. Yet magnets can make certain objects move toward or away from themselves.

This attracting or pushing away happens because a magnet has two ends, or poles: a north pole and a south pole. Opposite poles of magnets attract each other. Like poles repel, or push away from each other.

Magnets create a field, or area, of force around them. Magnetic objects made of steel or iron get pulled toward the magnet when they come inside this force field. The following diagrams show what happens in a magnetic object.

Non-Magnetized Iron or Steel

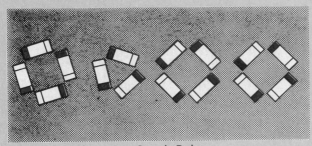

■ North Poles   □ South Poles

Tiny areas of magnetism in a magnetic object normally form closed "chains." The north and south poles cancel each other out.

But when a magnetic object is near a strong magnetic field, its areas of magnetism line up. Its poles all turn in the same direction. The object becomes a magnet.

Magnetized Iron or Steel

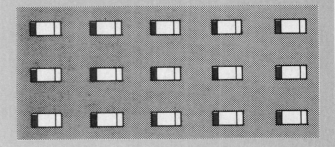

You can make a magnetic field. Rub a magnetic object with a magnet or run an electric current through it. The object will become a magnet.

Use the diagram and article to help you answer the following questions.

1. Will rubbing an old copper penny with a magnet change the penny into a magnet? Why or why not?

_____

_____

2. Read this paragraph from the article again:
"You can make a magnetic field. Rub a magnetic object with a magnet or run an electric current through it. The object will become a magnet."
Does this express a fact or an opinion? Explain your answer.

_____

_____

Super Train

Trains have been dying out as a means of transportation in the United States. Slow and noisy, trains have given way to airplanes as the choice of more and more people.

But this may soon change. New trains are being built that can go faster and run more quietly than ever before. These "super trains" run on magnets instead of fuel.

Powerful electromagnets in the train and on the track move the train. Because the magnets repel each other, the train rises above the track. It glides along, as if on air. Such a train can travel at speeds up to 150 miles per hour. It could make a trip from Chicago to New York in less than five hours.

Use the information above to answer these questions.

1. Super trains do not use wheels and tracks like regular trains. How did knowing about magnets help scientists build a train that is more comfortable to ride?

_____

_____

_____

_____

2. How might the use of super trains help control pollution in big cities?

_____

_____

_____

_____

Lasers

Lasers are one of the most exciting things to come from modern science. A laser is a tool that sends out a special light beam.

Lasers concentrate energy. They create a narrow beam of light that is extremely powerful. It can cut through diamonds and steel. Lasers are used to cut things when a precise, exact cut is needed.

Laser beams are precise because their light travels in only one direction. A laser's light does not spread out like ordinary light beams.

In ordinary sunlight, light waves move in many directions and have many lengths. In a laser's light, all the light waves move in matching wavelengths. The single wavelength makes the light beam precise.

Lasers are used in many stores. A clerk bounces a laser beam off the bands of a code on each product. A computer reads the code and figures the bill.

Lasers are also used to weld sheet metal parts. Laser beams can join glass and plastic parts. They can be used to cut cloth for garments or to cut metal. Doctors often use lasers to cut one part of the body without hurting others.

Write a few words to answer the questions.

1. What sentence in this article is an opinion? Copy it here.

_____

_____

2. What quality of lasers makes them useful in medical operations?

_____

_____

Bits, Bytes, and Chips

What does a computer eat? A bit of this, a byte of that. A few chips. That is a normal "diet" for a computer.

Computers work by carrying information back and forth. A person programs, or puts information into, the computer. The information is stored in the computer's memory. Another part of the computer—the processor—uses the stored information to work out problems.

Today's computers can put lots of information into very small places. Information is put into computers on computer "chips." A chip is a tiny piece of silicon. A silicon chip is about 3/16 inch square. It can fit through the eye of a needle.

A pattern for an electric circuit is etched, or drawn, onto a computer chip. This circuit pattern tells the computer what to do. Changes in the pattern are read by the computer. These changes represent information that was put into the computer program.

Each piece of information in a computer is called a "bit." Eight bits of information make up one "byte."

As computer chips get smaller and hold more information, smaller computers can be made. Today's computers do much more work and take up much less space than earlier computers.

Look at the difference in the size of the blocks in the following graph. This will give you an idea of the increase in the amount of information that could be put on a computer chip from 1970 to 1990.

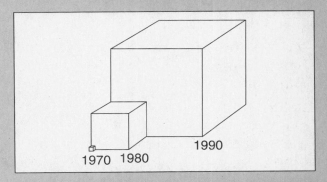

In 1970, scientists could put about 100 bits of information onto one chip. By 1980, many chips held 70,000 bits each. By 1990, chips could hold as many as 1,000,000 bits.

Write a few words to answer the following questions. Use the diagram to help you.

1. From 1970 to 1990, how did silicon chips change?

_____

_____

_____

2. Write *Fact* or *Opinion* before each statement.

_____ **a.** Computers are difficult to understand.

_____ **b.** Computers take up less space today than they did in 1970.

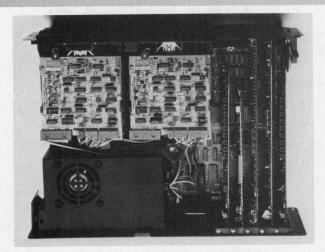

The inside of a personal computer. The circuit boards on the right side of the picture hold the computer chips.

Radios and Waves

The discovery of radio waves changed the way people communicate in this century.

Radio waves cannot be seen or felt. They are used in radios, radar, and satellites.

Here's how your radio uses radio waves. A radio wave is sent out from one place (the radio station) and picked up at another (your radio). Sound (voices or music) is put into a microphone at the radio station. The sound is changed into an electric current, or signal. This signal is sent out over the radio antenna and picked up by a receiver in your radio. Inside your radio, the signal is changed back into sound.

The signals at a radio station can change the frequency of waves (the number of waves that pass by). They can also change the amplitude (the height) of the waves.

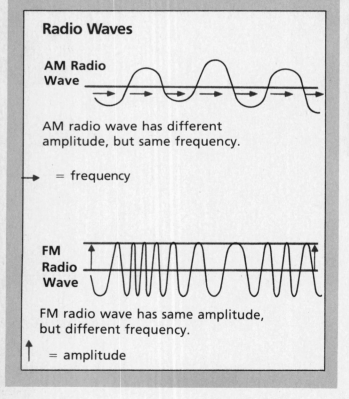

Radio Waves

AM Radio Wave

AM radio wave has different amplitude, but same frequency.

→ = frequency

FM Radio Wave

FM radio wave has same amplitude, but different frequency.

↑ = amplitude

Write a few words to answer the questions below. Use the diagram to help you.

1. Why can't you get an FM station on your AM radio?

_____

_____

2. What might a "radio jammer" do to interfere with your radio's reception?

_____

_____

The End of Cash?

Do you pay cash for items? More and more people do not. Today, many Americans pay for products by check or credit card.

Some experts say we are headed for a "cashless society"—one where no money is passed back and forth. All banking, buying, and selling will be done with computer cards.

Computers in stores would be linked up with bank computers. All sales would be added to or subtracted from the proper accounts by computer.

Now answer these questions.

1. *A cashless society is definitely in our future.* Is this a fact or an opinion? Explain your answer.

_____

_____

2. Name at least one advantage of a cashless society.

_____

_____

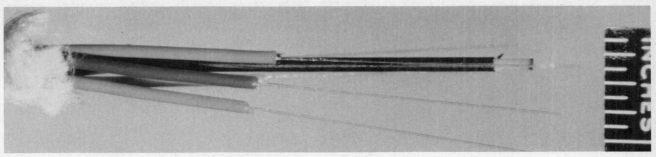

A telephone wire stripped open to show the optical fibers inside.

Fiber Optics and the Telephone

The use of optical fibers has brought the telephone into a new age. Tiny glass fibers are replacing copper coil for telephone wire in many places.

Lasers can work like transmitters. They can change telephone messages into tiny pulses of light. These light pulses travel along thin glass fibers to their destination. Then a receiver changes the message back into sound. This laser-based system is called fiber optics.

Optical fibers can transmit more phone calls faster than copper wires, which use electricity to carry phone calls. A single pair of optical fibers can carry thousands of phone calls. It would take 250 pairs of copper wires to carry the same number of calls.

Write a short answer to each question.

1. What invention helped make fiber optics possible?

_____

2. *All copper telephone wires should be replaced by optical fibers.* Is this statement a fact, an opinion, or a hypothesis? Why?

_____

_____

A Test-Taking Tip

Some multiple-choice questions may ask you to tell a fact from an opinion or a hypothesis. Many of the answer choices may look like they are true. But a true statement must be backed up by information from the article. Look for the answer choice that has been shown as fact based on what you read.

GED Warm-up

All of the following statements are facts except

(1) Copper telephone wires carry sound by electricity.

(2) Optical fibers carry more calls than copper wire.

(3) A single laser could be made to carry all the world's phone calls at once.

(4) Optical fibers transmit sound through light.

(5) Optical fibers transmit phone calls faster than copper wire.

Measuring What You've Learned

This test has four articles, a table, and a diagram from science. It will help you see how much you've learned. Read each article carefully. Then answer the questions about it. This test is not timed, so don't feel you have to hurry. When you've finished, you can check your answers on page 259.

Items 1–3 are based on the article below.

Falling Asleep at the Wheel

Scientists are taking a closer look at certain people who get sleepy when they drive. Recent studies show that these people cause more accidents.

Such persons are victims of "sleep apnea." They stop breathing for a few seconds on and off all night as they sleep. The apnea, or periods of non-breathing, happens because the person's airways are too narrow. Sleep apnea victims often make loud snoring noises, especially when they are sleeping on their backs.

Sleep apnea victims may also have trouble staying awake behind the wheel of a car. In one study, drivers with sleep apnea had seven times more accidents than drivers who did not have the condition.

Researchers say sleep apnea may affect about one percent of Americans. Some people with the condition can help control it by losing weight. All sleep apnea victims should take extra care when they drive and never drive when they are tired.

1. List three effects of sleep apnea.

_____

_____

_____

2. Which of the following best states the main idea of this article? Circle the best answer.

    a. People who snore have sleep apnea.

    b. People with sleep apnea cause more car wrecks than other people.

    c. Losing weight helps sleep apnea victims drive better.

    d. Scientists are studying drivers of automobiles.

    e. One out of 100 Americans have some sleep problem.

3. The article suggests that one reason some sleep apnea victims have trouble breathing is that they

    a. have a disease

    b. snore too loudly

    c. sleep on their stomachs

    d. have an allergy

    e. are overweight

Items 4–6 are based on the diagrams below.

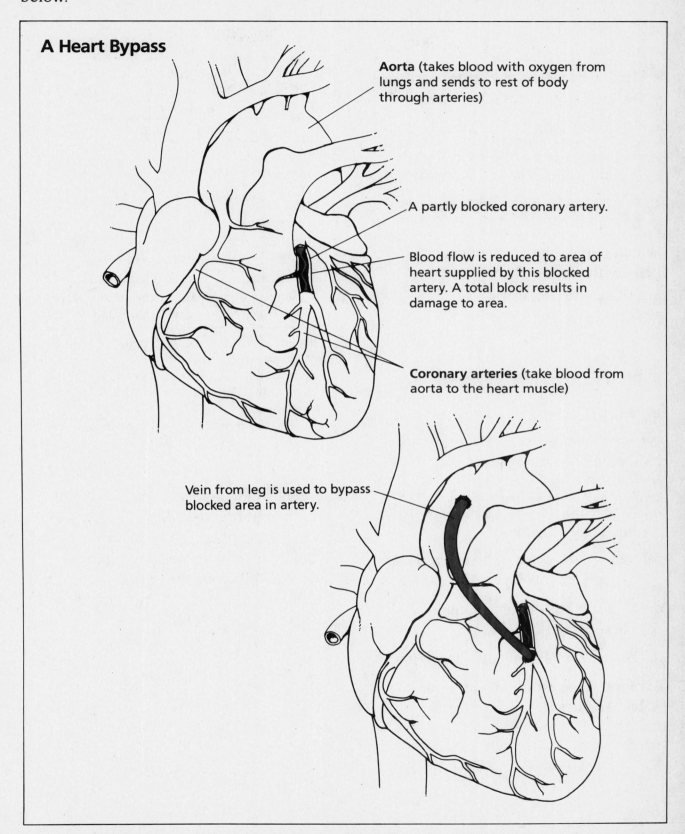

A Heart Bypass

Aorta (takes blood with oxygen from lungs and sends to rest of body through arteries)

A partly blocked coronary artery.

Blood flow is reduced to area of heart supplied by this blocked artery. A total block results in damage to area.

Coronary arteries (take blood from aorta to the heart muscle)

Vein from leg is used to bypass blocked area in artery.

4. What happens when the blood flow to a part of the heart is stopped?

   a. That part of the heart muscle is damaged.

   b. The heart works as normal because enough blood flows elsewhere.

   c. The heartbeat doubles to start the flow again.

   d. The heart no longer needs a bypass.

   e. Extra arteries open up to restore blood flow.

5. Which of the following supplies the body with blood?

   a. coronary artery

   b. vein

   c. aorta

   d. blocked artery

   e. heart muscle

6. When a blood vessel in the heart is partly blocked, the heart is not receiving enough oxygen because

   a. there is not enough blood flow from the lungs to the heart

   b. the blood is flowing too quickly through the heart

   c. the aorta has become completely blocked

   d. the person has difficulty breathing

   e. blood flows around and past a blocked vessel

Items 7–9 are based on the tables below.

Nutrition Labels

Vitamin A & D Grade A Pasteurized Homogenized Skim Milk	
Nutrition Information per Serving	
Serving size	1 cup
Serving per container	1
Calories	90
Protein	8 grams
Carbohydrates	11 grams
Fat	1 gram

Percentage of U.S. Recommended Daily Allowances (U.S. RDA)			
Protein	20	Niacin	0
Vitamin A	10	Iron	0
Vitamin C	4	Calcium	30
Thiamine (B1)	6	Vitamin D	25
Riboflavin (B2)	25		
Contains skim milk, Vitamin A palmitate, and Vitamin D.			

The nutrition label above shows the food value in a serving of skim milk.

The percentage of the Recommended Daily Allowance for each vitamin and mineral tells you how much of your daily need for each nutrient you can get in one serving.

7. How many grams of protein are in one cup of skim milk?

_____

8. In which of the following diets would skim milk be a better choice to give the nutrients needed?

   a. low calcium, low carbohydrate

   b. low protein, high fat

   c. high protein, low fat

   d. low carbohydrate, high fat

   e. high calorie, high fat

9. How many glasses of skim milk would you need to drink for the full recommended daily allowance of vitamin D?

Items 10–12 are based on the article below.

"Living Fossils" in the Sea

A fish once thought to have disappeared from the earth has been found alive and well in the ocean. In the waters off Africa, fishermen caught a strange-looking fish called a coelacanth. This fish was thought to have died out about 60 million years ago.

Coelacanths have an extra pair of fins. They use their fins differently from other fish. They move like crawling lizards. The front left fins move in coordination with the right rear fins.

Scientists were excited about finding this "living fossil." Some think ancestors of coelacanths may have evolved, or slowly changed into, land animals. These scientists hope the coelacanth will help them better understand how life moved from the sea to the land millions of years ago.

Another, more common "living fossil" is the horseshoe crab. Horseshoe crabs are not true crabs. They have not changed in 200 million years. The closest relatives of today's horseshoe crabs are scorpions and spiders.

10. You can conclude from information in the article that the ancestors of scorpions and spiders must have been

   a. true crabs

   b. horseshoe crabs

   c. crawling lizards

   d. coelacanths

   e. sea animals

11. The words "living fossil" are used in the article to mean

   a. a plant or animal that died out long ago

   b. an animal thought to have died out but which did not

   c. any living thing that lived for more than a century

   d. plant or animal remains that have hardened into rock

   e. old animal bones that are like those of modern animals today

12. Some scientists think that ancient relatives of coelacanths may have moved from the sea to land. Which fact below supports that idea?

   a. Coelacanths are living fossils.

   b. Coelacanths grow to more than 5 feet in length.

   c. Coelacanths are found near the coast of Africa.

d. The bones inside the extra fins of coelacanths are arranged like the bones of legs.

e. Coelacanths have an extra pair of fins.

Items 13–16 are based on the article below.

The Hottest Spot on Earth

Looking for the hottest spot on Earth? Go down—way down—to the very center of the earth. It's hotter than Hades down there!

Scientists have found new ways to "see" inside the earth. They think that the center, or core, of the earth is even hotter than some sunspots on the surface of the sun. The core is also very dense. This super-hot, tightly packed core is under great pressure. This pressure keeps the core solid.

Around the earth's core is a layer of melted rock. On top of this melted rock is a thick layer of solid rock called the mantle. On top of this mantle rests the outer "skin" of the earth, the earth's crust.

Some scientists believe that at times the earth's inner core builds up too much pressure. Then "heat waves" push out from the inner core. These waves go through the hot melted rock of the earth's outer layer, causing it to move.

In turn the melted rock pushes into the mantle, and the mantle moves the crust. The "waves" eventually create changes in the earth's surface.

13. Which of the following is the best summary of the passage?

a. The center of the earth is hotter than the sun. This heat causes pressure. The pressure keeps the earth's core packed tightly together.

b. The earth is made of three layers. The middle layer contains melted rock. Sometimes this hot rock moves into the inner layer, or core, of the earth.

c. There is a hot center core in the earth. Because of this, waves move up through the earth. This creates waves in the ocean.

d. The center of the earth is very hot. Increased pressure here can cause movement in the three outer layers. This can result in changes on the earth's surface.

e. The earth's center, or core, is the hottest spot on earth. Pressure and heat in the core cause solid rock to melt and flow into the outer layers.

14. The extreme pressure of the earth's inner core keeps it in a solid state. Which statement below best explains why this happens?

a. The particles of matter in the core are spread far apart from one another.

b. The particles of matter in the core are so tightly pressed together that they cannot move from place to place.

c. The pressure inside the earth's core pushes out all liquid, leaving only solid matter.

d. Particles of solid matter change to liquid under pressure.

e. Pressure increases the movement of particles within a solid.

15. All of the following might occur as a result of melted rock moving within the earth <u>except</u>

    a. earthquakes

    b. volcanoes

    c. tidal waves

    d. changes in shapes of mountains

    e. heat waves

16. What is meant by the earth's crust?

    a. the earth's middle layer of melted rock

    b. the outer layer, or surface, of the earth

    c. dry edges of the earth's deserts

    d. places on earth where there is no water

    e. high tops of mountain ranges

<u>Items 17–19</u> are based on the article below.

Radon Watch

Caution! Your home may be dangerous to your health! Scientists say the threat comes from radon. It causes lung cancer.

Radon is a radioactive gas found in soil. Radon has no color or odor. It leaks into homes through cracks and crawl spaces. Sometimes the gas comes in through sump pumps or foundations.

Researchers think the radon threat has become worse in recent years. The reason is the way homes are now sealed to save energy.

Radon gets into people's lungs through the air they breathe in the home. These days more people seal windows and doors against the cold. Less inside air can move to the outside. More radon builds up inside the home.

Homeowners can help keep the level of radon in their homes lower. They can vent crawl spaces and sump pumps. All cracks in the foundation and on basement floors should be sealed. An indoor air cleaner that removes dust also helps.

17. In your own words, write the main idea of the article "Radon Watch."

_____

_____

_____

18. Read the following statement.

Radon is a dangerous substance.

Support that conclusion with information from the article. Use two facts from the article to show the conclusion is a good one.

_____

_____

_____

_____

19. Name two ways the radon level in a home can be lowered.

_____

_____

Your Results

Did you know many of the answers to the questions on this test? If you had trouble with a question, the table below will help you. You may also want to review some lessons in the book to sharpen your skills.

The table tells you the question numbers and the skills needed to answer those questions. Look to the right to see which lessons in Part B of the book can help you review those skills.

If you missed four or more questions, be sure to review the lessons listed in the chart. If you missed less than four questions, you are ready to go on to study for the GED Test. Good luck with your GED studies.

Question	Skill	Lesson
1	Seeing patterns of ideas	1
2	Stating the main idea	9
3	Drawing conclusions	4
4	Interpreting a diagram	2
5	Interpreting a diagram	2
6	Cause and effect	4, 7
7	Interpreting a table	3
8	Applying ideas	5
9	Interpreting a table	3
10	Drawing conclusions	4
11	Understanding vocabulary	1–11*
12	Assessing supporting data	10
13	Summarizing	9
14	Cause and effect	7
15	Cause and effect; Using what you know	4, 7, 8
16	Understanding vocabulary	1–11*
17	Stating the main idea	9
18	Identifying facts	11
19	Supporting data	10

*For help with vocabulary skills, review Working with Words in each lesson.

Measuring What You Know
(pages 2–5)

1. decides what he or she feels about what others see. The numbers in the article tell you the order of the steps a child takes. Find the step that follows the one that the question describes.

2. A child sees himself or herself as the child thinks others see him or her. Often the main idea of an article is in either the first or the last sentence. Here the words "In short" tell you that the last sentence sums up the main idea.

3. a. Parents help mold their child's character. Parents are part of the "others" so important to Cooley's ideas.

4. other people. As with a looking glass, or mirror, the child looks to others to see himself or herself.

5. cotton. The 1980 bar for cotton is taller than those for wheat and corn.

6. cotton. Compare the 1800 and 1980 bars for each crop. You can see that the difference between the bars for cotton is greatest.

7. 1980. Notice *Production* in the title of the graph. This word tells you that the graph should help you reach conclusions about production of crops, not just hours of labor. Since crops took less time to grow, a farmer could plant more acres in 1980.

8. traffic jams. A cause and its effect often follow each other in a passage. In this case, the effect "traffic jams" follows its cause—"drive too slowly."

9. a. Laws keep peace and order. Choice b is a detail in the passage. Choice a, however, is the main idea that b supports.

10. The driver may hit the person. Here the author expects you to put together the facts and then to predict the outcome of unsafe driving.

11. duties. Notice in the reading that the word *responsibilities* is followed by a comma and the words *or duties*. A comma and the word *or* sometimes come after an unfamiliar word. These are signs that the word's meaning follows.

12. b. English lawmakers. The key to this answer is careful reading. It shows that the point of view of French Americans is not discussed. It also tells you that the main concern of English colonists was land, not the Native Americans. Finally, it shows that English lawmakers passed a law to stop fighting with the Native Americans.

13. They were ruled by England but lived in America. The second paragraph helps you figure out the meaning of *colonists.*

14. West Africa. The map says 75% of slaves came from West Africa. This is larger than any other group.

15. the West Indies and South America. The widest arrows point to these two regions of the map.

16. 5%. Only one arrow points to the southern United States. It points to Charleston. The arrow is labeled 5%.

The Active Reader
Working It Out
(page 9)

1. She rubbed him with soap, cleaned his creases with cotton balls, and then rinsed him with a warm washcloth.

2. She dried him, rubbed oil on him, and dressed him.

Part A / Lesson 1

Reading on Your Own
Carried Babies
(page 12)

1. The picture shows babies tied and strapped like pieces of clothing to their parents.

2. because they feel more sure of their parents' love. Discuss the reasons for your answer with someone.

What's Wrong with Today's Youth?
(page 12)

Your answers may be similar to the following:

1. Children learn to do what is done to them.

2. "Taking care of children is tiring. Sometimes I say and do things I don't mean. At home, I tell my children how sorry I am."

Typical Swings in Behavior
(page 13)

1. At two, children are well balanced. Then six months later, they are unstable. By three, they are fairly well balanced again.

2. Diagrams will vary. Be sure you can explain your diagram to someone else.

Showing Love
(page 13)

1. Talking with children about their feelings helps them feel loved.

2. Do the words you wrote show the daughter that her mother cares? Then you answered correctly.

Daily Calorie Needs
(page 14)

1. For the first ten years, boys and girls need about the same amount of food. You can see on the diagram that daily calorie needs for boys and girls are the same at ages 1–3, 4–6, and 7–10 years. Only at ages 11–14 years do boys need more calories.

2. In general, fourteen-year-old boys are taller than fourteen-year-old girls. On the diagram for 11–14 years, boys are 63 inches tall and girls are 62 inches tall. So the boys are taller than the girls.

Secrecy Breeds Dis-ease
(page 14)

1. Her husband was seeing another woman. A clue is that a woman called and asked for her husband.

2. Secrets confuse teenagers. It's better to tell them the truth. The last paragraph sums this up.

3. Give reasons for your answer.

Friends vs. Parents
(page 15)

1. Most fifth graders ask for help from parents. Most ninth graders get advice from both parents and friends.

2. parents. The graph shows that the younger the students the more likely they are to ask only parents to help.

The Day Care Debate
(page 15)

1. Some experts say children under three should not be in day care. Others say day care won't harm these children.

2. because they come into contact with other children who may be sick

3. a small center with only a few children and with one adult for every two to three children

Finding a Good Day Care Center
(page 16)

1. a. Children learn to get along with others.
b. Children improve movement and vision with toys.
c. Children start to learn numbers and reading.

2. Sample answer:
They might not be able to pay for a large staff.
They might take in more children than they can take care of.

GED Warm-up
(page 16)

(1) The article says children need personal attention. The checklist mentions warm and friendly adults. Answer (2) could also be true, but it is not mentioned anywhere in the article.

The Active Reader Working It Out
(page 18)

1. *Transportation* is a means of going from one place to another.

2. In general, they look for well-known labels rather than for well-made goods.

3. Show-offs brag, they tell the price of their homes and furniture, they buy cars to show off, and they look for well-known labels.

Part A / Lesson 2

Reading on Your Own A Successful Writer
(page 21)

1. success. The first paragraph says this.

2. Be sure to give reasons for your answer. Answers will vary. You may want to discuss this question with other members of your class.

3. Your answers may be similar to these:
hardworking—He worked so hard at the printing office that his eyes went bad.
studious—He told Dick that he had a "taste for reading and study."
clever—He used what he read to invent a machine.
Secure would not be a correct answer because the young

Whitney didn't even know where his next meal was coming from.

A Secure Way of Life
(page 22)

1. No, because the village people did things as their parents did them. They did not value change.

2. probably not. They had little desire to change their life. In Horatio Alger's books, the characters' main goal was to improve their life.

Birth Order and Personality
(page 22)

1. Answers will vary. Perhaps parents expect the oldest child to help with the other children.

2. Answers will vary. Perhaps the middle child has had to deal with older and younger children in the family.

3. Answers will vary. Perhaps the youngest child was taken care of for a longer time by parents and older children.

The Responsible Oldest
(page 23)

1. serious and responsible. The author wrote that taking care of her brothers and sisters made her "serious, and quite responsible."

2. To answer this question, put yourself in the place of the younger children. They might have been thankful for their older sister's care. Then they would describe her as helpful or loving. Or they may have thought she was bossy.

What Being Shy Can Do
(page 23)

1. Talk loudly enough to put your message across. The author writes that shy people don't speak up, so talking loudly may help them.

2. Take a dancing or acting class. A class might help shy people overcome the fear of meeting people and trying new things.
According to the passage, shy people already hide their feelings, such as anger, so (1) cannot be an answer. The author also writes that shy people are "wrapped up" in how they feel, so (4) is not a good suggestion.

Using Eyes to Overcome Being Shy
(page 24)

1. b. The passage states: "The less you like someone, the more you avoid looking at them."

2. This answer should be based on what you have experienced and seen.

Unhappy People
GED Warm-up
(page 25)

1. (1) The passage tells you that the Empty Shell blows up when "life slows down." The Martyr probably would not have the energy to throw things.

2. (2) The Empty Shell shops constantly, so she could not be the correct answer. The Martyr, on the other hand, thinks everything is ugly. So he is less likely to want to look at clothing or even at himself.

The Active Reader
Working It Out
(page 27)

1. Section 2: Power tools for the home workshop

2. Section 1: Hand tools: How to choose and use them

3. Section 3: Fasteners, hardware, and adhesives

4. Section 2: Power tools for the home workshop

5. Section 1: Hand tools: How to choose and use them

6. Section 3: Fasteners, hardware, and adhesives

7. Section 3: Fasteners, hardware, and adhesives

8. Section 2: Power tools for the home workshop

9. Section 3: Fasteners, hardware, and adhesives

Part A / Lesson 3

Reading on Your Own
Moral Development in Children
(page 30)

1. Be sure to give a reason for your answer.

2. You probably chose *selfish*. The boy thought that Heinz should do what helped him most. The boy did not seem interested in how the wife felt.

3. Base your answer on your own experience. Ask yourself: Would I have answered question 1 the same way at age 6? at age 14? Have my views on right and wrong changed over the years?

Lawrence Kohlberg's Levels of Moral Development in Children
(page 31)

1. Level I. Timmy wanted to avoid being punished.

2. Level III. Duty to his friends came first with Stash.

3. Level II. Janet acted to please her mother.

A Woman's Point of View
(pages 31–32)

1. In her book, Gilligan said women view right and wrong differently from men. The women's view is the "different voice."

2. Your answer may depend on what you value more—justice or caring.

3. Gilligan's main idea is that men and women make moral decisions from different points of view. Men think in terms of rights and justice. Women think in terms of caring and responsibility.

4. Be sure to give a reason for your answer.

Authoritarian and Democratic People
(page 32)

1. democratic. The speaker respects children's ideas as if the children were equals.

2. authoritarian. This speaker views people as either good or bad.

3. Answers will vary. You might say that democratic people don't get things done as quickly.

4. Answers will vary. You might say that authoritarian people are too fearful of others.

People Who Carry Orders Too Far
(page 33)

1. authoritarian. The reading before pointed out that authoritarian individuals like to take orders. Most of the subjects obeyed orders even when they thought they were hurting someone.

2. Officers might order soldiers to do something against the rules of war. For example, the officers might order the soldiers to shoot civilians.

Leaders Make or Break Boys' Clubs
(page 33)

1. democratic. The democratic leaders let the boys plan their work. They also allowed the boys to discuss their work. This gave the boys chances to decide things for themselves.

2. Base your answer on your own values. Unsure of what you think? Then ask: Do you like being told what to do? Do you like finishing as much work as possible? Then you would prefer an authoritarian boss. Do you like working on your own? Do you like a relaxed workplace? Then your choice would be the democratic boss.

The Foreman
GED Warm-up
(page 34)

1. (3) He told the workers to stop talking. In the last article, you read that authoritarian leaders did not let the boys talk to each other in the boys' club. The foreman in this article is treating his workers the same way.

2. (2) They hung their heads. Perhaps they felt the foreman was being unfair. But no one

said so. They did not feel on an equal footing with the foreman.

3. Answers will vary. You might say that the worker was being treated like a child, so he began to feel like a child.

4. Answers will vary. Be sure to give reasons for your answer. You might want to discuss your answer with other students in your class.

5. Answers will vary. You might want to discuss this question with other students.

The Active Reader
Working It Out
(page 37)

1. the rowhouse

2. the apartment

3. The fast-food industry grew.

4. No one had time to cook dinner.

Part A / Lesson 4

Reading on Your Own
Budgeting for Goals
(page 40)

Belinda sets money aside to use each week, so her goal is short-term. Ed is saving $40 a month for a motorcycle. It likely will cost thousands of dollars, so his goal will take a few years to reach. Barb is saving for retirement, at least 30 years away. So you would number the goals this way:
1. 2
2. 1
3. 3

Bill's Monthly Budget
(page 40)

1. 3 years. To find the answer, divide $1,500 by $40. This gives you the number of months Bill will need to save $1,500. Then divide this number by 12, the number of months in a year. The answer will be just over 3 years.

2. clothing. Most likely Bill can get by with the clothing he already has. But if he fails to pay the rent, he may lose his apartment.

3. Answers will vary. You might say a budget helps Bill see that he has $40 extra he can save each month.

4. Answers will vary. Be sure to give a reason for your answer.

Buy Now, Pay Later
(page 41)

1. Sally probably charged many things she bought rather than paying by check. The only check she had to pay for was the one to the credit card company.

2. Washington most likely charged more than he could pay for each month. As a result, his payment covers only the interest.

3. Don't charge it. Tell your friend that she would end up paying interest on her charge. This would raise the "real" price of the coat.

Credit Card Slaves
(page 42)

1. The man looks greedy and the woman looks frightened. The rest of your answer is based on what you think. But it may be like the following: The man is eager to buy

things. He's willing to sign away his future earnings. The woman has already gone through that stage. Now she is scared. She doesn't know how she will pay the bills she has run up.

2. They have taken on too much debt.

3. against. He shows the cards as traps.

Buying a Used Car
(page 42)

To finish the sentences, you had to look at the tips in the article. You should have found those which discussed the same subjects as the sentences.

1. He pleased his past customers.

2. He accepted a 50/50 warranty.

Checking Warranties
(page 43)

1. The article tells you that an implied warranty is the unwritten promise that a product will work as it is supposed to.

2. The written warranty is better. It is easier to prove if something goes wrong with the product. The promises are on paper. But you cannot prove what was said to you at the time you bought the goods.

Comparing Costs of Living
(page 43)

1. The West. Families in the West spent $10,142 on housing.

2. The Midwest ($1,654) and the West ($1,619).

3. The South ($1,116).

4. The South and the Midwest. Added together, costs in these areas are several thousand dollars less than in the Northeast and the West.

Buying a House
GED Warm-up
(page 44)

1. (3) All the answers should sound familiar. The passage discussed them all. Think to yourself: What does each answer describe? Look at the passage for help. You'll see that (1) describes a loan application. Choice (2) describes a survey. And (3) describes a mortgage.

2. (1) Did you use the test-taking tip when you answered this question? The key words are *keeps, returns,* and *doubles.* The passage tells you that the bank *keeps* the money.

3. (2) The passage does not tell you the answer to this question directly. But careful reading will show that the survey and title search are handled before the closing. At the closing, you sign papers that protect the bank. You also give a down payment to the seller. Therefore, (2) makes the most sense.

The Active Reader
Working It Out
(page 46)

1. Pamela is written on the woman's purse. You can see this in the picture.

2. The woman is wearing a "Vote Kowalski" button. This is also in the picture.

3. b. If she already knew these facts, she probably read them in the newspaper.

4. a. You know the word could not mean 60 seconds because the sentence says that *months* of planning are over.

5. b. Victory party is more likely, because she has been helping her husband run for office.

Part A / Lesson 5

Reading on Your Own
American Voters Over the Years
(page 49)

1. white men over 21 who own property. The first entry on the time line is about white men.

2. Answers will vary.

Voting Power
(page 49)

1. They represent, or speak and act for, the people who elect them.

2. The author believes you can elect leaders who will work for your interests.

3. Be sure to give a reason for your answer.

A Voter's Registration Card
(page 50)

1. her address, because it determines where she can vote and who she votes for

2. Precinct 15. Counties and states are generally larger than cities. However, precincts are divisions of a city.

Why Many People Don't Vote
(page 50)

Your answers should be based on your own ideas and experiences. The following answer is only an example:

2. I don't agree. Government officials spend the taxes I pay. My vote gives me a say in how my taxes are used.

How Many People Vote?
(page 51)

1. 1960. More people voted in 1960 than in any other year shown on the graph.

2. because they have to register

3. Be sure to give a reason for your answer.

Saving Wildlife
(page 51)

1. a. by promising to vote for representatives who supported them. You can draw this conclusion because this is the usual way citizen groups work to make changes through government.

2. b. Other runways never were added on to the first. You can predict this because the article says the government stopped the building of the airport.

An Indiana Mayor
(page 52)

1. Other people used the streets and were protected by the new workers in the fire and police departments.

2. because he would not benefit from the federal tax money spent in Gary

Winning Civil Rights
(page 52)

1. a. to not deal with a business. This meaning describes what African Americans did to protest the way the Montgomery bus company treated Parks.

2. The bus company probably allowed African Americans to sit wherever they wanted. A ruling of the Supreme Court is like the law of the land. If the bus company went against the ruling, they could have been sued.

Huey Long of Louisiana
GED Warm-up
(page 53)

1. (1) Choice (2) is unlikely because Longfellow's poem was set in Louisiana, so it probably was a favorite of its people. The reading tells you that Long already was known in northern Louisiana, so (3) also is unlikely.

2. (2) Wealthy taxpayers would not want taxes raised to pay for all that Long seemed to promise. Current officeholders probably did not like Long pointing out how little they did for the voters. However, parents probably were glad to hear that Long was concerned about their children's schools.

3. (3) You could have used the test-taking tip to rule out (1). World War II came after 1924. Careful reading rules out (2). Long did not praise the oak in his speech. But (3) sums up Long's message, so it is the correct choice.

The Active Reader
Working It Out
(page 55)

1. bar graph; Japan

2. table; Indonesia

3. table; 93,527,000

4. bar graph; Japan, Switzerland, Taiwan, United States

5. bar graph; farms

Part A / Lesson 6

Reading on Your Own
Different Economic Systems
(page 58)

1. planned. *Party leaders* should say "government" to you. And the government directed a planned economy according to the reading.

2. traditional. The clue words here are "the same way their parents and grandparents did." The reading connects traditional economies with families.

3. market. The example tells how buyers caused more running shoes to be made. According to the reading, those who buy and sell answer economic questions.

4. planned. Again, a government is acting here, so the answer is a planned economy.

5. market. This is an example of a failed market economy. The words *sell* and *buy* are the tip-offs.

The Economic Cycle in a Market Economy
(page 59)

2. People buy. You know that ads try to get people to buy. If the ads work, more people buy the product.

6. Workers are hired. In step 5, work increases. Who is going to do this work? More workers.

9. People spend more for wants. What do most people do with at least some of the extra money they make? Spend it, of course.

The Changing U.S. Economy
(page 59)

1. There are fewer jobs in factories. There are more jobs in services.

2. An autoworker may not have enough education to get a service job that pays well.

Quality of Life
(page 60)

1. Japan has a higher quality of life than Afghanistan. According to the reading, the death rate for infants in a country is a measure of its quality of life. The country with the lower death rate probably has the higher quality of life.

2. Taiwan, because the reading states that literate people can learn to make a wide range of goods.

3. Afghanistan. The life expectancy of men is 44 years, but for women it's 43 years.

4. Japan. In Japan people live the longest. Fewer infants die. About 99% of its people can read. And it has the lowest number of people per hospital bed.

Jobs and Status
(page 61)

1. Sweden. Doctors are not listed in the top twenty jobs for Sweden, so you can conclude that doctors have a lower status in Sweden than they do in the United States, where they are ranked second.

2. You can draw several conclusions. Perhaps people value education more in Sweden than in the United States. Perhaps teachers are paid more in Sweden.

Annual Income by Educational Level
(page 61)

1. On the average, a high school graduate makes $15,364 more than a grade school graduate. You find the answer by subtracting.

$28,060
$-12,696$
_____
$15,364

2. The more education a person has, the higher the income that person will make.

Income of Households, 1980 and 1990
(page 62)

1. 42 percent. You can get this answer by adding the percentage under $10,000 (15 percent) to the percentage between $10,000 and $24,999 (27 percent).

2. It decreased slightly, by 1 percent.

3. $25,000–$49,000. In both 1980 and 1990, this bar is the longest one.

4. You probably will say that they stayed about the same. The percentage of households in each category below $50,000 decreased by 2 percent or less. And even though the percentage of households in the upper group rose by 5 percent, this group still makes up only one-fourth of all the households in the country.

Are Americans Getting Richer?
GED Warm-up
(page 62)

(3) Americans in general were better off in the 1980s than in the 1970s. The article points out that incomes generally dipped in the 1970s, so (1) is not likely. The article does not support (2) because it talks only about money spent. It does not talk about money earned. Houses are mentioned, but not many facts are given. Thus, (4) is not the answer. However, (3) is close to the idea the article ends with: Americans were richer in the 1980s than in the 1970s.

The Active Reader
Working It Out
(page 64)

1. The electors vote for the candidates. This is the second step on the flow chart.

2. The House of Representatives chooses the President from the two or three candidates with the most votes. Find the triangle that asks, "Did any candidate receive more than half the votes?" Follow the arrow that says "No" to find the answer.

3. A President is elected. Whatever way you follow the flow chart, you always end up at this point.

4. 242 million. Find 1987 on the graph. Move your finger up to the dot above 1987. Then move your finger across to the number of people. It will fall between 240 and 245. Notice that these numbers stand for millions of people, so 242 million is a good estimate.

5. about 10 million. Find the number of Americans in 1991 the same way you did in ques-

tion 4 for 1987. The number is 252 million. Subtract 242 million from 252 million.

252 million (1991)
−242 million (1987)
   10 million

Part A / Lesson 7

Reading on Your Own
The Articles of Confederation
(page 67)

1. They probably had to carry different kinds of money when they went from state to state.

2. It could not raise money to pay for an army or other services by taxing the people.

Changing the American Plan of Government
(page 67)

1. This answer should be based on your own ideas.

2. Your answer may be like the following one. The thirteen states could do almost whatever they wanted. It was like having thirteen leaders and no followers.

Representing the People
(page 68)

1. The House of Representatives has increased because there are more states and there are more people in each state today. The article says that the number of representatives depends on the number of people in a state, therefore, as a state's population grows larger, the number of representatives for that state will grow larger too.

2. The Senate has increased because the number of states has increased. The article says that each state has two senators. You can see on the graph that in 1790 there were 26 senators. This is because there were 13 states at that time and each state had two senators. The graph shows that in 1970 there were 100 senators. That is because by that time there were 50 states.

3. In 1850 there were 60 senators. In 1970 there were 100 senators. To find the first answer, find 1850 on the bottom of the graph. Move your finger up to the point on the line directly above 1850. Then move your finger over to the left to find the number of senators for that year. It will be at 60. You can find the second answer in the same way.

Watergate and the Constitution
(pages 68–69)

1. Judges of the Supreme Court are picked by the president. This is one way the president has power over the court. The president can pick judges that agree with the president's thinking.

2. Congress can impeach the president. This answer is in the last paragraph of the article. It shows that Congress has the power to put the president on trial if the president breaks a law.

3. Watergate showed that a president's power is limited. The legislative branch (Congress) can force him or her to resign if he or she breaks the law. The judicial branch (the Supreme Court) can tell the president he or she is breaking the law.

The Rights of the Accused
(page 69)

1. because it is named after a court case involving Ernesto Miranda. It was in this case that the Supreme Court said police must tell accused people their rights.

2. The Supreme Court ruled that people have these rights because the U.S. Constitution gives these rights to all Americans. This answer is in the second paragraph of the article.

Passing an Amendment
(page 70)

1. They might let members of Congress or their state legislatures know whether they are for or against the amendment.

2. It probably takes a long time to go through all the steps. A lot of people have to agree to pass an amendment, so few amendments make it into the Constitution.

Women in the Central Government
(page 70)

1. a. Sandra Day O'Connor becomes the First Woman Supreme Court Justice. Notice details in the cartoon. The dress the woman is wearing is dark and long, like a judge's robes. The name of the building includes J-U-S, the beginning of the word *justice*. You even may have known that the talking statue stands for "blind (equal) justice." Also, the scales the statue is holding are a symbol for justice.

2. b. Gail Sheehy. The cartoonist seems to feel, as Gail Sheehy does, that women can handle high office.

The Equal Rights Amendment
(page 71)

1. a. both sexes were equal under the law. This is a paraphrase of the one sentence the amendment contains. Choices b, c, and d describe what some people feared would happen if the ERA passed.

2. Give a reason for your answer.

GED Warm-up

1. (3) You have to know that the United States has 50 states. The reading tells you that $\frac{3}{4}$ of the states needed to approve the amendment to make it part of the Constitution. So take $\frac{3}{4}$ of 50. The answer is between 36 and 38. So 38 is the best answer.

The Active Reader Working It Out
(page 75)

1. southern United States. Use the title to find this answer.

2. Texas. Use the compass rose to help you find this answer.

3. Texas and Florida. Use the compass rose to help you find this answer.

4. Nashville. Use the key to help you. The city in Tennessee with a star by it is the state capital.

5. about 600 miles. The scale shows that 1 inch stands for 300 miles. The distance from Montgomery to Richmond is about 2 inches. 300 miles × 2 = 600 miles.

6. Texas. The map shows that Texas borders on Mexico, so it would be easy for immigrants from Mexico to enter the United States through Texas.

Reading on Your Own
A Population Map
(page 78)

1. the Northeast. Notice the many clusters of dots in this small part of the country.

2. Two answers are correct: *water* and *major cities.* There are more dots clustered near the ocean coasts and lakes. There are also many dots near major cities such as Denver, Dallas, Chicago, and New York.

How Standard Time Began
(page 79)

1. Your answer may be like the following. Travel between time zones probably was so slow that timetables showed days rather than hours of arrival and departure.

2. Except in the places that broadcast the shows, the shows would start at odd times such as 9:50 or 2:12.

A Time Zone Map
(page 79)

1. To find your time zone, you may have to compare the time zone map with a political map showing a city you live in or near.

2. 5 P.M. New York is three time zones east of San Francisco, so its time is three hours ahead of San Francisco time.

3. You would set your watch back two hours. Denver is two time zones west of New York.

Raising Cotton Down South
(page 80)

1. Machines help the farmers produce more.

2. Most likely machines now do the jobs that early farmworkers did, For that reason farmworkers and their families have moved to cities to find jobs.

Houses in New England
(pages 80–81)

1. Traders and sea captains were wealthy enough to build fine houses, so their businesses must have been profitable. Because much of the Northeast lies along the ocean, these businesses are most likely still important.

2. rainy and snowy with cold winters. The way the colonists built their houses gives clues to the kind of climate in New England.

Missions in California
(page 81)

1. warm. Again, the way the friars and Native Americans built their houses suggests the climate was warm. You might also guess it was dry. Why? In a rainy climate, the houses made of dry mud might wash away. Also, if many trees were nearby, the friars and Native Americans might have used wood instead of adobe. But most likely the climate was not rainy enough for many trees to grow.

2. cities such as San Francisco and Santa Barbara. Many of the mission names are the same as those of large California cities.

Tornadoes in the Midwest
(page 82)

1. Kansas and Missouri. The key tells you that the darkest

shading on the map covers the places where tornadoes are most likely to occur.

2. hardly ever occur. Find the northern part of the map, using the compass rose. Look for the area around the Great Lakes. This area has the lightest shading. The key tells you that means tornadoes rarely occur there.

The West: Natural Vegetation
(page 82)

1. a. Nevada is the only choice without any grasslands for cattle to graze on. The key on the map is your best help here.

2. c. Denver is the only choice in the mountains. The key shows you where the mountain areas are.

GED Warm-up

(1) Seattle is the only choice surrounded by forests. The other cities are in deserts.

The Active Reader Working It Out
(page 84)

1. to scare the Aztecs. You can infer that Cortés wanted to scare the Aztecs because he wanted the cannons to make a great noise. He probably knew that the Aztecs had never seen cannons or horses before.

2. yes, because the Spaniard wrote that the Indians were frightened. You'll find this in the last sentence of the paragraph written by the Spaniard.

3. clever. They knew the cannons were not magical, so they would not think Cortés was

amazing. But they would think he was clever to scare the Aztecs this way.

4. They viewed him as amazing. The Aztec paragraph shows they saw the Spaniards as strange and powerful.

5. b	7. d
6. c	8. a

Part A / Lesson 9

Reading on Your Own Voyages of Columbus
(page 87)

1. c. third. The line that stands for the third voyage goes along the northern coast of South America.

2. b. the Caribbean Islands. During every voyage Columbus traveled through the Caribbean Islands. None of the lines on the map go near Florida or Mexico's eastern coast.

A Case of Mistaken Identity
(page 87)

1. Columbus reached the Caribbean Sea, not the Indian Sea.

2. San Salvador was a small island, not a continent.

3. Columbus was not near China.

The Arawak Indians
(page 88)

1. friendly, they "show as much love as if they were giving their hearts"

2. generous, "of anything they have, if you ask for it, they never say no"

3. honest, "they are so artless"

The Amazing Aztec City
(page 88)

1. to find gold. The reading tells you that Cortés thought that the Aztecs had gold.

2. the great towers, temples, and buildings rising from the waters. The word *amazed* in the reading gives the answer away. The meaning of *amazed* is close to the meaning of *surprised.*

Where Early Native American Groups Lived
(page 89)

1. **c.** Chinook, because they lived near the ocean

2. **b.** Powhatan, because they were on the coast closest to Europe

Eastern Woodland Indians
(pages 89–90)

1. ''Often chiefs became clan leaders because their fathers and grandfathers were chiefs.'' The sentence is in the third paragraph.

2. Even the chief of a tribe could not make laws on his own. Before deciding anything, he had to talk with a council. This information is in the last paragraph.

Diagram of Woodland Society
(page 90)

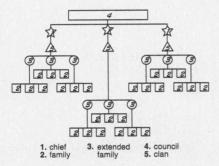

1. chief 3. extended 4. council
2. family   family   5. clan

The Pilgrims' First Year
(page 90)

1. **a.** The Pilgrims suffered hardships. Most of the paragraph tells about sickness and fire.

2. **b.** The Pilgrims had to learn new ways. The fact about the peas supports this main idea. It explains in part why the Pilgrims had to learn new ways.

Life in a New Land
(page 91)

1. the rich soil. Much of the Irish settler's letter tells about the crops he and his father have grown. From this, you can guess that he is excited about the rich soil in America.

2. the hard work and the high cost of the trip. The first part of his letter describes how hard people have to work. The second part describes how much money it costs to get there from Germany.

3. Sample answer: Perhaps the Irish settler was used to hard work in Ireland. Perhaps the Irish settler was rich and could afford to pay for the trip and buy land. Maybe the German was poor.

GED Warm-up
(page 91)

(4) The Irish settler says much the same thing as (1) in the first sentence of his letter. He also would agree with (2). He does not want to keep his good fortune to himself. He wants to share it with his friend. The German immigrant would disagree with (1) and (2). He writes that no matter how hard people work they will not do as well as in Germany. For these same reasons, the German immigrant would agree with (3). We know the Irish settler would not because he seems happy. However, both the Irish settler and German immigrant would agree that living in America takes work, so (4) is the correct answer.

The Active Reader Working It Out
(page 93)

equality: ''to protect them, not only as equals before the law;'' ''the right to be full sharers''
freedom: ''to protect . . . their liberties as men, as workers, and as citizens.''
high standard of living: ''to protect workers in their inalienable rights to a higher and better life;'' ''to secure to them . . . the right to be full sharers in the abundance.''

1. Coolidge probably would approve.

2. Gompers would be angry that Reagan did not bargain with the strikers.

Part A / Lesson 10

Before You Read
(page 94)

The blanks should be filled in with these words:

1. services

2. providing

3. machines

4. hand

Reading on Your Own A Factory Worker
(page 96)

1. The worker disliked her job because it was monotonous, or boring.

2. the amount of goods produced; the workers were given little time to rest.

Early Women Workers
(page 96)

1. "Most of the time they were not given the same pay as men."

2. "Most women accepted this as normal."

Rise of Labor Unions
(page 97)

1. b. wanted better working conditions. The article says that, during a strike, sometimes new workers were brought in who were happy to get a job. But the strikers wanted better working conditions, among other demands.

2. a. talk failed to produce change. The reading tells you that employers listened to the workers. But they did not always make the changes that workers asked for.

Women Workers Die in Fire
(page 97)

1. to protest the long hours, low wages, and unfair ways that employers treated them and to demand the right to join a union

2. To regain power lost in the strike, the managers locked out union leaders. As a result, the workers could not escape the fire.

Some Early Events in the History of American Labor
(page 98)

1. The federal government sided *against* workers in **1877,** when federal troops broke a strike. The federal government

helped workers in **1935,** when the National Labor Relations Act was passed, and in **1938,** when the Fair Labor Standards Act was passed.

2. Samuel Gompers. Workers looked to unions rather than to employers for leadership.

A. Philip Randolph, Labor Leader
(page 98)

1. the part that promises to protect them as *equals* before the law. The union did not treat all workers as equals when it barred African Americans from joining.

2. to protect the workers and to secure their rights

Unemployment Compensation
(page 99)

1. no. The reading says that workers cannot collect benefits if they lose their jobs through their own fault.

2. no. According to the reading, a person with full-time work cannot collect.

3. yes. Pedro lost his job through no fault of his.

Migrant Workers in the 1930s
(page 99)

1. The growers did not pay enough to cover the workers' costs.

2. From an early age, migrants' children were working rather than going to school. Therefore, they would not be prepared to get better jobs.

The Migrant Workers' Grape Strike
GED Warm-up
(page 100)

1. (2) Choice (1) is wrong because the reading says that the workers are innocent, not the bosses. The reporter who wrote the passage sides with the workers. This suggests that (3) is unlikely. Choice (4) is wrong because the reading tells you that the leaders were weak. The reading describes the growers as powerful, which suggests rich, so (5) is also wrong.

The reading tells you "The workers had been too poor and too frightened to make the strike last." You can infer that, if they were poor, they did not want to lose wages. Also, if they were poor, what would frighten them? The possibility of not earning anything in the future would be frightening. So (2) is the best answer.

2. (4) Chavez certainly had (1), (2), and (3), and he recognized (5) in the workers. But he devoted his life to justice, or (4).

3. (5) Choice (1) is wrong because the Spanish are not even discussed. Cesar Chavez, Peter Matthiessen, and the United Farm Workers oppose the bracero system, so (2) and (3) cannot be right. But the grape growers want to keep the system because it helps them get their crops picked cheaply.

The Active Reader
Working It Out
(page 102)

1. Sample answers: aircraft manufacturing workers, technicians, businesspeople, and boat workers. Some sentences and phrases in the reading include: "center for small high-tech companies"; "The largest employer in the Seattle area is Boeing, the aircraft company"; and "Seattle is a center of trade and shipping."

2. Sample answers: camping, hiking, mountaineering, fishing, boating, swimming, and diving. Some sentences and phrases in the reading are: "nearby outdoor recreation opportunities"; "large body of water by which Seattle is located"; and "just a half hour by car from the Cascade Mountains and a two-hour drive from the Pacific Ocean."

3. The answer to this question depends on what you do for a living and what you think is fun.

Part A / Lesson 11

Before You Read
(page 103)

1. subway

2. lead

3. noise

4. water

5. computer

Reading on Your Own
Pollution in Early Cities
(page 105)

1. Possible answers: "City people always have had problems." Or "In a city such as New York, manure caused more than eye and nose pollution."

2. "Now, people thought, cities would become quieter, cleaner, and healthier places to live."

3. Draw on your own experience to answer this question.

What's on City Streets?
(page 105)

1. Salt is spread to make winter streets safe for driving.

2. Sample answer: Cities might keep cars off the streets after snows rather than spreading salt. Or they might treat the sewer water before it runs into the water supply.

Lead Poisoning and City Children
(page 106)

1. b. The article says most lead in the air comes from gas in cars.

2. a. The article says new laws have limited the lead in gasoline.

3. c. The article reports on a study of Boston children that suggests lead poisoning is causing learning problems.

Art or Vandalism?
(page 106)

1. stealing paint

2. they wanted people to see their art. Ali says this in the last sentence.

Computer Crime
(page 107)

1. Sample answers: Perhaps workers do not like the way they are being treated. Or the large amounts of money they can steal are worth the risk.

2. Sample answers: by keeping the account numbers secret and by checking on the few employees who know the account numbers

Measuring Sounds of the City
(page 107)

1. Listening to heavy trucks may cause ear damage.

2. Employers can use the scale to find out if the noises on the job are harmful and then correct any problem.

Noise Exposure Limits
(page 108)

1. yes. A carpenter probably would work eight hours on a construction site. More than two hours on a construction site is enough to cause hearing loss.

2. yes. A traffic officer is in city traffic for up to eight hours. After one hour his or her hearing may be harmed.

3. no. A restaurant is noisy only at mealtimes. So a waitress probably would not be exposed long enough to suffer hearing loss.

4. yes. Listening to a live band for less than 2 minutes can cause hearing loss. So a concert of one to three hours would certainly cause some loss of hearing.

5. depends. The table says a screaming child can reach 110 decibels and cause hearing loss after $3\frac{3}{4}$ minutes. So if a child screamed for a long time, you might suffer hearing loss.

6. depends. If you rode the subway for more than 30 minutes at a time, it could cause hearing loss.

7. no. You would have to use a hair dryer for 4 hours to suffer hearing loss.

8. depends. If you used a power lawn mower for 30 minutes, you could suffer hearing loss.

Reston: A Planned Community
(page 109)

1. b. The major streets bypass the homes. The map shows that **a** and **c** are false. People can't take the train to work because the train does not go past housing. Neighborhoods can be reached by roads, not just walkways. You can guess from clues such as the many roads that **d** is also wrong. On the other hand, the map shows that **b** is correct. Only circle or dead-end streets go into the housing clusters.

GED Warm-up

(4) By carefully studying the map, you can see that (1) and (3) are wrong because they are false. Factories are not near a lake, and the railroad runs north of town. (2) and (5) state facts. The church is across from the school, and housing is built near Rt. 606. But these would not affect pollution, so (2) and (5) are not the answers. Keeping factory wastes far from homes is a good way to keep people from breathing or drinking them in. So (4) is the correct answer.

Measuring What You've Learned
(pages 110–115)

1. d. The key to the answer is time order. In the passage, look for each event from the answer choices. When does it happen? You'll find the only possible answer is **d.**

2. Sample answer: It is better to be wise than it is to be proud. The story calls the dog proud and the cat wise. The cat comes out on top, so wisdom seems to be better than pride.

3. b. The cat was old, but it wasn't the one fooled, so **a** is wrong. The dog was young and good-looking. Yet it has a lot to learn. So **c** and **d** are wrong. The dog looked long for its food. Yet it failed to keep it. So **e** is not correct. The dog was proud, and he lost his food. Both these facts point to **b.**

4. e. Except for **b**, the choices give different meanings for *wise*. However, **e** is the meaning that best fits the story.

5. a. The question states an effect. The answer should be the cause. The reading says immigrants from Norway and Sweden farmed for a living. It also says America's plains were good land for farming. So you can infer that they settled there because they wanted to farm.

6. b. Look at the details in the reading. Ask: Which choice do all these details support? The answer is **b.**

7. e. Common sense tells you that most Chinese immigrants sailed from Asia and landed on the West Coast. That's why many settled in California. Their descendants probably still live in the West.

8. d. Immigrants are people who came here from other countries.

9. Canada has the tallest light bar, so Canada sends the most dollars worth of goods to the United States. In other words, the United States buys more goods from Canada than from any other country shown on the graph.

10. Japan is the only country with a light bar about two spaces taller than its dark bar. Notice that each space is equal to $5 million, so two spaces would equal $10 million.

11. d. Compare the bars above *Mexico.* The dark one rises to about $32 million. The light one rises to about $12 million.

$32 million
− 12 million
$20 million

12. d. The Americans traded goods for deerskins. They must have viewed the hides as valuable.

13. d. The reading does not support **b.** Common sense tells you that **c** is false. Since the Americans traded away buttons, they probably did not value them much. Therefore, **e** is false. Another girl wanted to trade a horse for the buttons. This suggests that **a** is false and that **d** is the correct choice.

14. e. Details in the reading suggest that **a, b, c,** and **d** are false. Because the people used willow root and hunted deer, **e** is the best answer.

15. a. Careful reading shows that the *War for Independence* was between Spain and Mexico.

16. b. Check the map key to find out what a state boundary looks like.

17. d. Always check the map's compass rose. The tops of most maps are north. But some are not.

18. e. You had to use the distance scale to answer this question.

19. Sample answer: The Native Americans in Indiana were made to leave. They suffered hardships as a result.

20. This question has no one right answer. The answer to the first part should be your opinion. The part that follows should include facts from the passage to support your opinion.

Part B

Answers

Measuring What You Know
(pages 118–121)

1. **c.** The article tells you about all the different causes of headaches.

2. Sample main idea: Headaches are a common illness with many different causes.

3. Since so many headaches are caused by tension, you can conclude that people would have fewer headaches if they relaxed more.

4. **a.** A tumor and disease are examples of things that can go wrong with the brain. Therefore, you can guess that *disorder* means "something wrong with the brain."

5. 20 minutes

6. A cup of milk contains more calories than a slice of bread. You can see from the graph that it takes 32 minutes to burn off the calories in a cup of milk and only 13 minutes to burn off the calories in a slice of bread. This tells you there are more calories in the milk than there are in the bread because it takes more work to burn them up.

7. 19 minutes. It would take 6 minutes to burn up the calories in the salad and 13 minutes to burn up the calories in the bread. To burn up the calories in both; you would need to add 6 plus 13 for 19.

8. **b.** The article tells mostly about the fact that scientists do not know why whales beach.

9. because the water is least likely to be deep enough for whales to swim back out into the open sea during low tide

10. Dolphins and whales, unlike other mammals, live their lives in the water.

11. In the sentence *beach* means "to swim up onto a beach."

12. **b.** The first choice contains true facts, but summary (b) gives more information that tells you what the article was mainly about.

13. **a.** You may already know that there must be a certain amount of moisture in the air for rain to fall.

14. You can expect cooler temperatures and less than normal rainfall.

15. **c.** In the sentence *correlation* means that when one thing changes, another thing changes also, as in soil temperatures and rainfall. There is a relationship between the two things.

The Active Reader
Working It Out
(page 125)

1. The cause-and-effect words are *reason* and *cause* (third sentence), *so* (fourth sentence), and *result* (fifth sentence).

2. **a.** *Effect:* The result was beef that has fewer calories than chicken. This is *what happened.* The breeding tests were *why it happened* (the cause).
b. *Cause:* fat in red meat. The word *cause* signals that the fat

in red meat makes something happen—heart problems and extra weight.

Part B / Lesson 1

Before You Read
(page 126)

1. These foods are usually thought to be better for your health: fruit juice, broiled chicken, and yogurt.

2. Fruit juice, broiled chicken, and yogurt are all lower in fat or sugar than the other foods. They are better for your heart and are less fattening.

3. Soda pop, fried chicken, and candy bars have fat or sugar. They can cause health problems.

Reading on Your Own
Ideal Weight
(page 128)

1. No, she is not overweight. Ideal weight for a woman 5'6" is listed as 120–160 pounds, and 135 pounds is within this range.

2. gender and height. You can see this on the table and read it in the article.

3. **b.** weights on the table are too low.
c. it's better to be a few pounds heavier.

Popular Diets
(page 129)

1. Eat healthful foods but in smaller amounts.

2. Protein can easily turn to fat. Fat might cause you to gain weight.

3. **Kinds of Foods** **Example**
  1. protein — meat or milk
  2. fats — margarine, oils, meat, or milk
  3. carbohydrates — fruits, bread, or vegetables

Obese Children
(page 130)

1. Children who watch TV are less active, and they snack as they watch TV.

2. Possible reasons include heredity, overeating habits passed down in the family, and the lack of exercise practiced in the family.

The Changing Eating Habits of Americans
(pages 130–131)

1. People eat more chicken, fish, margarine, and low-fat milk, and they eat less beef, butter, and whole milk.

2. Packaged foods are easier to make and take less time. This answer is not given in the article, but you can use your experience and judgment to think of this answer.

3. b **4.** a **5.** a
6. b **7.** a

Cholesterol
(page 131)

1. High in cholesterol: liver, fried chicken, eggs, and pep-peroni pizza. Liver and eggs are animal parts. Fried chicken and pepperoni pizza have animal fat. Pepperoni pizza also has pork, a fat meat, and cheese. Low in cholesterol: oatmeal and skim milk. Skim milk has no fat. Oatmeal is a grain, and has no cholesterol.

2. Juan's breakfast is foods that are all high in cholesterol. Eggs and butter are mentioned in the article. Bacon is a fat meat. Juanita's breakfast is all low-cholesterol foods. It also includes oatmeal, which helps get rid of cholesterol.

Planning a Menu
(page 132)

Check the guidelines for meal planning to be sure your menu is healthful.

Anorexia
GED Warm-up
(page 132)

(2) This is the reason anorexics have such a problem eating properly. Many people exercise each day, but they eat well to keep their proper weight.

The Active Reader
Working It Out
(page 134)

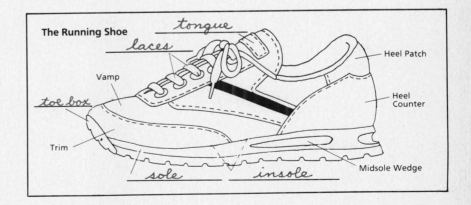

The Running Shoe — tongue, laces, Vamp, toe box, Trim, sole, insole, Heel Patch, Heel Counter, Midsole Wedge

Part B / Lesson 2

Before You Read
(page 136)

Sample sentence with *blood pressure:* Get your blood pressure checked often to make sure it is not too high.

Sample sentence with *transplant:* These days doctors can transplant kidneys, livers, and even hearts.

Other possible examples of things similar to blood vessels are a hose carrying water and the roots of plants taking up water.

Reading on Your Own
Your Heart: How to Keep It Healthy
(page 137)

1. eat the right foods
watch your weight
don't smoke
check your blood pressure
exercise

2. Sample answer: male; older; history of heart disease in the family; overweight; smoker; doesn't exercise

3. c. The fifth paragraphs helps you understand what blood pressure is. Blood *pressure* and *force* of blood have the same meaning.

Warning Signs of a Heart Attack
(pages 137–138)

1. pain in the chest, sweating, shortness of breath, an upset stomach, weakness

2. no. Most often, or 90% of the time, people are asleep, resting, or doing their daily routine when a heart attack occurs.

Artificial Hearts
(pages 138–139)

1. The heart constantly takes in and pumps out blood.

2. transplant

3. Smoking cuts down the amount of oxygen in the lungs. The heart must work harder to get more oxygen from the blood.

Hardening of the Arteries
(page 139)

1. b. The other choices are also definitions of a vessel, but they do not apply to this article.

2. fat and calcium deposits

3. a. 2 Fat has begun to collect in the artery.
b. 1 The vessel is clear and open.
c. 4 Only a tiny opening is left.
d. 3 Fat has built up, narrowing the passage.

Smoking and Its Effects on the Lungs
(page 140)

1. Nicotine keeps the bronchi from opening as they should, so air cannot move in and out easily. Carbon monoxide enters the blood as well as oxygen. And the air sacs eventually break down.

2. Smoke is taken in with the air a smoker breathes. The carbon monoxide in smoke cuts down the amount of oxygen in the blood. When there is less oxygen in the blood, a person has less energy.

3. Both the nose and the mouth let air into the windpipe. Therefore, even if your nose is blocked, you can continue to breathe through your mouth.

Aerobics
(page 141)

1. The heart and lungs are strengthened.

2. Possible reasons aerobics could be a fad: People get bored with the same type of exercise and want a change. Many people do aerobics only because it's popular; these people may stop aerobics when a new exercise fad begins.
Possible reasons aerobics is here to stay: People care about their health and realize that aerobics keeps the heart and lungs healthy. You don't need special equipment to do aerobic exercises. Aerobics can be fun.

How Exercise Affects the Bones
(page 141)

1. a. weaker **b.** more dense **c.** more calcium **d.** faster bone loss

GED Warm-up
(page 141)

1. (2) The article helps you see that regular exercise helps keep bones strong.

The Active Reader Working It Out
(page 143)

1. 0.05 percent, and the person has mood swings. Run your finger down the first column to 2, then over to the two columns on the right.

2. 5 drinks. Run your finger up the left side of the graph ("Level of Alcohol in Blood"). Stop at 0.10 percent. Now run your finger across until your finger touches the line on the graph. Run your finger down to the bottom line ("Number of Drinks in One Hour"). There is your answer.

3. The more a person drinks, the more affected his or her behavior becomes. He or she becomes less and less aware.

Part B / Lesson 3

Reading on Your Own Alcoholism—Get the Facts
(pages 146–147)

1. a chemical problem in the body. This answer is found in the paragraph before the graph.

2. "Won't" means the person does not want to stop drinking; "can't" means the person is not able to stop drinking.

3. __3__ liver disease
__2__ other diseases
__1__ drunk driving
__7__ drownings
__5__ other accidents
__6__ suicide
__4__ murder

Alcohol's Effect on the Brain
(pages 147–148)

1. Short-term effects, any two of these: information to the brain is unclear (not "sorted" correctly); cannot see clearly; clumsy movements; brain no longer in full control of the muscles; person can become unconscious (parts of the brain "stop working" for a time)

Long-term effects, any two of these: brain cells are changed; many brain cells die and are not replaced; memory loss; cannot recall current events (no "new memory"); blackouts; senses dulled

2. The arrows point in both directions to show that chemical messages travel back and forth between the brain and body parts and between the brain and the senses.

Cocaine
(pages 148–149)

1. It changes chemicals in the body to make the brain's pleasure center produce a feeling of pleasure, or a high. This answer is in the fifth paragraph.

2. because the chemicals that carry messages to the pleasure center drop off after fifteen to thirty minutes. This cause-and-effect relationship is explained in the fifth paragraph.

3. This question asks for your opinion. Sample answers: because some people don't think the bad effects will happen to them; because some people care more about feeling good than about other things in life

Effects of Drug Abuse
(page 149)

1. friends: Harry saw his friends less and less.

2. job: Harry lost his job.

3. feelings: Harry was depressed, irritable, and frightened.

4. money: All of Harry's money went to buy cocaine

Drug Abuse Cases
(page 150)

1. New York. This city has the tallest bar.

2. about 5,500. Run your finger to the top of the bar for Chicago, then over to the scale on the left. The mark for 5,000 is midway between 4,000 and 6,000. The bar for Chicago reaches about midway between 5,000 and 6,000.

3. The bar for Washington, D.C., should reach midway between about the 5,000 mark (the line midway between 4,000 and 6,000) and the 6,000 mark. The bar for Miami should reach about midway between the 4,000 mark and the 5,000 mark.

GED Warm-up
(page 150)

(2) Detroit has about the same number of drug abuse cases in a much smaller population. That probably means a higher percent of people use drugs in Detroit than in Los Angeles.

The Active Reader
Working It Out
(page 153)

1. yes. Weed seeds travel well and don't need much soil. Therefore, they could reach the dirt piles and grow.

2. "Therefore, city weeds are made for survival." (This is the first sentence of the last paragraph.) The word *therefore* is the signal word.

3. The author thinks city weeds show toughness and beauty. To the author, living plants in such an unpleasant place are special.

Part B / **Lesson 4**

Reading on Your Own
Help from Pets
(page 156)

1. mental; physical. The second paragraph shows how a pet helps the mental health of its owner. The third paragraph explains how the pet helps physical health.

2. Sample answer: Pet owners help their pets by feeding them, giving them shelter, and caring for their health.

Social Order
(pages 156–157)

1. The queen mates and lays eggs. Her role makes sure there will be new bees or ants.

2. "Lower in the pecking order" means that a person has less power and is less important than another.

3. The monkey that is groomed by all the others is at the top of the social order in its group. You can conclude this because lower monkeys groom monkeys above them.

Animal Instincts
(page 157)

1. The trigger is the baby's feeling something against its face.

2. The instinct is to suck.

3. The instinct to suck helps the baby eat and therefore survive.

How Animals Learn
(page 158)

1. a. imitation
   b. reinforcement
   c. individual ideas and actions

2. Every time the dog sat when you said, "Sit," you would reward it with a treat. (You might even slightly push the dog down as you said, "Sit.") The reward would reinforce its sitting.

A Gorilla Who "Speaks"
(pages 158–159)

1. **Food**
   banana
   apple

   Emotions
   happy
   sad
   mad

   Action
   hug

   Animal
   kitten

2. because the hands of a gorilla can make the signs that stand for ideas in sign language. Only a few animals—primates—could be used in such an experiment.

3. You know that gorillas *and* humans are primates. You can conclude that primates are a special group of animals. You also learn that primates have five fingers that move well and grasp objects.

How Bees Communicate
(page 159)

1. to show other bees where food is located

2. because a bee shows the location of food in relation to the position of the sun. At night the sun is not out, so the bee could not dance at a particular angle up the hive.

3. B. The angle of the food matches the angle of the bee's dance.

Animals on the Move
(page 160)

1. the cheetah. According to the graph, the cheetah can reach a speed of 70 mph.

2. 4 times. In water a human can swim up to 5 mph. A human can reach up to 20 mph running on land. That is 4 times the speed in water.

3. a turtle. A sea turtle can swim 20 mph, but a land turtle can crawl only 1/10 mph.

GED Warm-up
(page 160)

(1) in the air. Look at the three sections of the graph. By far the animals that move through air (birds) can move faster than land or sea animals. The fastest animal of all is the duck hawk. It can fly up to 180 mph.

The Active Reader Working It Out
(page 162)

1. Activated charcoal should be used because it would be dangerous to make the victim vomit.

2. Ipecac should be used because it causes vomiting. Vomiting is not dangerous in this situation.

3. No ipecac or activated charcoal should be used with an unconscious person.

4. The number likely decreased to about 100. That decrease follows the pattern of 1987 and 1988.

Part B / Lesson 5

Reading on Your Own Pollution Problem for Fish
(page 165)

1. Thermal pollution is heat pollution.

2. probably. The article tells you catfish can live in warm or cool water. If garfish are like catfish, they can probably live in the warm water.

3. Using water from streams saves money. If a company had to find other ways to cool its products, it could cost a lot of money.

A Food Chain
(page 165)

1. First, the small fish eats plants. Second, the big fish eats the small fish. Third, the man catches and eats the big fish.

2. The man would not catch a fish. With no plants, there would be no fish living in the pond.

3. Some examples of other food chains: A bird eats insects. Then a cat eats the bird. A chicken eats corn. Then a person eats the chicken.

Photosynthesis—How Plants Make Food
(page 166)

1. Water, carbon dioxide, and light energy from the sun.

2. Less water for the soil means less water to use to make food. If the weather is dry too long, the plant will not be able to make food at all. It will die.

3. A plant puts out oxygen during photosynthesis. Humans and other animals breathe oxygen.

4. Fewer trees mean fewer green plants for photosynthesis. That means less oxygen in the air to breathe.

Algae as Food
(page 166)

1. Algae can provide food to eat. They would take up little room on the spaceship.

2. In Africa. The need for food is greater there than in North America.

The People Problem
(page 167)

1. The number of people in the world keeps getting larger.

2. The amount of farmland and forestland keeps getting smaller.

3. There will be less food for more people. More people may go hungry.

Plants That Save Lives
(page 167)

1. no longer living; having died out

2. They could teach us about the use of plants to heal. We could make medicine from them.

3. Some people with high blood pressure will no longer have medicine that was made from this plant. They would have to find other treatment.

An Island Laboratory
(page 168)

1. because the number of plants decreased. There was less food to support a large moose population.

2. The moose population seems to increase a little, probably because there are fewer wolves to eat moose.

3. The moose population would probably decrease again because of lack of food.

4. The wolf population would likely decrease too. The wolves feed on the moose.

Disappearing Animals
(page 169)

1. The animals that depend on that animal for food may have problems. These animals may even become extinct.

2. The animals that feed on that kind of animal would have problems finding food. The numbers of all these other animals may decrease too.

3. Humans can destroy the homes of animals. They cut down forests, for example. This destruction can also cause the extinction of animals.

GED Warm-up
(page 169)

(3) The number and kind of living things in an area tend to stay the same. The second paragraph begins with the idea of upsetting "the balance of na-ture." The rest of the para-graph explains that the bal-ance is upset when the numbers of animals change.

The Active Reader Working It Out
(page 173)

1. Sample questions: How did the men travel? What hap-pened during the race? Who reached the South Pole first?

2. Sample answers: The sec-ond paragraph answers the second question. The last sen-tence of the third paragraph answers the third question.

3. Sample answer: The first question was not answered.

4. a. What the South Pole is was not explained.

5. "But the Norwegians had reached the Pole earlier—on December 14, 1911."

Part B / Lesson 6

Reading on Your Own Solids, Liquids, and Gases
(page 176)

1. In a steel building the mol-ecules are packed more tightly. The steel is a solid. In liquid steel, the molecules are not so tightly packed. In *any* solid, the molecules are packed more tightly than in a liquid of the same material.

2. Solid margarine melts to become liquid. The molecules move further apart from each other.

Heat on the Move
(page 177)

1. The higher the tempera-ture of an object, the faster its particles move.

2. The faster particles push into the slower ones. The slower particles begin to speed up. The faster particles also lose energy, so they slow down.

3. Heat moves from the hot coffee molecules to the cold molecules in the milk. Finally, they all become the same temperature.

How Does a Pond Freeze?
(page 177)

1. A frozen pond may or may not be safe to walk on. Since water freezes from the top, the pond may look as if it is frozen. But it may still be water underneath. By poking a hole in the ice, you can see if the ice is thick enough to walk on.

2. Water expands in the ice tray as it freezes. The ice cubes take up more room than the water used to make them.

Don't Catch Cold!
(page 178)

1. no, because a cold temperature will not make you sick.

2. People use refrigerators and freezers to cool and freeze foods. They also heat food by cooking it. The germs can't live in the cold or hot food.

How a Pressure Cooker Works
(page 178)

1. When the steam builds up too high in a pressure cooker, some can escape through the escape valve. If the extra steam did not escape, the pot could explode.

2. If your car overheats, you should not remove the radiator lid right away. Built-up steam will escape, and you could get burned.

Inside a Refrigerator
(page 179)

1. The temperature goes down because heat is lost to the air. This answer is in the third paragraph.

2. When you open the door to a refrigerator, you let in warm air. Then the refrigerator turns on to cool the inside again.

A Watched Pot
(page 179)

1. The boiling point is the temperature at which a particular liquid boils.

2. It will take less time to heat tea to boiling in the mountains because you do not need to reach as high a temperature as at sea level.

Super Cool Science
GED Warm-up
(page 180)

1. (1) Superconductors pass electricity very easily at low temperatures. The molecules were not expected to behave this way. (2) is true, but it's not important for this question.

2. (1) The other statements tell things that happen because of the use of cryogenics. Cryogenics is used to freeze foods, not to thaw them.

The Active Reader
Working It Out
(page 182)

1. No rain and temperatures over 90° are the two causes.

2. A dangerous water shortage is the effect.

3.

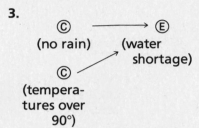

4. "The result was" is the clue to the cause-and-effect relationship.

Part B / Lesson 7

Reading on Your Own
Weather and Climate
(page 185)

1. Weather is the conditions of temperature, wind, and so on that change from day to day. Climate is the kind of weather a place generally has over a long period of time.

2. The equator gets more direct rays from the sun. Direct rays give more heat.

3. The poles get slanted sun rays. Slanted rays give less heat.

4. You would expect the climate of England to be fairly warm. Air over the Gulf Stream is warmed by the ocean's warmth. This warm air blows across England.

5. There is more of a temperature difference between summer and winter in Idaho than in the Caribbean. The climate of a Caribbean island is kept mild by the ocean around it. Idaho does not get this effect.

Weather Forecasting
(page 186)

1. a cold front. The symbol for a cold front is just east of Seattle on the map.

2. warm and rainy, with a temperature of 75°. A warm front is near New York, and the symbol for rain is over the city. The temperature forecast is near the name of the city.

3. because low-pressure areas are usually warm and cloudy. A warm front marks the edge of a warm air mass.

Rain, Snow, Sleet, and Hail
(page 187)

1. 1, 2, 4, 5, 3, 6. These causes and effects are explained in the fourth paragraph.

2. It will fall as snow. The table gives you this answer.

3. The hailstones were formed in the clouds in the sky, where it must be below freezing. If the hailstones were large, they would not melt completely on the way down, even in warm air.

Hurricanes
(page 188)

1. Strong winds and floods due to rain and waves cause damage to property during a hurricane. The first two paragraphs mention these causes.

2. Hurricanes occur most often in late summer and early fall because that is when the surface of the ocean is warmest. A warm ocean surface provides the heat and moist air a hurricane needs to start.

3. The center, or eye, of the hurricane becomes calm, with clear skies.

4. The hurricane can move over land, or it can move onto a cool part of the ocean. Both these events take away the source of warm, moist air a hurricane needs.

Is the Earth Getting Warmer?
(page 189)

1. Carbon dioxide and water vapor act as a seal in the atmosphere to create the greenhouse effect.

2. Cars put more carbon dioxide into the air. The added carbon dioxide creates an even thicker seal, so even more heat is trapped.

GED Warm-up
(page 189)

(3) If the ocean rises several inches, cities on the shore will be flooded with the extra water.

The Active Reader
Working It Out
(page 191)

1. probably another 4.5 or 5 billion years. A middle-aged person is in the middle of an average life. He or she will live to be about twice as old as he or she is now. If the sun is middle-aged at 4.5 billion years, it will probably live for another 4.5 or 5 billion years.

2. When fuel for a car runs out, it "dies"; it can no longer run. When fuel for a fire runs out, the fire dies; it no longer burns. The same will be true of the sun when its fuel runs out. It will cool off and "die."

Part B / Lesson 8

Before You Read
(page 192)

telescopes, rockets, moon, weightless, Earth, sun

Reading on Your Own
The Solar System
(page 194)

1. Saturn is colder because it is farther away from the sun's heat.

2. Mars has the larger orbit because it is farther away from the sun.

Gravity and Orbits
(pages 194–195)

1. The force of gravity keeps objects in orbit.

2. If a planet did not get pulled toward the sun, it would keep going in a straight line away from the sun and out into space.

3. The moon closer to a planet moves faster because it has more pull from the planet's gravity.

Sun and Earth, Day and Night
(page 195)

1. People thought the sun moved around the Earth because the sun appears to rise, move through the sky, and set.

2. When you see the sun rise and set, you are actually moving in and then out of view of the sun. Your spot on Earth is spinning toward the sun and then away from the sun.

Phases of the Moon
(page 196)

1. Moonlight is really sunlight reflected by the moon.

2. After half of its orbit, the moon is a full moon. It looks like a full, glowing circle.

The Making of a Moon
(page 197)

1. **a.** The last two sentences explain that gravity pulled the pieces together to make the moon.

2. **c.** If the moon were caused by a crash 4½ billion years ago, the Earth would have to be at least that old.

What Is Mars Really Like?
(page 197)

1. You may know that canyons and gorges on the earth are created by rivers wearing away the land. If there are canyons and gorges on Mars, they were likely created by rivers too.

2. The air on Mars does not seem right; it is mostly carbon dioxide. You might also have mentioned that there is probably not enough water.

Discoveries from Space
(page 198)

1. True. Saturn appears to have seven rings or bands. *Voyager II* showed that the seven rings are actually made up of many small rings.

2. False. The fourth paragraph tells you the rings and moons of Uranus are made up of a black material *and* ice.

The Asteroid Belt
GED Warm-up
(page 198)

1. **(1)** Asteroids and planets both orbit the sun.

2. **(3)** One idea is asteroids may have come from the explosion of a planet. Reading closely, you see that this planet would have been between Mars and Jupiter. Mars and Jupiter themselves did not crash.

The Active Reader
Working It Out
(page 200)

1. **c.** Spray-can gas is not good for the air. That is the most important idea of the *whole* article.

2. **b.** Spray-can gas harms the earth's ozone. **d.** Without the ozone, the sun would burn people badly. These two ideas help explain the main idea. They tell *why* spray-can gas is not good.

3. Sample summary: Spray-can gas is not good for the air because it harms the earth's ozone. Without the ozone, the sun would burn people badly.

Part B / Lesson 9

Before You Read
(page 201)

1. landfill—A landfill is a place where cities dump and bury their garbage.

2. smog—Smog is a kind of air pollution. The word is a combination of *smoke* and *fog*.

3. poison—Lead injures the brain and even kills, if taken in great amounts.

4. rain—Acid rain is unhealthy rain caused by air pollution.

5. wildlife—Wild forest animals are often harmed by pollution from cities.

Reading on Your Own
Acid Rain
(page 203)

1. People can make new kinds of fertilizer that do not put acid-making chemicals into the air. They can also cut down on pollution from factories and cars.

2. Sample summary: Acid rain is a serious problem caused by polluting gases. It can destroy animal and plant life.

Getting the Lead Out
(page 204)

1. Inner-city children are at risk of being poisoned by lead because they often live in homes that still have lead paint on the walls. They sometimes eat paint that peels off the walls.

2. They have made cars that use unleaded gas.

Fossils in the Dump
(page 204)

1. because there are many fossils that are hard to find elsewhere

2. Sample summary: In western Germany, some fossils may be lost if the hole where they were found becomes a garbage dump.

"No Waste" Waste
(page 205)

1. **Old ways:** dumps, landfills, burning. **New ways:** recycling, using garbage.

Noise Pollution
(page 205)

1. 95 decibels; yes. The graph tells you the noise in a subway train is 95 decibels loud. Since this is above the line where danger begins, and the article says loud noise can make people lose their hearing, you know the subway can harm your hearing.

2. Noise pollution is a growing problem. Cities and the need for bigger machines are creating more noise that may even harm people.

Pollution Fallout
(page 206)

1. Chemicals carried to the island by the wind caused birth defects in the animals. You can draw this conclusion from information in the second paragraph.

2. People in one country may get angry if pollution from another country is blown onto their land.

Ozone Alert
(page 206)

1. A large city would have more ozone than the country because there are many more factories and cars in the city. Exhaust from cars and factories helps make ozone.

2. Ozone is helpful when it is 20 to 30 miles up in the atmosphere because it shields us from harmful solar rays.

Air Pollution in Cities
(page 207)

1. Either: smoke and gases from cars and factories; or dust. These causes are listed in the second paragraph.

2. Any two: eats away materials; makes it hard for sunlight to get through; burns eyes and noses; gives headaches; causes colds and lung diseases. These effects are listed in the first, third, and fourth paragraphs.

3. Air pollution in cities is a serious problem. It has many bad effects, but people may not always realize them.

GED Warm-up
(page 207)

1. (1) People don't see pollution as a problem because they don't see the effects right away. The question starts, "According to the article." This reason was given at the end of the article.

The Active Reader Working It Out
(page 209)

1. no. Even if all snakes are thin, this does not prove that snake livers could make people thin. Snakes could be thin for reasons that have nothing to do with their livers. Also, what makes a snake thin might not make a person thin.

2. no. One person losing weight with Fat-Off is not enough to prove Fat-Off is a good diet aid. Thousands of people would have to try Fat-Off to determine if it would help most people lose weight.

3. no. Relying on what "everybody knows" is not a scientific way of gathering facts.

Part B / Lesson 10

Reading on Your Own Using the Scientific Method
(page 212)

1. All three activities are parts of the scientific method.

2. You could do an experiment to see if it is below freezing outside. You could take out a container of water. If it freezes, then you know that the temperature is below freezing.

Alchemists—Mad Scientists
(page 212)

1. True. The alchemists never made gold or silver because their idea of "sick" and "well" metals was wrong.

2. True. Scientists often get new ideas from experiments that fail.

3. True. The alchemists learned to make alcohol and acids. They learned how to separate zinc from other particles.

Getting Down to Basics
(page 213)

1. A nucleus is made up of protons and neutrons. Protons have a positive charge, and neutrons have no charge of electricity.

2. An electron is a particle in an atom which has a negative charge. You can see in the diagram that electrons circle the nucleus of the atom.

3. 26. The last paragraph of the article states that an atom has the same number of electrons as protons. An iron atom has 26 protons, so it must have 26 electrons also.

Atoms in Combination
(page 213)

1. True. Look again at the last sentence of the first paragraph. Combinations of atoms make new substances.

2. False. Look again at the first two sentences. Atoms of elements are found mostly combined with other elements, not alone.

Power from Atoms
(page 214)

1. When the nucleus of a uranium atom is split, a huge amount of energy is released.

2. A chain reaction occurs when neutrons from one split nucleus split another nucleus, and so on.

3. People worry that the chain reaction will get out of control, and they worry about radioactive waste.

Radioactivity and the Curies
(page 215)

1. After coming across some unexpected findings, Marie Curie's next step was to do more experiments. Because of the new experiments, she discovered radium.

2. b. A radioactive element has a nucleus that breaks down.

Magnetism and Michael Faraday
(page 215)

1. The work of an earlier scientist showed Faraday that magnetism could be made from electricity. This gave him the idea to do an experiment to see if it worked the other way around.

2. A result of Michael Faraday's discovery of electricity made from magnetism was that electricity could be made in large amounts.

A Perpetual Motion Machine?
GED Warm-up
(page 216)

1. (4) Being able to repeat an experiment with the same results is part of the proof that an idea is true.

2. (3) A machine needs more energy when parts that rub or push against each other use up energy.

The Active Reader
Working It Out
(page 218)

1. yes. It could be proved that sounds don't bounce off the walls. As a test, you could make a noise in the gym. If there's no echo, then you know the sound didn't bounce. You could also read in a science book that cork keeps sound waves from bouncing.

2. hypothesis. It could be true that the students will play better. But it hasn't been proved yet. To test this hypothesis, you could compare basketball scores after the gym was built with earlier scores.

3. opinion. Whether or not the gym is worth the money spent on it is a personal judgment. It can't be tested or proved.

Part B / Lesson 11

Reading on Your Own
Power from Magnets
(page 221)

1. No, a copper penny cannot

become magnetized. Only objects made of iron or steel can become magnetized.

2. It's a fact because it can be proved.

Super Train
(page 222)

1. Scientists knew that magnets can repel each other. A super train uses the energy of magnets repelling each other to move. With no bumping of wheels against tracks, the ride on a super train is smoother than a ride on a regular train.

2. If more people ride super trains, there will be less car exhaust put into the air. And super trains, which use magnetism for power, do not pollute like ordinary trains do. They also do not make noise.

Lasers
(page 222)

1. "Lasers are one of the most exciting things to come from modern science." The word *exciting* makes the sentence an opinion.

2. Lasers are precise or exact. In an operation, a laser can cut in one place without hurting other parts.

Bits, Bytes, and Chips
(page 223)

1. Silicon chips changed from 1970 to 1990 in the amount of information that they could hold. In 1970, a chip could hold 100 bits of information. By 1990, that amount had increased 10,000 times.

2. a. Opinion. This statement is a personal judgment; it cannot be proved.
b. Fact. This statement can be proved by comparing the sizes

of older computers with newer computers.

Radios and Waves
(page 224)

1. The waves of FM and AM signals are different. They need different receivers to change them back into sound.

2. A radio jammer jams, or mixes up, radio signals. The radio waves can't be changed back into their proper sounds.

The End of Cash?
(page 224)

1. Opinion. No one can *prove* what will happen in the future. Therefore, the statement can't be a fact.

2. In a cashless society, buying and selling would be faster and easier. There would be fewer checking mistakes because people would not add and subtract from their own checking accounts. People would not need to carry large sums of money.

Fiber Optics and the Telephone
(page 225)

1. The invention of the laser made fiber optics possible. The second paragraph tells you so.

2. This is an opinion. Many people believe that copper wire should be replaced by optical fibers. But that is a personal judgment. It cannot be proved.

GED Warm-up
(page 225)

(3) The other statements are facts. You can find them in the article. This statement is an

idea that is possible but has never been proved true. It is a hypothesis.

Measuring What You've Learned
(pages 226–231)

1. Any three of the following effects: short stops in breathing, loud snoring, falling asleep while driving, and higher rate of accidents.

2. b. This statement best describes the main idea of the *entire* article. Three out of the four paragraphs are about sleep apnea, not just drivers of cars.

3. e. The fourth paragraph tells you that losing weight helps some people with sleep apnea. You can conclude that they must be overweight and that their weight may be one reason they have problems breathing.

4. a. When blood flow to an area of the heart is stopped, that area would be damaged.

5. c. You can get this answer directly from the diagram.

6. a. The blood that comes from the aorta has oxygen from the lungs in it. Part of the heart does not receive this oxygen if its artery is blocked.

7. 8 grams. You can find this answer in the top part of the chart.

8. c. Skim milk is fairly high in protein and low in fat.

9. 4 glasses. One glass gives you 25 percent of what you need. So four glasses would give you 100 percent ($4 \times 25 = 100$), or all that you need.

10. e. The article tells you that at some point animals moved from the sea to the land. You can conclude that the ances-

tors of land animals such as scorpions and spiders once lived in the sea. They were *related* to horseshoe crabs, but they were not horseshoe crabs.

11. b. A fossil is the remains of a plant or animal that died long ago. A "living fossil" is an animal that was thought to have died out, but didn't.

12. d. If the bone arrangement of the fins is like that in legs, you can conclude that perhaps at one time they developed into legs for land animals.

13. d. The first summary is true, but it deals with just one paragraph of the passage. Choice (4) summarizes the *entire* passage.

14. b. This statement best explains why the core of the earth is solid. Particles that are packed tightly together cannot move.

15. e. All the other choices can result from the movement of melted rock under the earth's crust. Heat waves *above* the earth's surface are weather conditions, not physical changes.

16. b. You can get this meaning from the third paragraph.

17. Sample main idea: Radon is a dangerous substance that can seep into homes from the ground and remain there.

18. These two facts from the article help support the conclusion that radon is dangerous: Radon is radioactive, and radon causes lung cancer.

19. Any two of these: vent crawl spaces and sump pumps; seal cracks in the foundation and basement floors; use an indoor air cleaner. You can find these ways in the last paragraph.

Answer Key

Part A

Measuring What You Know
(pages 2–5)

1. decides what he feels about what others see

2. A child sees himself as he thinks others see him.

3. a. Parents help mold their child's character.

4. other people

5. cotton

6. cotton

7. 1980

8. traffic jams

9. a. Laws keep peace and order.

10. The driver may hit the person.

11. duties

12. b. English lawmakers

13. They were ruled by England but lived in America.

14. West Africa

15. the West Indies and South America

16. 5%

Part A

Measuring What You've Learned
(pages 110–115)

1. d.

2. It is better to be wise than it is to be proud.

3. b.
4. e.
5. a.
6. b.
7. e.
8. d.
9. Canada
10. Japan

11. d.
12. d.
13. d.
14. e.
15. a.
16. b.
17. d.
18. e.

19. Sample answer: *The Indians in Indiana were made to leave. They suffered hardships as a result.*

20. Answers will vary.

Part B

Measuring What You Know
(pages 118–121)

1. c.

2. Sample main idea: Headaches are a common illness with many different causes.

3. People would have fewer headaches if they relaxed more.

4. a.

5. 20 minutes

6. A cup of milk contains more calories than a slice of bread.

7. 19 minutes

8. b.

9. because the water is least likely to be deep enough for whales to swim back out into the open sea during low tide

10. Dolphins and whales, unlike other mammals, live their lives in the water.

11. "to swim up onto a beach"

12. b.

13. a.

14. You can expect cooler temperatures and less than normal rainfall.

15. c.

Part B

Measuring What You've Learned
(pages 226–231)

1. Any three of the following effects: short stops in breathing, loud snoring, falling asleep while driving, and higher rate of accidents.

2. b.
3. e.
4. a.
5. c.
6. a.
7. 8 grams
8. c.
9. 4 glasses

10. e.
11. b.
12. d.
13. d.
14. b.
15. e.
16. b.

17. Sample main idea: Radon is a dangerous substance that can seep into homes from the ground and remain there.

18. Radon is radioactive. Radon causes lung cancer.

19. Any two of the following: vent crawl spaces and sump pumps; seal cracks in the foundation and basement floors; use an indoor air cleaner.

Two-Letter State Abbreviations

Alabama	AL	Kentucky	KY	Ohio	OH
Alaska	AK	Louisiana	LA	Oklahoma	OK
Arizona	AZ	Maine	ME	Oregon	OR
Arkansas	AR	Maryland	MD	Pennsylvania	PA
American Samoa	AS	Massachusetts	MA	Puerto Rico	PR
California	CA	Michigan	MI	Rhode Island	RI
Colorado	CO	Minnesota	MN	South Carolina	SC
Connecticut	CT	Mississippi	MS	South Dakota	SD
Delaware	DE	Missouri	MO	Tennessee	TN
District of Columbia	DC	Montana	MT	Trust Territory	TT
Florida	FL	Nebraska	NE	Texas	TX
Georgia	GA	Nevada	NV	Utah	UT
Guam	GU	New Hampshire	NH	Vermont	VT
Hawaii	HI	New Jersey	NJ	Virginia	VA
Idaho	ID	New Mexico	NM	Virgin Islands	VI
Illinois	IL	New York	NY	Washington	WA
Indiana	IN	North Carolina	NC	West Virginia	WV
Iowa	IA	North Dakota	ND	Wisconsin	WI
Kansas	KS	No. Mariana Islands	MP	Wyoming	WY

Acknowledgments *continued*

Company, 1988, p. 12. **60** Adapted from INVITATION TO ECONOMICS, Teacher's Annotated Ed., Third Ed., by Lawrence Wolken and Janet Glocker. Scott, Foresman and Company, 1988, p. 464. **71** Adapted from AMERICA PAST AND PRESENT by Joan Schreiber et al. Scott, Foresman and Company, 1983, pp. 385, 386. **79** Adapted from AMERICA YESTERDAY AND TODAY, Teacher's Annotated Ed. Worksheets. Scott, Foresman and Company, p. 45. **80** Adapted from GEOGRAPHY: OUR COUNTRY AND OUR WORLD by Barbara J. Winston. Scott, Foresman and Company, 1988, p. 188. **82** Adapted from GEOGRAPHY: OUR COUNTRY AND OUR WORLD by Barbara J. Winston. Scott, Foresman and Company, 1988, p. 219. **83** Spanish account of Cortés and Aztec description as cited in THE FREE AND THE BRAVE: THE STORY OF THE AMERICAN PEOPLE, 4th Ed, by Henry F. Graff. Chicago: Riverside Publishing Company, 1980. **88** Joan Schreiber et al., REGIONS OF OUR COUNTRY AND OUR WORLD. Glenview, Il.: Scott, Foresman and Company, 1985, p. 81. From THE BROKEN SPEARS: THE AZTEC ACCOUNT OF THE CONQUEST OF MEXICO. Ed. by Miguel León-Portilla. Translated by Lysander Kemp. Boston: Beacon Press, 1962. **89** Adapted from WESTERN HEMISPHERE: LATIN AMERICA AND CANADA, Teacher's Ed., by Joan Schreiber et al. Scott, Foresman and Company, 1986, pp. 106, 107. **91** Letters of Robert Parke and a German immigrant, as cited in THE FREE AND THE BRAVE: THE STORY OF THE AMERICAN PEOPLE, 4th Ed., by Henry H. Graff. Chicago: Riverside Publishing Company, 1980. **94** Adapted from AMERICA PAST AND PRESENT by Joan Schreiber et al. Scott, Foresman and Company, 1983, p. 22. **96** Adapted from AMERICA PAST AND PRESENT by Joan Schreiber et al. Scott, Foresman and Company, 1983, p. 307. **97** Adapted from AMERICA PAST AND PRESENT by Joan Schreiber et al. Scott, Foresman and Company, 1983, p. 305. **99** Ruth Holland, THE FORGOTTEN MINORITY: AMERICA'S TENANT FARMERS AND MIGRANT WORKERS. Copyright © 1970 by Ruth Holland. Reprinted with permission of the Macmillan Publishing Company, p. 138. **100** Ruth Holland, THE FORGOTTEN MINORITY: AMERICA'S TENANT FARMERS AND MIGRANT WORKERS. Copyright © 1970 by Ruth Holland. Reprinted by permission of the Macmillan Publishing Company, p. 143. **100** Excerpt from SAL SI PUEDES by Peter Matthiessen. Copyright © 1969 by Peter Matthiessen. Reprinted by permission of Random House, Inc. **105** Adapted from AMERICA PAST AND PRESENT by Joan Schreiber et al. Scott, Foresman and Company, 1983, p. 317. **105** Adapted from POLLUTION by Geraldine and Harold Woods. Copyright © 1985 by Geraldine and Harold Woods. Reprinted by permission of Franklin Watts Inc. **106** From THE NEW YORK TIMES by Michael T. Kaufman. **110** Richard L. Allington et al., ROUGH AND READY. Glenview, Il.: Scott, Foresman and Company, 1985, p. 107. **111** Adapted from REGIONS OF OUR COUNTRY AND OUR WORLD by Joan Schreiber et al. Scott, Foresman and Company, 1986, p. 104. **113** Adapted from CALIFORNIA HISTORY: THE STUDY OF OUR STATE by Joan Schreiber et al. Scott, Foresman and Company, 1984, p. 50. **115** Adapted from REGIONS OF OUR COUNTRY AND OUR WORLD by Joan Schreiber and Kathleen Kain. Scott, Foresman and Company, 1985, p. 206. **172–173** Adapted from ROUGH AND READY by Richard L. Allington et al. Scott, Foresman and Company, 1985, pp. 462, 464. **180** Adapted from PHYSICAL SCIENCE by Jay M. Pasachoff et al. Scott, Foresman and Company, 1983, p. 397. **180** Adapted from PHYSICAL SCIENCE by Jay M. Pasachoff et al. Scott, Foresman and Company, 1983, p. 145. **205** Adapted from EARTH SCIENCE by Jay M. Pasachoff et al. Scott, Foresman and Company, 1983, p. 469. **213** Adapted from SCIENCE by Michael R. Cohen et al. Scott, Foresman and Company, 1984, pp. 172, 173. **222** Adapted from PHYSICAL SCIENCE by Jay M. Pasachoff et al. Scott, Foresman and Company, 1982, p. 415. Dictionary entries are from SCOTT, FORESMAN BEGINNER, INTERMEDIATE, and ADVANCED DICTIONARY by E.L. Thorndike and Clarence L. Barnhart. Copyright © 1983 by Scott, Foresman and Company.

Index